THE DAILY STUDY BIBLE

THE REVELATION
of
JOHN

Volume 1

THE REVELATION

of

JOHN

Volume 1

(Chapters 1 to 5)

Translated,
with an Introduction and Interpretation
by

WILLIAM BARCLAY

THE WESTMINSTER PRESS
PHILADELPHIA

First published by The Saint Andrew Press
Edinburgh, Scotland
First Edition, May, 1959
Second Edition, June, 1960

Library of Congress Catalog Card No. 61–8293

Typeset in Great Britain
Printed in the United States of America

GENERAL INTRODUCTION

IT may truly be said that this series of Daily Bible Studies began almost accidentally. A series which the Church of Scotland was using came to an end, and another series was immediately required. I was asked to write a volume on *Acts*, and, at the moment, had no intention beyond that. But one volume followed another, until the demand for one volume became a plan to write on the whole New Testament.

The translation which is given in each volume claims no special merit. It was included in order that the reader might be able to carry both the text of the New Testament and the comments on it wherever he went, and that he might be able to read it anywhere. While I was making the translation, the translations of Moffatt, Weymouth, and Knox were ever beside me. *The American Revised Standard Version, The Twentieth Century New Testament,* and *The New Testament in Plain English,* by Charles Kingsley Williams, have been in constant use. Since its publication, I have consistently consulted *The Authentic New Testament,* translated by Hugh J. Schonfield.

I cannot see another edition of these books going out to the public without expressing my very deep and sincere gratitude to the Church of Scotland Publications Committee for allowing me the privilege of first beginning, and then continuing, this series. And in particular I wish to express my very great gratitude to the convener, Rev. R. G. Macdonald, O.B.E., M.A., D.D., and to the committee's secretary and manager, Rev. Andrew McCosh, M.A., S.T.M., for constant encouragement and never-failing sympathy and help.

As these volumes went on, the idea of the whole series developed. The aim is to make the results of modern scholarship available to the non-technical reader in a form that it does not require a theological education to understand; and then to seek to make the teaching of the New Testament books relevant to life and work to-day. The whole aim of these books is summed up in Richard of Chichester's famous prayer; they are meant to enable men and women to know Jesus Christ more clearly, to love Him more dearly, and to follow Him more nearly. It is my prayer that they may do something to make that possible.

FOREWORD

WITH the publication of this volume our task is very near an end, for with it we have reached the last book of the New Testament. When in 1952 I undertook to write a volume of Daily Bible Readings on *Acts*, I never meant to go beyond that volume. At that time I little thought that my part in the series would in the end cover the whole New Testament. I do not think that I would ever have carried through this task without the constant encouragement of so many friends. I am deeply grateful to the many people who throughout these years have written to me. I am grateful alike for their thanks which so often uplifted me, and for their criticism from which I always benefited. For myself these years of study of the whole New Testament have been an experience the value of which is beyond words to tell. While often the production of these volumes has been a heavy task, I have nothing but regret that now I have come almost to the end of it. I cannot do other than express my heartfelt gratitude to those who began with *Acts* and who have persevered in the journey with me through the New Testament to this final volume.

The *Revelation* is notoriously the most difficult book in the New Testament. But it is supplied with a magnificent assembly of commentaries, some of which are among the great commentaries of the world. The two volume commentary by R. H. Charles in *The International Critical Commentary* is a mine of information, and is completely indispensable. That by H. B. Swete in the *Macmillan Commentaries* combines scholarship and devotion, as

Swete always succeeded in doing in every commentary he wrote. That by I. T. Beckwith is of first-class importance. F. J. A. Hort's commentary was never completed, but even the fragment is precious. That by James Moffatt in the *Expositor's Greek Testament* is still valuable. All these commentaries are on the Greek text.

On the English text W. H. Simcox's volume in *The Cambridge Bible for Schools and Colleges* is brief, and now somewhat old—it was published in 1890—but is still useful, as is that of Martin Kiddie in *The Moffatt Commentary*. *The Book of Revelation* by E. F. Scott is not a commentary, but it is a lucid and illuminating exposition. R. C. Trench's *Commentary on the Epistles to the Seven Churches* has all that author's usual width of learning and spirit of devotion.

As we have said in this commentary, the *Revelation* is unique in the New Testament, but it is far from being unique of its kind, for it is a specimen of the Apocalyptic Literature which flourished so greatly between the Old and the New Testaments. For the study of that literature R. H. Charles' massive two volume work *The Apocrypha and Pseudepigrapha of the Old Testament* is completely indispensable. In 1958 there was published by far the best English commentary on the *Revelation*, that by Thomas S. Kepler, which does more to make the *Revelation* intelligible to English readers than any other commentary on the English text. Along with it *The Book of the Unveiling* by M. R. Newbolt is well worth reading. Austin Farrer's *A Rebirth of Images* is a work of scholarship and of importance, but is sometimes as difficult as the *Revelation* itself.

There are many who would like to read the *Revelation*, but who have found it so difficult that it is next to impossible; and who have abandoned the struggle. It is my hope and my prayer that this volume of studies will do something to unlock the wealth of what is one of the greatest and most dramatic books of the New Testament.

WILLIAM BARCLAY.

TRINITY COLLEGE,
  GLASGOW, *December*, 1958.

CONTENTS

CONTENTS

CONTENTS

CONTENTS

THE REVELATION OF JOHN

INTRODUCTION

The Strange Book

When a student of the New Testament embarks upon the study of the *Revelation* he feels himself projected into a new and a different world. Here is something quite unlike the rest of the New Testament. Not only is the *Revelation* different; it is also notoriously difficult for a modern mind to understand. The result is that the *Revelation* has sometimes been abandoned as quite un-intelligible, and it has sometimes become the playground of religious eccentrics, who use it to map out celestial time-tables of what is to come, or who find in it evidence for their own eccentricities. One despairing commentator said that there are as many riddles in the *Revelation* as there are words, and another said that the study of the *Revelation* either finds a man mad or leaves him mad. Luther would have denied the *Revelation* a place in the New Testament at all. Along with *James*, *Jude*, *2 Peter* and *Hebrews* he relegated it to a separate list at the end of his New Testament. He declared that in it there are only images and visions such as are found nowhere else in the Bible. He complained that, notwithstanding the obscurity of his writing, the writer had the boldness to add threats and promises for those who kept or disobeyed his words, while no one knows what he means. In it, said Luther, Christ is neither taught or acknowledged; and the inspir-ation of the Holy Spirit is not perceptible in it. Zwingli is equally hostile to the *Revelation*. " With the *Apocalypse*," he writes, " we have no concern, for it is not a biblical book. ... The *Apocalypse* has no savour of the mouth or the mind of John. I can, if I so will, reject its testimonies." Most voices have stressed the unintelligibility of the *Revelation*; some voices have even questioned its right to a place in the New Testament at all. On the other hand there are those in every generation who have loved this book. T. S. Kepler, the *Revelation's* latest editor quotes

I

the verdict of Philip Carrington on the *Revelation*, and makes that verdict his own: " In the case of the *Revelation* we are dealing with an artist greater than Stevenson or Coleridge or Bach. St. John has a better sense of the right word than Stevenson; he has a greater command of unearthly super-natural loveliness than Coleridge; he has a richer sense of melody and rhythm and composition than Bach. . . . It is the only masterpiece of pure art in the New Testament. . . . Its fulness and richness and harmonic variety place it far above Greek tragedy."

We shall no doubt find this book difficult and bewilder-ing; but equally doubtless we shall find it infinitely worth-while to wrestle with it until it gives us its blessing, and opens its riches to us.

Apocalyptic Literature

In any study of the *Revelation* we must begin by remem-bering one basic and essential fact. Although the *Revelation* is unique in the New Testament, it is nonetheless the New Testament representative of a kind of literature which was the commonest of all literatures between the Old and the New Testaments. The *Revelation* is commonly called the *Apocalypse*. Its title in Greek is *Apokalupsis*. Between the Old and the New Testament there grew up a great mass of what is called *Apocalyptic Literature*. Apocalyptic Litera-ture was the product and result of an undefeatable and indestructible Jewish hope.

The Jews could not forget that they were the Chosen People of God. To them that fact involved the certainty that some day they must arrive at world supremacy. Some day their enemies must be destroyed, and they them-selves must enter into the pre-eminence and the glory which was theirs by right. In their early history they looked forward to the coming of a king of David's line who would reunite the nation and lead them to greatness. There was to come forth a rod from the stem of Jesse (*Isaiah* II.I,I0).

THE REVELATION OF JOHN

God would raise up a righteous branch to David (*Jeremiah* 23.5). Some day the people would serve David their king (*Jeremiah* 30.9). David would be their shepherd and their king (*Ezekiel* 34.23; 37.24). The tabernacle of David would be repaired (*Amos* 9.11); out of Bethlehem there would come a ruler who would be great to the ends of the earth (*Micah* 5.3-5).

But the whole history of Israel gave the lie to their hopes. After the death of Solomon, the kingdom, small enough to begin with, split into two under Rehoboam and Jeroboam, and so lost its unity. The northern kingdom with its capital at Samaria, vanished in the last quarter of the eighth century B.C. before the assault of the Assyrians, and never again reappeared in history, and is now the lost ten tribes. The southern kingdom, with its capital at Jerusalem, was reduced to slavery and exile by the Babylonians in the early part of the sixth century B.C. It was later to be the subject state of the Persians, the Greeks and the Romans. History for the Jews was a catalogue of disasters, from which it became clear that no human deliverer could rescue them.

The Two Ages

Jewish thought stubbornly held to the conviction of the chosenness of the Jews, but it had to adjust itself to the facts of history. It did so by working out a scheme of history. The Jews divided all time into two ages. There was *this present age*. This present age is wholly bad; it is beyond redemption; it cannot be reformed; for it there can be nothing but total destruction and obliteration. The Jews, therefore, waited for the end of things as they are. There was *the age which is to come*. The age which is to come was to be wholly good and wholly righteous; it was to be the golden age of God; in it there would be peace, prosperity and righteousness; and in it God's chosen people would at last be vindicated, and would receive the place that was theirs by right.

3

The obvious question is, How was this present age to become the age which is to come? How was the change to be brought about? The Jews believed that this could never happen by human agency; and, therefore, they looked for the direct intervention of God. God Himself would descend into the arena of events; God Himself would come striding on to the stage of history; He would blast this present world out of existence, and bring in His own golden time. The day of the coming of God was called *The Day of the Lord.* And the Day of the Lord was to be a terrible time of terror and destruction and judgment, in which things as they are would be shattered out of existence, and the new age tempestuously born. The Day of the Lord would be the birthpangs of the new age.

All apocalyptic literature deals with these events. It deals with the sin of the present age; with the terrors of the time between; and with the blessings of the time to come. It is entirely composed of dreams and visions of the end. That means that all apocalyptic literature is necessarily cryptic. It can only use symbols and pictures. It is necessarily trying to express in human terms such things as the eye has not seen, and the ear has not heard, and which have never entered into the minds and hearts of men. Apocalyptic literature is continually attempting to describe the indescribable, to say the unsayable, to paint the unpaintable. It is always dealing with events about which no human being knows, and to express things which are beyond human words and speech to express.

This was further complicated by another fact. It is only natural that these apocalyptic visions should flame the more brightly in men's minds when men were living under tyranny and oppression and enslavement. The more some alien power held them down, the more they dreamed their dreams of the destruction of that power and of their own coming vindication. But it would only have worsened the situation, if the oppressing power could have understood

4

these dreams, and if such books fell into the hands of their tyrannous masters. Such writings would have seemed the works of rebellious revolutionaries. It, therefore, followed that such books were frequently written in code; they were deliberately couched in language which was unintelligible to the outsider; and there are many cases in which they must remain unintelligible because the key to the code no longer exists. But it does follow that the more we know about the historical background and situation of such books, the better we can interpret them, and grasp their meaning.

The Revelation

All this is the precise picture of our *Revelation*. There are any number of Jewish Apocalypses—*Enoch*, *The Sibylline Oracles*, *The Testaments of the Twelve Patriarchs*, *The Ascension of Isaiah*, *The Assumption of Moses*, *The Apocalypse of Baruch*, *Fourth Ezra*. All these are Jewish Apocalypses; our *Revelation* is a Christian Apocalypse, the only one in the New Testament, although there were many others which did not gain admission to the New Testament. It is written exactly on the Jewish pattern; it follows the basic conception of the two ages. There is this present age, wholly bad, doomed to destruction, under the domination of satanic powers; there is the golden age to come, the age of the new heavens and the new earth, when God will have made all things new. The only difference is that for the day of the Lord the Christian Apocalypse substituted the Coming in Power of Jesus Christ. Not only is the pattern the same; the details also are the same. The Jewish apocalypses had a standard apparatus of events which were to happen at the last time; these events all have their place in our *Revelation*. But before we go on to outline that pattern of events, another question arises. Both *apocalyptic* and *prophecy* deal with the events which are to come. What, then, is the difference between them?

Apocalyptic and Prophecy

The difference between the prophets and the apocalyptists was very real. There were two main differences, one of message and one of method. (i) The prophet thought in terms of this present world. His message was often a cry for social, economic, political justice; and his message was always a summons to men to obey God and to serve God within this present world. To the prophet it was this world which was to be reformed and remade; it was in this world that God's will would ultimately be done, and that God's kingdom would come. It has been put in another way which means the same—the prophet believed in history. He believed that in the events of history within time and within the world God's will and God's purpose were being worked out under the guidance of God. In one sense the prophet was an optimist, for, however sternly he condemned things as they are, he nonetheless believed that they could be mended, if men would accept the will and the commandments of God. But to the apocalyptist the world was beyond mending; it was wholly given over to evil, and dominated by evil. The apocalyptists believed, not in reformation, but in the dissolution of this present world. They did not look forward to a recreation of this world; they looked forward to the creation of a new world, when this world had been shattered into destruction by the avenging wrath of God. In one sense, therefore, the apocalyptist was a pessimist, for he did not believe that things as they are could ever be cured. True, he was quite certain that the golden age would come, but only after this world had been blasted out of existence by the fire of God. (ii) The prophet's message was spoken; it was delivered to men by word of mouth; the prophet personally, in speech, and in his own name confronted men with the message from God. On the other hand, the message of the apocalyptist was always written. Apocalyptic is a literary production. Had it been delivered by word of mouth, it is quite clear that men would never have understood it. It is difficult, involved, often unintelligible; it smells of the lamp; it has to be pored over in the study before it can be understood. Further, the prophet always spoke under his own name; all apocalyptic writings—except our one New Testament Apocalypse—are pseudonymous; that is to say, they are written under names other than that of the real author. They are put into the mouth of the great ones of the past, and are issued as the words of Noah, Enoch, Isaiah, Moses, The Twelve Patriarchs, Ezra, Baruch. There is something pathetic about this. The men who wrote the apocalyptic literature had the feeling that greatness was gone from the earth; they were too self-distrusting to put their names to their works; they attributed them to the great figures of the past, as if thereby seeking to give them an authority which their own names would never have given. As Jülicher put it: " Apocalyptic is prophecy turned senile."

The Apparatus of Apocalyptic.

As we have already said, apocalyptic literature has a pattern; it seeks to describe the things which will happen at the last times, and the blessedness which will follow; and the same pictures occur in it over and over again. It always, so to speak, worked with the same materials; and these materials find their place in our Book of the Revelation. We may briefly and summarily set out the material of apocalyptic.

(i) In apocalyptic literature the Messiah is a divine, pre-existent, otherworldly figure of power and glory, waiting to descend into the world to begin his all-conquering career. He existed in heaven before the creation of the world, before the sun and the stars were made, and he is preserved in the presence of the Almighty (*Enoch* 48.3, 6; 62.7; 4 *Ezra* 13.25, 26). He will come to put down the mighty from their seats, to dethrone the kings of the earth, and to break the teeth of sinners (*Enoch* 42.2-6; 48.2-9; 62.5-9; 69.26-29). In apocalyptic there is nothing human and

THE REVELATION OF JOHN

nothing gentle about the Messiah; he is a divine figure of
avenging power and glory before whom the earth trembles
in terror.

(ii) The coming of the Messiah was to be preceded by the
return of Elijah who would prepare the way for him
(*Malachi* 4.5, 6). Elijah was to stand upon the hills of
Israel, so the Rabbis said, and announce the coming of the
Messiah with a voice so great that it would sound from one
end of the earth to the other.

(iii) The last terrible times were known as " the travail
of the Messiah." The coming of the Messianic age would
be like the agony of birth. In the Gospels Jesus is depicted
as foretelling the signs of the end, and He is reported as
saying: " All these things are the beginnings of sorrows "
(*Matthew* 24.8; *Mark* 13.8). The word for *sorrows* is *ōdinai*,
and it literally means *birthpangs*.

(iv) The last days will be a time of terror. Even the
mighty men will cry bitterly (*Zephaniah* 1.14); the inhabitants of the land shall tremble (*Joel* 2.1); men will be
affrighted with fear, and will seek some place to hide, and
will find none (*Enoch* 102.1, 3). The apocalyptist thought
much of the terror to come.

(v) The last days will be a time when the world will be
shattered; it will be a time of cosmic upheaval when the
universe, as men know it, will be disintegrated. The stars
will be extinguished; the sun will be turned into darkness
and the moon into blood (*Isaiah* 13.10; *Joel* 2.30, 31;
3.15). The firmament will crash in ruins; there will be a
cataract of raging fire, and creation will become a molten
mass (*Sibylline Oracles* 3.83-89). The seasons will lose their
order, and there will be neither night nor dawn (*Sibylline
Oracles* 3.796-806). The earth will be shattered into pieces,
and the accepted order of things will be destroyed.

(vi) The last days will be a time when human relationships will be destroyed. Hatred and enmity will reign upon the earth. Every man's hand will be against his neighbour (*Zechariah* 14.13). Brothers will kill each other; parents will murder their own children; from dawn to sunset they shall slay one another (*Enoch* 100.1, 2). Honour will be turned into shame, and strength into humiliation, and beauty into ugliness. The man of humility will become the man of envy; and passion will hold sway over the man who once was peaceful (2 *Baruch* 48.31-37). The earth will be shattered; the closest human relationships will be disrupted; there will be nothing left but chaos.

(vii) The last days will be a time of judgment. God will come like a refiner's fire, and who may abide the day of His coming? (*Malachi* 3.1-3). It is by the fire and the sword that God will plead with men (*Isaiah* 66.15, 16). The Son of Man will destroy sinners from the earth (*Enoch* 69.27), and the smell of brimstone will pervade all things (*Sibylline Oracles* 3.58-61). The sinners will be burned up as Sodom was long ago (*Jubilees* 36.10, 11). In the last days the destroying wrath of God will walk the earth.

(viii) In all these visions the Gentiles have their place, but it is not always the same place. (*a*) Sometimes the vision is that the Gentiles will be totally destroyed. Babylon will become such a desolation that there will be no place for the wandering Arab to plant his tent among the ruins, no place for the shepherd to graze his sheep; it will be nothing more than a desert inhabited by the beasts (*Isaiah* 13.19-22). God will tread down the Gentiles in His anger (*Isaiah* 63.6). The Gentiles will come over in chains to Israel (*Isaiah* 45.14). (*b*) Sometimes there is depicted one last gathering of the Gentiles against Jerusalem, and one last battle in which they are destroyed (*Ezekiel* 38.14-39.16; *Zechariah* 14.1-11). The kings of the nations will throw themselves against Jerusalem; they will seek to ravage the shrine of the Holy One; they will place their thrones in a ring round the city, with their infidel people with them; but it will only be for their final destruction (*Sibylline Oracles* 3.663-672). (c) Sometimes there is the picture of the conversion of the Gentiles through the light of Israel. God has given Israel for a light to the Gentiles, that she may be God's salvation unto the ends of the earth (*Isaiah* 49.6). The isles wait upon God (*Isaiah* 51.5); the ends of the earth are invited to look to God and to be saved (*Isaiah* 45.20-22). The Son of Man will be a light to the Gentiles (*Enoch* 48.4, 5). Nations shall come from the end of the earth to Jerusalem to see the glory of God (*Psalms of Solomon* 17.34). Of all the pictures in connection with the Gentiles the commonest picture is that of the destruction of the Gentiles and the exaltation of Israel.

(ix) In the last days the Jews who have been scattered and exiled throughout the earth will be ingathered to the Holy City again. They will come back from Assyria and from Egypt and will worship the Lord in His holy mountain (*Isaiah* 27.12, 13). The hills will be removed, and the valleys will be filled in, and even the trees will gather to give them shade, as they come back (*Baruch* 5.5-9). Even those who died as exiles in far countries will be brought back.

(x) In the last days the New Jerusalem, which is already prepared in heaven with God (4 *Ezra* 10.44-59; 2 *Baruch* 4.2-6), will come down among men. It will be beautiful beyond compare with foundations of sapphires, and windows of agate, and gates of carbuncles, on borders of pleasant stones (*Isaiah* 54.12, 13; *Tobit* 13.16, 17). The glory of the latter house will be greater than the glory of the former (*Haggai* 2.7-9).

(xi) An essential part of the apocalyptic picture of the last days is the resurrection of the dead. " Many of them that sleep in the earth shall awake, some to everlasting life, and some to shame and everlasting contempt " (*Daniel* 12.2, 3). Sheol and the grave will give back that which has been entrusted to them (*Enoch* 51.1). The scope of the resurrection of the dead varied in different conceptions of it. Sometimes it was to apply only to the righteous in Israel; sometimes to all Israel; and sometimes to all men everywhere. Whichever of its forms this hope took, it is true to say that now for the first time we see emerging a strong hope of a life beyond the grave.

(xii) There were differences of belief as to how long the Messianic kingdom was to last. The most natural view is to think of it as lasting for ever, and, indeed, that is the most usual view. The kingdom of the saints is an everlasting kingdom (*Daniel* 7.27). There were some who believed that the reign of the Messiah would last for four hundred years. They arrived at this figure from a comparison of *Genesis* 15.13 and *Psalm* 90.15. In the *Genesis* passage Abraham is told in advance that the period of affliction of the children of Israel will be four hundred years; the psalmist's prayer is that God will make the nation glad according to the days wherein He has afflicted them, and the years wherein they have seen evil. In the *Revelation* itself the view is that there is to be a reign of the saints for a thousand years; then the final battle with the assembled powers of evil; then the golden age of God.

Such, then, were the events which the apocalyptic writers expected and pictured in the last days; and it can be seen that practically all of them find their place in the pictures and the scenes of the New Testament *Revelation*. To complete the picture we may briefly summarize the picture of the blessings of the coming age.

The Blessings of the Age to Come

(i) The divided kingdom would be united again. The house of Judah would walk again with the house of Israel (*Jeremiah* 3.18; *Isaiah* 11.13; *Hosea* 1.11). The old divisions would be healed and the people of God would be one.

(ii) There would be in the world an amazing fertility. The wilderness would become a field (*Isaiah* 32.15), it would become like the garden of Eden (*Isaiah* 51.3); the desert would rejoice and blossom as the rose (*Isaiah* 35.1). The earth will yield its fruit ten thousandfold; on each vine there will be a thousand branches, on each branch a thousand clusters; in each cluster a thousand grapes; and each grape will give a cor (120 gallons) of wine (2 *Baruch* 29.5-8). There would be a plenty such as the world had never known, and the hungry will rejoice.

(iii) A consistent part of the dream of the new age was that in it all wars would cease. The swords would be beaten into ploughshares and the spears into pruning-hooks (*Isaiah* 2.4). Great will be the peace of the children of God (*Isaiah* 54.13). There will be no sword or battle-din. There will be a common law for all men and a great peace throughout the earth, and king will be friendly with king (*Sibylline Oracles* 3.751-760).

(iv) One of the loveliest ideas concerning the new age was that in it there would be no more enmity and estrangement between the beasts and between man and the beasts. The leopard and the kid, the cow and the bear, the lion and the fatling will play and lie down together (*Isaiah* 11.6-9; 62.25). There will be a new covenant between man and the beasts of the field (*Hosea* 2.18). Even a child will be able to play where the poisonous reptiles have their holes and their dens (*Isaiah* 11.6-9; 2 *Baruch* 73.6). In all nature, between man and man, between people and people, between beast and beast, and between man and beast, there will be a universal reign of friendship, in which none will wish to do the other any harm.

(v) The coming age will bring the end of weariness, of sorrow and of pain. The people will not sorrow any more

(*Jeremiah* 31.12); everlasting joy will be upon their heads (*Isaiah* 35.10). There will be no such thing as an untimely death (*Isaiah* 65.20-22); no man will say: " I am sick " (*Isaiah* 33.24); death will be swallowed up in victory and God will wipe all tears from their faces (*Isaiah* 25.8). Disease will withdraw; anxiety, anguish and lamentation will pass away; childbirth will have no pain; the reaper will not grow weary and the builder will not be toilworn (*2 Baruch* 73.2-74.4). The age to come will be an age when what Virgil called " the tears of things " will be no more.

(vi) The age to come will be an age of righteousness. There will be perfect holiness and perfect righteousness among men. Mankind will be a good generation, living in the fear of the Lord in the days of mercy (*Psalms of Solomon* 17.28-49; 18.9, 10).

The *Revelation* is the New Testament representative of all these apocalyptic works which tell of the terrible time before the end of time, and of the blessings of the age to come; and we can see that it uses all the familiar pictures and all the familiar imagery. It may often be difficult and even unintelligible to us, but for the most part it was using pictures and ideas which those who read it, when it was first written, would know and understand.

The Author of the Revelation

We must now go on to see what we can find out about the writer of the *Revelation*.

(i) The Revelation was written by a man called John. He begins by saying that God sent the visions which he is going on to relate to His servant John (1.1). He begins the body of his book by saying that it is from John to the Seven Churches which are in Asia (1.4). He speaks of himself as John the brother and companion in tribulation of those to whom he writes (1.9). " I John," he says, " saw these things and heard them " (22.8).

THE REVELATION OF JOHN

(ii) This John was a Christian who lived in Asia in the same sphere as the Christians of the Seven Churches to whom he wrote. He calls himself the brother of those to whom he writes; and he says that he too shares in the tribulations through which they are passing (1.9). He is certainly not writing from a distance; he is writing out of the situation in Asia Minor in which his readers were.

(iii) It is fairly safe to say that he was most probably a Jew of Palestine who had come to Asia Minor late in life. We can deduce that from the kind of Greek which he wrote. He writes vivid, powerful, and pictorial Greek; but from the point of view of grammar and correctness it is easily the worst Greek in the New Testament. He can make mistakes in grammar and syntax which no schoolboy who knew Greek could make. Greek was certainly not his native language; and it is often clear that he is writing in Greek and thinking in Hebrew. It is certainly true that he was steeped in the Old Testament. He quotes, or alludes to, the Old Testament 245 times. These quotations come from about twenty Old Testament books; his favourite books are *Isaiah, Daniel, Ezekiel, Psalms, Exodus, Jeremiah, Zechariah.* Not only did he know the Old Testament intimately; he was also familiar with the Jewish apocalyptic books which were written between the Testaments.

(iv) His claim for himself is that he is a prophet, and it is on that fact that he rests his authority and his right to speak. The command of the Risen Christ to him is that he must prophesy (10.11). It is through the spirit of prophecy that Jesus gives His witness to the Church (19.10). God is the God of the holy prophets, and sends His angel to show His servants what is going to happen in the world (22.6). The angel speaks to him of his brothers the prophets (22.9). His book is characteristically prophecy, or the words of prophecy (22.7, 10, 18, 19).

14

It is here that John's authority lies. He does not call himself an apostle, as Paul does when he wishes to underline his authority and his right to speak. He has no " official " or administrative post or position in the Church; he is a prophet. He writes what he sees; and since what he sees and hears comes from God, his word is faithful and true (1.11, 19).

When John was writing, the prophets had a very special place in the Church. John was writing, as we shall see, about the year A.D.90. By that time the Church had two kinds of ministry. There was the local ministry; those who were engaged in it were settled permanently in one Church and congregation. The local ministry consisted of the elders, the deacons, and the teachers. And there was the wandering and itinerant ministry of those whose sphere of labour was not confined to any one place or congregation, but embraced the Church at large. In it there were the apostles, whose writ ran throughout the whole Church; and there were the prophets, who were wandering preachers, who had left all to listen to God, and to speak for God. The prophets were greatly respected; to question the words of a true prophet was the sin against the Holy Spirit, as the *Didache* says (11.7). The accepted order of service for the celebration of the Eucharist is laid down in the *Didache*, but at the end of it there comes the sentence: " But allow the prophets to hold the Eucharist as they will " (10.7). The prophets were regarded as uniquely the men of God, and John was a prophet.

(v) It is not likely that he was an apostle. It is not likely that he would so stress the fact that he was a prophet, if he had in fact been an apostle. And further, he speaks of the apostles, as it were, from the outside, and as if he was looking back on them as the great founders and foundations of the Church. He speaks of the twelve foundations of the wall of the Holy City, and then says, " and on them were

the names of the twelve apostles of the Lamb " (21.14).
That would hardly be likely, if he himself was one of the
apostles. That is much more the way in which one who
looked back on the apostles would speak.

This is rendered even more likely by the title of the book.
In the Authorised Version and in the Revised Version the
book is called *The Revelation of St. John the Divine*. It is
true that in the American Revised Standard Version, in
Moffatt's and in J. B. Phillips' translations, the word *the
Divine* are omitted, because they are absent from the
majority of the oldest Greek manuscripts; but, even so,
they go very far back. The Greek for *Divine* in this title is
theologos; and the word is here used in the sense in which
we speak of " the Puritan divines," and means, not John
the saintly, but, John the theologian; and the very
addition of that title seems to distinguish this John from the
John who was the apostle.

As long ago as A.D.250 Dionysius, the great scholar who
was head of the Christian school at Alexandria, saw that
it was well nigh impossible that the same man could have
written the *Revelation* and the Fourth Gospel, if for no
other reason than that the Greek is so different that the
same man could not have written both books. The Greek
of the Fourth Gospel is simple but correct enough; the
Greek of the *Revelation* is rugged and virile and vivid, but
notoriously incorrect. Further, the writer of the Fourth
Gospel studiously avoids any mention of his own name;
the John of the *Revelation* repeatedly mentions his own
name. And still further, the ideas of the two books are
different. The great ideas of the Fourth Gospel, light, life,
truth, grace, do not dominate the *Revelation*. At the same
time we can say this, that there are enough resemblances in
thought and language to make it clear that the Fourth
Gospel and the *Revelation* come from the same centre and
from the same school and from the same world of thought.

Both were written in Ephesus, and, although it is to all intents and purposes certain that the same man did not write both, they are nonetheless kindred books.

The Date of the Revelation

We have two sources which enable us to fix the date when John wrote the *Revelation*.

(i) There is the account of the writing of the book which tradition gives to us. The consistent tradition is that John was banished to Patmos in the time of Domitian; that he saw his visions in Patmos; that at the death of Domitian he was liberated and came back to Ephesus, and there set down the visions which he had seen. Victorinus, who wrote towards the end of the third century A.D., says in his commentary on the *Revelation*: " John, when he saw these things, was in the island of Patmos, condemned to the mines by Domitian the Emperor. There, therefore, he saw the revelation . . . When he was afterwards set free from the mines, he handed down this revelation which he had received from God." Jerome is even more detailed: " In the fourteenth year after the persecution of Nero, John was banished to the island of Patmos, and there wrote the *Revelation* . . . Upon the death of Domitian, and upon the repeal of his acts by the senate, because of their excessive cruelty, he returned to Ephesus, when Nerva was emperor." Eusebius says: " The apostle and evangelist John related these things to the Churches, when he had returned from exile in the island after the death of Domitian." Tradition makes it certain that John saw his visions, when he was in exile in Patmos; the only thing that is doubtful—and it is not important—is whether he wrote them down during the time of his banishment, or, when he returned to Ephesus. On this evidence we will not be wrong, if we date the *Revelation* sometime about A.D. 95.

(ii) The second line of evidence is the evidence of the material in the book itself. In the *Revelation* there is a completely new attitude to Rome and to the Roman

Empire. In the story of *Acts* it is true that the tribunal of the Roman magistrate was often the safest refuge of the Christian missionaries against the hatred of the Jews and the fury of the mob. Paul was proud that he was a Roman citizen, and again and again claimed the rights of citizenship to which every Roman citizen was entitled. In Philippi he brought the local magistrates to heel by revealing that he was a Roman citizen (*Acts* 16.36-40). In Corinth Gallio dismissed the complaints against Paul with impartial Roman justice (*Acts* 18.1-17). In Ephesus the Roman authorities were careful for the safety of Paul against the rioting mob (*Acts* 19.13-41). In Jerusalem the Roman tribune rescued Paul from what might have become a lynching (*Acts* 22.30-40). When the Roman tribune in Jerusalem heard that there was to be an attempt on Paul's life on the way to Caesarea, he took every possible step to ensure Paul's safety (*Acts* 23.12-31). When Paul despaired of justice in Palestine, he exercised his right as a citizen and appealed direct to Caesar (*Acts* 25.10, 11). When Paul wrote to the Romans, he urged upon them obedience to the powers that be, because these powers were ordained by God, and were a terror only to the evil, and not to the good (*Romans* 13.1-7). Peter's advice is exactly the same. Governors and kings are to be obeyed, for their task is given to them by God. It is a Christian's duty to fear God and to honour the emperor (I *Peter* 2.12-17). In writing to the Thessalonians it is likely that Paul points to the power of Rome as the one thing which is controlling the threatening chaos of the world (2 *Thessalonians* 2.7). But in the *Revelation* there is nothing but blazing hatred for Rome. Rome is a Babylon, the mother of harlots, drunk with the blood of the saints and the martyrs (*Revelation* 17.5, 6). John looks and hopes for nothing but the total destruction of Rome.

What is the explanation of this change in attitude? The explanation lies in the wide development of Caesar worship;

and Caesar worship with its accompanying persecution is the background of the *Revelation*. We must, therefore, see what Caesar worship was, how it arose, what it demanded, and how it affected the Christian Church.

By the time the *Revelation* was written Caesar worship was the one religion which covered the whole Roman Empire; and it was because of their refusal to conform to its demands that Christians were persecuted and killed. The essence of Caesar worship was that the reigning Roman Emperor, as embodying the spirit of Rome, was divine. Once a year everyone in the Empire had to appear before the magistrates in order to burn a pinch of incense to the godhead of Caesar, and to say: " Caesar is Lord." After he had done that, a man might go away and worship any god or goddess he liked, so long as that worship did not infringe decency and good order; but first of all he must go through the ceremony in which he acknowledged the Emperor as a god. The reason for all this was very simple. Rome had a vast heterogeneous empire, stretching from one end of the known world to another. It had in it many tongues, many races, many traditions, many countries. The problem was how to weld this varied mass into a self-conscious unity. There is no unifying force like the force of a common religion. None of the national religions, and none of the local gods, could conceivably have become universal. But Caesar worship could. It was the one common act and common belief which turned the Empire into a unity. And to refuse to burn the pinch of incense, and to refuse to say: " Caesar is Lord," was not an act of irreligion; it was an act of political disloyalty. If a man refused to go through the annual ceremony, the Romans did not regard him as an irreligious man; they regarded him as a bad and dis-affected citizen who refused to acknowledge the greatness of Caesar and the divinity of Rome. That is why the Romans dealt with the utmost severity with the man who would not say: " Caesar is Lord." And no Christian could be persuaded to give the title Lord to any one other than Jesus Christ. For the Christian—it was the centre and essence of his creed—Jesus Christ, and Jesus Christ alone is Lord.

But we must see how this Caesar worship developed, and how it was at its peak in the time when the *Revelation* was written.

One basic fact must be noted. Caesar worship was not imposed on the people by the government from above. It arose from the people; it might even be said that it arose in spite of efforts of the early Emperors to stop it, or at least to curb it. And it is to be noted that of all the people in the Empire only the Jews were exempt from it.

Caesar worship began as a spontaneous outburst of gratitude to Rome. The people of the provinces well knew what they owed to Rome. Impartial Roman justice had taken the place of capricious and tyrannical oppression. Security had taken the place of insecurity. The great Roman roads spanned the world; and the roads were safe from brigands and the seas were cleared of pirates. Roman justice was a reality; the *pax Romana*, the Roman peace, was the greatest thing which ever happened to the ancient world. As Virgil had it, Rome felt her destiny to be " to spare the fallen and to cast down the proud." Life had a new security and a new order about it. E. J. Goodspeed writes: " This was the *pax Romana*. The provincial under Roman sway found himself in a position to conduct his business, provide for his family, send his letters, and make his journeys in security, thanks to the strong hand of Rome."

Caesar worship did not begin with the deification of the Emperor. It began with the deification of Rome. The spirit of the Empire was deified under the name of the goddess Roma; Roma was Rome personified. She stood for all the strong and benevolent power of the Empire. The first temple to Roma was erected in Smyrna as far back as 195 B.C. It was no great step to think of the spirit of Rome being incarnated in one man, in the Emperor. It was the Emperor who embodied and personified Rome. The worship of the Emperor began with the worship of Julius Caesar after his death. In 29 B.C. the Emperor Augustus granted to the provinces of Asia and Bithynia permission to erect temples in Ephesus and Nicaea for the joint worship of the goddess Roma and the deified Julius Caesar. At these shrines Roman citizens were encouraged and even exhorted to worship. But then another step was taken. To provincials who were *not* Roman citizens Augustus gave permission to erect temples in Pergamum in Asia, and in Nicomedia in Bithynia, for the worship of Roma and *himself*. At first, then, the worship of the reigning Emperor was considered to be something permissible for provincial non-citizens, but not for those who had the dignity of the citizenship.

But there was an inevitable development. It is human to worship a god who can be seen rather than a spirit which is after all only an abstraction. And bit by bit men began more and more to worship the Emperor himself instead of the goddess Roma. It still required special permission from the senate to erect a temple to the living Emperor, but by the middle of the first century that permission was more and more freely given. Bit by bit Caesar worship was becoming the universal religion of the Roman Empire. Some men might worship some gods; but all men began to join in the worship of Caesar. A priesthood developed; the worship was organised into presbyteries, whose officials were held in the highest honour.

It is to be noted, as we have already indicated, that this worship was never intended to be exclusive. It was not meant to wipe out other religions. Rome was essentially tolerant. A man might worship Caesar *and* his own god. But more and more Caesar worship became a test of political loyalty; it became the bond which held all loyal citizens together; it became, as it has been said, the recognition of the dominion of Caesar over a man's life, and, indeed, over his soul. Let us, then trace the development of this worship under the Emperors up to, and immediately beyond, the writing of the Revelation.

(i) Augustus, who died in A.D. 14, allowed the worship of Julius Caesar, his great predecessor. He allowed non-citizens in the provinces to worship himself, but he did not permit citizens to do so; and he certainly made no attempt to enforce this worship.

(ii) Tiberius (A.D. 14-37) entered into a situation in which he could not halt Caesar worship. He forbade temples to be built, and priests to be appointed, for his own worship. And in a letter to Gython, a Laconian city, he definitely refused divine honours for himself. So far from enforcing Caesar worship, he actively discouraged it.

(iii) Caligula (A.D. 37-41), the next Emperor, was an epileptic, a madman, and a megalomaniac. He insisted on divine honours. He attempted to enforce Caesar worship even on the Jews, who had always been, and who always were to remain, exempt from it. He planned to place his own image in the Holy of Holies in the Temple in Jerusalem, a step which would certainly have provoked unyielding rebellion. Mercifully he died before he could carry out his plans. But in his reign we have an episode when Caesar worship became an imperial demand.

(iv) Caligula was succeeded by Claudius (A.D. 41-54). Claudius completely reversed the insane policy of the mad Caligula. He wrote to the governor of Egypt—there were a million Jews in Alexandria—fully approving of the Jewish refusal to call the Emperor a god, and granting them full liberty to enjoy their own worship and their own religion. On his accession to the throne, he wrote to Alexandria saying: " I deprecate the appointment of a High Priest to me, and the erection of temples, for I do not wish to be offensive to my contemporaries, and I hold that sacred fanes and the like have been by all ages attributed to the immortal gods as peculiar honours." Once again, Claudius sought to control rather than to encourage Caesar worship.

(v) Nero (A.D. 54-68) did not take his own divinity seriously, and did nothing to insist on Caesar worship. It is true that he persecuted the Christians; but he did not persecute them because they would not worship himself; he persecuted them because he had to find scapegoats for the great fire of Rome, for which, it is almost certain, he himself was responsible.

(vi) On the death of Nero there were three Emperors in eighteen months—Galba, Otto and Vitellius, and in such a time of chaos the question of Caesar worship did not arise.

(vii) The next two Emperors Vespasian (A.D. 69-79) and Titus (A.D. 79-81) were wise and sound rulers, who still made no insistence on Caesar worship.

(viii) But with the coming of Domitian (A.D. 81-96) there came a complete change. Domitian was a devil. He was the worst of all things—a cold-blooded persecutor. With the exception of the mad Caligula, he was the first Emperor to take his divinity seriously, and to *demand* Caesar worship. The difference was that Caligula was an insane devil; Domitian was a sane devil which is much more terrifying. He erected a monument to " the deified Titus son of the deified Vespasian." He began a campaign of bitter persecution against all those who would not worship the ancient gods—" the atheists " as he called them. In particular he launched his hatred against the Jews and the Christians. When he arrived in the theatre with his empress, the crowd were urged to rise and shout: " All hail to our Lord and his Lady!" He enacted that he himself was a god. He informed all provincial governors that government announcements and proclamations must begin: " Our Lord and God Domitian commands . . ." Everyone who addressed him in speech or in writing must begin: " Lord and God."

Here is the background of the *Revelation*. All over the Empire men and women must call Domitian god—or die. Caesar worship was the deliberate policy; all men must say: " Caesar is Lord." There was no escape.

What were the Christians to do? What hope had they? They had not many wise and not many mighty. They had no influence, no power, no prestige. Against them there had risen the might of Rome which no nation and no people had ever stood against. They were confronted with the absolute choice—Caesar or Christ. It was to encourage men in times like that that the *Revelation* was written. In a time of mounting terror John did not shut his eyes to the terrors; he saw dreadful things and he saw still more dreadful things on the way; but beyond them he saw the bliss and the glory for those who defied Caesar for the love of Christ. The *Revelation* comes from one of the most heroic ages in all the history of the Christian Church. It is true that Domitian's successor Nerva (A.D. 96-98) repealed the savage and the penal laws; but the damage was done; the Christians were outlaws; and the *Revelation* is the clarion call to be faithful unto death in order to win the crown of life.

The Book worth Studying

No one can shut his eyes to the difficulty of the *Revelation*. It is the most difficult book in the Bible; but it is infinitely worth studying for it contains the blazing faith of the Christian Church in the days when life was an agony, when men expected the end of the heavens and the earth as they knew them, and when they still believed that beyond the terror there was the glory, and that above the raging of men was the power of Almighty God.

REVELATION

GOD'S REVELATION TO MEN

Revelation I.1-3

> This is the revelation revealed by Jesus Christ, the revelation which God gave to Him to show to His servants, the revelation which tells of the things which must soon happen. This revelation Jesus Christ sent and explained through His angel to His servant John, who testified to the word sent to him by God and attested by the witness borne by Jesus Christ, everything which he saw.

THIS book which we are to study is called sometimes the *Revelation* and sometimes the *Apocalypse*. The Authorized Version begins with the word: "The Revelation of Jesus Christ." The meaning of that phrase is not the Revelation which tells *about* Jesus Christ, but the Revelation which was given *by* Jesus Christ. The Greek word for *revelation* is *apokalupsis*, from which we get the word *Apocalypse*, and which is a word with a history.

(i) The word *apokalupsis* is composed of two parts. *Apo* means *away from*, and *kalupsis* means a *hiding* or a *veiling*. *Apokalupsis*, therefore, means an *unhiding, the taking away of a veil, a revealing*. It was not originally a specially religious word; it meant simply the revealing or the disclosure of any fact. There is an interesting use of it in Plutarch (*How to tell a Flatterer from a Friend*, 32). Plutarch tells how once Pythagoras severely rebuked a devoted disciple of his in public, whereat the young man went out and hanged himself. "From that time on Pythagoras never admonished anyone when anyone else was present. For error should be treated as a foul disease, and all admonition and *disclosure* (*apokalupsis*) should be in secret." *Apokalupsis*, then, is an unveiling, a revealing, a disclosure of that which is hidden and secret. But the word became very specially a Christian word.

25

(ii) It is used for the revealing of God's will to us for our actions. Paul says that he went up to Jerusalem by *apokalupsis*. He went because God told him that that was what He wanted him to do (*Galatians* 2.2).

(iii) It is used of the revelation of God's truth to men. Paul received his gospel, not from men, but by *revelation*, *apokalupsis*, from Jesus Christ (*Galatians* 1.12). In the Christian assembly the message of the preacher is an *apokalupsis*, a *revelation* (I *Corinthians* 14.6).

(iv) It is used of God's revealing to men of His own mysteries, especially of the revelation of God which came in the Incarnation of Jesus Christ (*Romans* 16.25; *Ephesians* 3.3). The coming of Jesus Christ into the world is the unveiling of the God who by His very majesty had been hidden from the eyes of men since the beginning of the world.

(v) It is specially used of the revelation of the power and the holiness of God which is to come at the last days, at the end of things, and at the Second Coming. That will be an unveiling of judgment (*Romans* 2.5); but for the Christian who knows and has accepted the merits of Jesus Christ it will be an unveiling of praise and glory (I *Peter* 1.7); of grace (I *Peter* 1.13); of joy (I *Peter* 4.13).

Before we go on to look at the more technical use of the word *apokalupsis*, we may note two things.

(i) This revelation, this unveiling, this giving of knowledge is connected specially with the work of the Holy Spirit, who is the Spirit of revelation (*Ephesians* 1.17).

(ii) We are bound to see that here we have a picture of the whole of the Christian life. There is no part of it which is not lit by the revelation of God. God reveals to us what we must do and what we must say; in Jesus Christ God reveals Himself to us, for he who has seen Jesus has seen the Father (*John* 14.9); and life moves on to the great and final consummation and revelation, in which there is judgment for those who have not submitted to God, but grace and glory and joy for those who are in Jesus Christ. Revelation is no technical theological idea; it is that which God is offering to all who will listen.

Now we must look at the technical meaning of the word *apokalupsis*, for that meaning is specially connected with the book which we are studying.

The Jews had long since ceased to hope that they would be vindicated as the chosen people by human means. They hoped now for nothing less than the direct intervention of God in human affairs in their favour. To that end they divided all time into two ages. There was *this present age*, which is wholly bad, and wholly given over to evil; and there was *the age to come*, in which there will be a new heaven and new earth, and which will be the age of God. Between the two there was to be a time of terrible trial and trouble, when the present world would be disintegrated and destroyed, and when judgment would come. In between the Old and the New Testament the Jews wrote many books which were visions of the dreadful time before the end, and visions of the blessedness that would be. These books were called *Apokalypses*; that was the technical name for them. We still possess many of these books— *The Sibylline Oracles, the Book of Enoch, The Testaments of the Twelve Patriarchs, The Apocalypse of Baruch, Fourth Ezra*. This is exactly what our *Book of the Revelation* is. It is not an isolated book, although there is nothing like it in the New Testament. It belongs to a class of literature which was common between the Testaments. All these books are wild and unintelligible, for they are all visions of a time in which no man knew what would happen, and they are all trying to describe the indescribable and to put into words that which is beyond words. An *Apocalypse* was a vision of the terrible end of this world, and the glorious beginning of the new world. Many such books circulated in the ancient world; and our book is one of them; and the very subject with which it deals is the reason why it is so difficult to understand.

THE MEANS OF GOD'S REVELATION

Revelation I.I-3 (*continued*)

THIS short section gives us a concise account of how revelation comes to men. The revelation of the truth was given by God to Jesus, and Jesus sent it through His angel to John.

(i) Revelation begins with God. God is the fountain and the source of all truth. Every truth which men discover is two things at one and the same time—it is a discovery of the human mind, and it is a gift of God. But it must always be remembered that men never *create* the truth; they *receive* the truth from God. We must also remember that that reception of the truth from God comes in two ways. It comes from *earnest seeking*. God gave men minds, and it is often through our minds that God speaks to us. Quite certainly God does not grant His truth to the man who is too lazy to think. It comes from *reverent waiting*. But at the same time God sends His truth to the man who not only thinks strenuously, but to the man who waits quietly in prayer and in devotion. But it must be remembered that prayer and devotion are not simply passive things. They are the intense, dedicated, concentrated listening for the voice of God.

(ii) God gives this revelation to Jesus Christ. The Bible never allows us to forget the majestic loneliness of God. The Bible never, as it were, makes a second God of Jesus. Rather it stresses the utter dependence of Jesus on God. " My teaching," said Jesus, " is not mine, but His that sent me " (*John* 7.16). " I do nothing of myself; but, as the Father hath taught me, I speak these things " (*John* 8.28). " I have not spoken of myself, but the Father which sent me, He gave me a commandment, what I should say and what I should speak " (*John* 12.49). It is God's truth that Jesus brings to men; and that is precisely why the teaching of Jesus is unique and final, because it is based in the very being of God Himself.

(iii) Jesus, as the writer of the *Revelation* says (I.I), sent that truth to John through His angel. Here the writer of the *Revelation* was a child of his day. At this time in history men were specially conscious of what is called the transcendence of God. That is to say, they were impressed above all things with the difference and the distance between God and man. So much did they stress this difference, that they came to feel that direct communication between God and man was impossible, that there must always be some intermediary. In the Old Testament story Moses received the Law directly from the hands of God. In the Old Testament story (*Exodus* 19 and 20) there is no question of any intermediary. It is directly from God that Moses receives the Law. But twice in the New Testament it is said that the Law was given by angels (*Acts* 7.53; *Galatians* 3.19). When we think of the time at which the New Testament was being written, we must think of a time when men were so conscious of the immense distance of God that they felt that some intermediary between Him and man must be necessary. And that is the reason for the introduction of the angel into the story.

(iv) Finally, the revelation is given to John. One of the most uplifting things to remember is the part that men play in the coming of the revelation of God. God must find a man to whom He can entrust His truth. God must find a man into whose mind He can pour His truth, and whom He can use as His mouthpiece to men.

(v) Let us note the *content* of the revelation which came to John. It was the revelation of " the things which *must quickly* happen " (I.I). There are two important words there. There is the word *must*. History is not haphazard; in life and in the world there is purpose; and that purpose is being necessarily worked out. There is the word *quickly*. Here is the proof that it is quite wrong to use the *Revelation* as a kind of mysterious celestial timetable of what is going to happen thousands of years from now. As John saw it, the events in it were working themselves out in the immediate happenings and events which were coming upon the world. If the *Revelation* is to be interpreted at all, it must be interpreted against the background of its own time.

SERVANTS OF GOD

Revelation 1.1-3 (continued)

TWICE the word *servant* appears in this passage. The revelation sent by God was sent to His *servants,* and it was sent through His *servant* John. In Greek the word is *doulos* and in Hebrew *ebedh.* Both these words are difficult fully to translate. The normal translation of *doulos* is *slave.* The real *servant* of God is, in fact, the *slave* of God. A servant can leave his service when he likes; a servant has stated hours of work and stated hours of freedom; a servant works for pay and for a wage; a servant has a will and mind of his own, and can bargain as to when, and for what, he will give and withhold his labour. A slave can do none of these things; a slave is the absolute possession of his owner, with neither time nor a will of his own. The words *doulos* and *ebedh* bring out how absolutely we must surrender life to God.

It is of the greatest interest to note to whom these words are applied in Scripture.

Abraham is the servant of God (*Genesis* 26.24; *Psalm* 105.42). Oftener than anyone else Moses is called the servant of God (*Exodus* 14.31; *Numbers* 12.7; *Deuteronomy* 34.5; *Joshua* 1.1, 2, 7, 13, 15; 8.31; 11.12; I *Chronicles* 6.49; 2 *Chronicles* 24.6; *Nehemiah* 1.7; 10.19; *Psalm* 105.26; 132.10; 144.10; *Daniel* 9.11). Jacob is the servant of God (*Isaiah* 44.1, 2; 45.4; *Ezekiel* 37.25). Caleb and Joshua are the servants of God (*Numbers* 14.24; *Joshua* 24.9; *Judges* 2.8). David is second only to Moses as characteristically the servant of God (I *Kings* 8.66; 11.36; 2 *Kings*

19.34; 20.6; I *Chronicles* 17.4; in the titles of *Psalms* 18
and 36; *Psalm* 89.3; *Ezekiel* 34.24). Elijah is the servant of
God (2 *Kings* 9.36; 10.10). Isaiah is the servant of God
(*Isaiah* 20.3). Job is the servant of God (*Job* 1.8; 42.7).
The prophets are the servants of God (2 *Kings* 21.10;
Amos 3.7). The apostles are the servants of God (*Philippians* 1.1; *Titus* 1.1; *James* 1.1; *Jude* 1; *Romans* 1.1;
2 *Corinthians* 4.5). A man like Epaphras is the servant of
God (*Colossians* 4.12). All Christians are the servants of
God (*Ephesians* 6.6).

Two things emerge from this.

(i) The greatest men regarded as their greatest honour
the fact that they were servants of God. There was no
higher title to which they could aspire. The summit of their
ambition was the service of God. The motto of the Prince
of Wales, beneath the crest of the three feathers is, " I
serve." No man can be anything greater than the servant
of God.

(ii) We must note the width of this service. Moses, the
law-giver; Abraham, the adventurous pilgrim; David,
shepherd boy, sweet singer of Israel, king of the nation;
Caleb and Joshua, soldiers and men of action; Elijah and
Isaiah, prophets and men of God; Job, faithful in misfortune; the apostles, who bore to men the story of Jesus;
every Christian—all can aspire to the title *servant of God*.

There is none whom God cannot use, if he will submit
himself to His service.

THE BLESSEDS OF GOD

Revelation 1.1-3 (*continued*)

THIS passage ends with a threefold blessing.

(i) The man who reads these words is blessed. The
reader here mentioned is not the private reader, but the man
who publicly reads the word in the presence of the congregation. The reading of Scripture was an essential part of

any Jewish service (*Luke* 4.16; *Acts* 13.15). It was, in fact, the centre of any Jewish service. In the Jewish synagogue Scripture was read to the congregation by seven ordinary members of the congregation, although if a priest or levite was present he took precedence. In the synagogue the ordinary man had the privilege and duty of reading Scripture to the people. The Christian Church took much of its service from the synagogue order, and the reading of Scripture remained a central part of the service. Justin Martyr gives us our earliest account of what a Christian service was like; and it includes the reading of " the memoirs of the apostles (i.e. the Gospels), and the writings of the prophets " (Justin Martyr, 1.67). The office of *reader* became in time an official office in the Church comparable with any other office. One of Tertullian's complaints about the heretical sects was the way in which a man could too speedily arrive at office without any training for it. He writes: " And so it comes to pass that today one man is their bishop, and tomorrow another; today he is a deacon who tomorrow is a *reader* " (Tertullian, *On Prescription against Heretics*, 41). It may well be that we have lost something valuable by taking from the laity the privilege and duty of reading the Scriptures in the assembly of the people.

The preacher and the teacher and the lay reader must never forget that one of the greatest privileges in the Church is to read Scripture to the assembled congregation. The Jews had a saying that he who teaches another the Law has as great a privilege as Moses had when he first received the Law from the hands of God.

(ii) The man who hears these words is blessed. We would do well to remember how great a privilege it is to hear the word of God in our own tongue. That was a privilege which was dearly bought. Men died to give it to us; and the professional clergy sought for long to keep it to themselves. There were martyrs who died that we might have God's word in our own tongue. To this day the task of giving men the Scriptures in their own tongue goes on. In 1958 The British and Foreign Bible Society alone had in progress the translation of the Scriptures into no fewer than two hundred and twenty-seven languages, and there are still many who have no word of Scripture in their own tongue. It is no small privilege to hear the word of God.

(iii) The man who keeps these words is blessed. To hear God's word is a privilege; to obey it is a duty. There is no real Christianity in the man who hears and forgets, or who hears and deliberately disregards. Every privilege brings with it a corresponding responsibility; and the privilege of hearing brings the responsibility of remembering and obeying.

That is all the more true because the time is short. The time, says John, is near (verse 3). The early Church lived in the vivid expectation of the coming of Jesus Christ at any moment, and, as it has been well put, that expectation was " the ground of hope in distress and constant heed to warning." Apart altogether from that, no man knows the hour when the call of God will come to him to take him from this earth, and, that he may meet God with confidence, he must add the obedience of his life to the listening of his ear.

We may here note that there are seven *blesseds* in the *Revelation*.

(i) There is the *blessed* which we have just studied. We may call it The Blessedness of Reading, Hearing and Obeying the Word of God.

(ii) Blessed are the dead which die in the Lord from henceforth (14.13). We may call it The Blessedness in Heaven of Christ's Friends on Earth.

(iii) Blessed is he that watcheth and keepeth his garments (16.15). We may call it The Blessedness of the Watchful Pilgrim.

(iv) Blessed are they which are called unto the marriage supper of the Lamb (19.9). We may call it The Blessedness of the invited Guests of God.

(v) Blessed and holy is he that hath part in the first resurrection (20.6). We may call it The Blessedness of the Man whom Death cannot touch.

(vi) Blessed is he that keepeth the sayings of this book (22.7). We may call it The Blessedness of the Wise Reader of God's Word.

(vii) Blessed are they that do His commandments (22.14). We may call it The Blessedness of those who Hear and Obey.

Such is the blessedness which is open to every Christian in Christ.

THE MESSAGE AND ITS DESTINATION

Revelation 1.4-6

> This is John writing to the seven Churches which are in Asia. Grace be to you and peace, from Him who is, and who was, and who is to come, and from the seven spirits which are before His throne, and from Jesus Christ, the witness on whom you can rely, the first-born of the dead, and the ruler of the kings of the earth. To Him who loves us and who set us free from our sins at the cost of His own blood, and who made us a kingdom, priests to His God and Father, to Him be glory and dominion for ever. Amen.

THE whole of the *Revelation* is a letter, and here is the beginning of the letter. It is written to the *seven Churches which are in Asia*. In the New Testament Asia is never the continent of Asia, but always the Roman province of Asia. The province had once been the kingdom of Attalus the Third, and he had willed it to the Romans at his death. It included the western sea-coast of Asia Minor, on the shores of the Mediterranean, with Phrygia, Mysia, Caria and Lycia in the hinterland; and its capital was the city of Pergamos. The Asia which the New Testament knew was a small part of Asia Minor, and not the vast continent of which we use the word.

He writes to the seven Churches, which in verse 11 he goes on to name—Ephesus, Smyrna, Pergamos, Thyatira, Sardis, Philadelphia, Laodicea. These were by no means the only Churches in Asia. There were Churches at Colossae (*Colossians* 1.2); Hierapolis (*Colossians* 4.12); Troas (2 *Corinthians* 2.12; *Acts* 20.5); Miletus (*Acts* 20.17); Magnesia and Tralles, as the letters of Ignatius, the Bishop of Antioch, show. Why, then, did John single out only these seven Churches from the whole province? There can be more than one reason for his selection.

(i) These seven Churches might be regarded as the centres of seven postal districts; they were all on a kind of ring road which circled round the interior of the province. If letters were delivered to them, they would circulate in the districts of which these towns were the centres. Troas was off the beaten track. But Hierapolis and Colossae were within walking distance of Laodicea; and Tralles, Magnesia and Miletus was close to Ephesus. Letters delivered to these seven cities would easily circulate in the surrounding areas; and it must be remembered that every letter had to be hand-written, and, therefore, each letter would need to be sent to the district where it would reach most easily the greatest number of people.

(ii) Any reading of the *Revelation* will show John's preference for the number seven. The number seven occurs fifty-four times in the *Revelation*. There are seven candlesticks (1.12), seven stars (1.16), seven lamps (4.5), seven seals (5.1), seven horns and seven eyes (5.6), seven thunders (10.3), seven angels, plagues and vials (15.6, 7, 8). The ancient peoples regarded the number seven as the perfect number, and it runs all through the *Revelation*. From this certain of the early commentators drew an interesting conclusion. Seven is the perfect number because seven stands for *completeness*. It is, therefore, suggested that, when John wrote to *seven* Churches, he was, in fact, writing to the *whole* Church in all its completeness. The first list of New Testament books is called The Muratorian Canon. It lists the books with brief explanatory notes about each. It says of the *Revelation*: " For John also, though he wrote in the *Revelation* to seven Churches, nevertheless speaks to them all." This is all the more likely when we remember how often John says: " He that hath an ear, let him hear what the Spirit is saying to the Churches " (2.7, 11, 17, 29; 3.6, 13, 22). John actually wrote to seven Churches, but the very completeness of the number seven indicates that his message is to the *whole Church*, and is still meant for us today.

(iii) Although the reasons we have adduced for the choice of these seven Churches may well be true, it may well be still truer that the reason why John chose these seven Churches is simpler than any of them. He may have chosen these seven Churches, because in them his writ specially ran, and in them he had a special place, a special influence, and a special authority. They were in a special sense *his* Churches, and by speaking to them he sent a message first to those who knew him and loved him best, and then through them to every Church in every place in every generation.

THE BLESSING AND ITS SOURCE

Revelation 1.4-6 (*continued*)

HE begins by sending them the blessing of God.

He sends them *grace*, and grace means all the splendour of the undeserved gifts of the wondrous love of God to men. He sends them *peace*, and R. C. Charles finely describes *peace* as " the harmony restored between God and man through Christ." The peace which we know is the result of the grace which God gave. But there are two extraordinary things in this greeting.

(i) John sends blessings from Him who is, and who was, and who is to come. That is in itself a common title for God. In *Exodus* 3.14 the word of God to Moses is " I am that I am." The Jewish Rabbis explained that by saying that God meant: " I was; I still am; and in the future

THE REVELATION OF JOHN

I will be." The Greeks spoke of "Zeus who was, Zeus who is, and Zeus who will be." The Orphic worshippers said: "Zeus is the first, and Zeus is the last; Zeus is the head and Zeus is the middle; and from Zeus all things come." This is what in *Hebrews* so beautifully became: "Jesus Christ, the same yesterday, today and for ever" (*Hebrews* 13.8).

But to get the full meaning of this we must look at it in the Greek, for John bursts the bonds of language and of grammar to show his reverence for God. We translate the first phrase that the blessing comes *from Him who is*; but that is not what the Greek says. The normal form of a Greek noun is the nominative case, when that noun is the subject of a sentence, but, when the noun is governed by a preposition it changes its case, and it *changes its form*. It is so in English. *He* is the subject of a sentence; *Him* is the object. When John says that the blessing comes *from Him who is* he should have put the phrase *Him who is* in the genitive case after the preposition; but quite ungrammatically he leaves it unchanged in the nominative. It is as if we said in English quite ungrammatically *from He who is*, and refused to change *He* into *Him*; that is precisely what John does. And why? Because he has such an immense reverence for God that he refuses to alter the form of the name of God, even when the rules of grammar demand an alteration. So much does John reverence the name of God, that that name must remain for ever and unalterably the same. It is impossible to show this in an English translation; but in Greek John's insistence on the unalterability of the name of God is very impressive.

But John is not finished with his amazing use of language. The second phrase is *from Him who was*. Literally, John says *From the He was*. The point is this; *who was* would be in Greek a participle. Now the odd things is that the verb *eimi* which means *to be* has no past participle. In place of that participle there is used the participle *genomenos* which is part of the verb *gignomai*; now *gignomai* means not only *to be*; it also means *to become*; *becoming* implies alteration and change; and John utterly refuses to apply any word to God that will imply any change; and so he uses a Greek phrase that is impossible in grammar and that no one ever used before—calling God *the He was*—because again he wishes to preserve the absolute changelessness of God. Such was the reverence of John for God that he defies grammar rather than alter the letters of the name of God, and rather than dare to use of God a word which implies that God could change in any way.

In the terrible days in which he was writing John stayed his heart on the changelessness of God, and used the defiance of grammar to underline his faith.

THE SEVENFOLD SPIRIT

Revelation 1.4-6 (*continued*)

ANYONE who reads this passage must be astonished at the form of the Trinity which we meet here. We speak of the Trinity in the form of the Father, the Son and the Holy Spirit. Here in John's form we have God, the Father, and we have Jesus Christ, the Son, but instead of the Holy Spirit we have *the seven Spirits which are before His throne*. What is the explanation of this strange phrase, and who, and what, are these seven Spirits? These seven Spirits are mentioned more than once in the *Revelation* (3.1; 4.5; 5.6). Three main explanations have been offered of them.

(i) The Jews talked of the seven angels of the presence, the angels whom they beautifully called " the seven first white ones " (I *Enoch* 90.21). They were what we call the archangels, and " they stand and enter before the glory of the Lord " (*Tobit* 12.15). Their names are not always the same, but they are often called Uriel, Rafael, Raguel, Michael, Gabriel, Saiquael and Jeremiel. These angels had the care of the elements of the world—fire, air and water—and they were the guardian angels of the nations, to which each of them was assigned. They were the most illustrious and the most intimate servants of God. Perhaps if we traced them far enough back into the primitive thoughts of men we would come to a time when men worshipped, not one, but seven gods, as, for instance, the Babylonians worshipped the seven star gods; and it may be that these seven archangels, if we go far enough back in religious thought, go back to that. As we have said, in Jewish thought they were closest of all to God; and some think that they are the seven Spirits mentioned here. But that cannot be; great as the angels were, they were still created beings. Not from them, but only from the uncreated God, could blessings come to men.

(ii) The second explanation connects this with the famous passage in *Isaiah* 11.2. There we have the promise: "The spirit of the Lord shall rest upon him, the spirit of wisdom and understanding, the spirit of counsel and might, the spirit of knowledge and piety; by this spirit he shall be filled with the fear of God." That is how the passage runs in the Septuagint, the Greek version of the Old Testament. It is this passage which is the basis of the great conception of *the sevenfold gifts of the Spirit*. It is of this that the hymn is thinking, when it sings:

> Come, Holy Ghost, our hearts inspire
> And lighten with celestial fire;
> Thou the anointing Spirit art,
> Who dost Thy sevenfold gifts impart.

The Spirit, as Beatus said, is one in name, but sevenfold in virtues. If, then, we think of the sevenfold gift of the Spirit, it is not difficult to think of the Spirit as, as it were, seven Spirits, each giving the great gifts to men. So, then, it is suggested that the famous conception of the sevenfold gifts of the Spirit gave rise to the idea of the seven Spirits before the throne of God.

(iii) The third explanation connects the idea of the seven Spirits with the fact of the seven Churches. In *Hebrews* 2.4 we read of God, as the Authorized Version has it, giving

" gifts of the Holy Ghost." The word which is translated
gifts is *merismos*, and it really means *shares*, as if the idea
was that God gives a share of His Spirit to every man. So
the idea here would be that the seven Spirits stand for the
share of the Spirit which God gave to each one of the seven
Churches. It would mean that there is no Christian fellowship and assembly left without the presence and the
visitation and the power and the illumination of the Spirit.

THE TITLES OF JESUS

Revelation 1.4-6 (*continued*)

IN this passage three great titles are ascribed to Jesus Christ.

(i) He is the witness on whom we can rely. It is a
favourite idea of the Fourth Gospel that Jesus is a witness
of the truth and the things of God. Jesus said to Nicodemus:
" Verily, verily, I say unto you, We speak that we do know,
and testify (literally *bear witness to*) that we have seen "
(*John* 3.11). Jesus said to Pilate: " For this cause came I
into the world, that I should bear witness to the truth "
(*John* 18.37). A witness is above all and essentially a person
who speaks from first-hand knowledge. A witness is a
person who tells what his eyes have seen, and what his ears
have heard. That is why Jesus is God's witness. Because
He came from God, because He identified Himself with the
will of God, He is able to speak at first-hand about God and
God's truth as no one else in all the world can. Jesus is
uniquely the person with first-hand knowledge about God.

(ii) He is the first-born of the dead. The word for *first-
born* is *prōtotokos*. This word can have two meanings. (*a*) It
can mean literally *first-born*. If it is used in this sense, the
reference must be to the Resurrection. Through His
Resurrection Jesus gained a new victory over death,
which all those who believe in Him may share. (*b*) Since
the first-born son was the son who inherited his father's
honour and power, *prōtotokos* comes to mean *one with power*

and honour, one who occupies the first place, a prince among
men. When Paul speaks of Jesus as being the first-born of
all creation (*Colossians* 1.15), he means that Jesus is the
Lord of the universe; to Him the first and the unique
place of honour and glory belongs. If we take the word in
this sense it means that Jesus is Lord of the dead as he is
Lord of the living. It is probably in this sense that we
ought to take the word. There is no part of the universe,
in this world or in the world to come, there is nothing in
life or in death of which Jesus Christ is not Lord; and,
therefore, nothing in life or in death can separate us from
Him.

(iii) He is the ruler of the kings of the earth. There
are two things to note here. (*a*) This is a quotation, or a
reminiscence of *Psalm* 89.27: " I will make Him my
first-born, higher than the kings of the earth." That was
always taken by the Jewish scholars to be a description
of the coming Messiah; and, therefore, to say that Jesus
is the ruler of the kings of the earth is to claim that He is
the Messiah, promised by God and long awaited. (*b*) Swete
very beautifully points out the connection between this
title of Jesus and the temptation story. In the temptation
story the devil took Jesus up into a high mountain and
showed Him all the kingdoms of the earth and the glory
of them, and said: " All these things will I give Thee, if
Thou wilt fall down and worship me " (*Matthew* 4.8, 9;
Luke 4.6, 7). It was the devil's claim that the kingdoms
of the earth were delivered into his power (*Luke* 4.6);
and it was his suggestion that, if Jesus would strike a bargain
with him, he would give Him a share in them. Now the
amazing thing is that what the devil promised Jesus—
and could never have given Him—Jesus won for Himself
by the suffering of the Cross and the power of the Resurrection. The Risen Christ is ruler of the kings of the earth
in virtue of His Cross and in virtue of His rising again, for
it was when He was lifted up on His Cross that He drew
all men unto Him (*John* 12.32). Not compromise with evil,

but the unswerving loyalty and the unfailing love which accepted the Cross brought Jesus His universal lordship.

WHAT JESUS DID FOR MEN

Revelation 1.4-6 (*continued*)

THERE are few passages which set down with such splendour what Jesus did for men.

(i) He loves us and He set us free from our sins at the cost of His own blood. We must first note here that the Authorized Version is certainly in error. It reads: " Unto Him that loved us and *washed* us from our sins in His own blood." The words *to wash* and *to set free* are in Greek very alike. *To wash* is *louein*; *to set free* is *luein*; and they are pronounced exactly in the same way. They are words which are very easy to confuse. But there is no doubt at all that the oldest and the best Greek manuscripts read *luein* which is *to set free*. Again the phrase *in His own blood* is a mistranslation. The word that is translated *in* is *en*, and, it is true that it can mean *in*; but here it is a translation of the Hebrew word *be* (the *e* is pronounced very short as the *e* in *the*), which means *at the price of*. What Jesus did, as John sees it, is that He freed us from our sins at the cost of His own blood. This is exactly what he says later on when he speaks of those who were redeemed to God by the blood of the Lamb (5.9). It is exactly what Paul meant when he spoke of us being *redeemed* from the curse of the Law (*Galatians* 3.13); and when he spoke of *redeeming* those who were under the Law (*Galatians* 4.5). In both cases the word he used is *exagorazein*, which means *to buy out from*, to pay the price of buying a person or a thing out of the possession of him who holds him or it in his power.

This is a very interesting and important correction of the Authorized Version. It is made in all the newer translations—the Revised Version, Moffatt, and the American

42

Revised Standard Version. And it means that the well-worn phrases which speak of being " washed in the blood of the Lamb " have little scriptural authority. They are phrases which, when we allow ourselves to think calmly of them, have in them a staggering picture; and it must come to many with a certain relief to know that what John said was that we are loosed from our sins at the cost of the blood, that is, at the cost of the life of Jesus Christ.

But there is another very significant thing here. We must carefully note the tenses of the verbs here. John says that Jesus *loves* us and *set us free* from our sins at the cost of His own blood. *Loves* is the *present tense*, and it means that the love of God in Christ Jesus is something which is continuous and which for ever goes on. *Set us free* is the *past tense*, the Greek aorist, which tells of one act completed and done in the past, and it means that in the one act of the Cross our liberation from sin was achieved. That is to say, what happened on the Cross was one availing act in time which was an expression of the continuous love of God. What happened on the Cross in a moment of time is a window into the eternal, unchanging, unceasing love of God.

(ii) Jesus made us a kingdom, priests to God. That is a quotation of *Exodus* 19.6: " Ye shall be unto me a kingdom of priests, and an holy nation." Jesus has done two things for us.

(*a*) He has given us royalty. Through Him we may become the true sons of God; and, if we are sons of the King of kings, then we are of lineage than which there can be none more royal. Our destiny is a royal destiny.

(*b*) He made us priests. The point about that is this. Under the old way, only the priest had the right of access to God. When a Jew entered the Temple, he could pass through the Court of the Gentiles, the Court of the Women, the Court of the Israelites—but there he must stop; into the Court of the Priests he could not go; no nearer the Holy of Holies could he come. Now it is to be noted that in the vision of the great days to come Isaiah said: " Ye shall be named the priests of the Lord " (*Isaiah* 61.6). In that day every one of the people would be a priest and every one would have access to God. That is what John means; he means that, because of what Jesus Christ did, access to the presence of God is not now confined to priests in the narrowest sense of the term, but that it is open to every man. Every man is a priest. There is a priesthood of all believers. We can come boldly unto the throne of grace (*Hebrews* 4.16), because for us there is a new and living way into the presence of God (*Hebrews* 10.19-22).

Jesus gave us the royalty of those who are sons of God; Jesus gave us the priesthood of those for whom the way to the nearer presence of God is always open.

THE COMING GLORY

Revelation 1.7

> Behold, He is coming with the clouds, and every eye shall see Him, and the people who pierced Him will see Him; and all the tribes of the earth shall lament over Him. Yea! Amen!

FROM now on in almost every passage with which we deal, however short, we shall have to note something. We shall have to note John's continuous use of, quotation of, and allusion to the Old Testament. John was soaked and saturated in the Old Testament, that it was almost impossible for him to write a paragraph without quoting it. Its thought and its language were interwoven into the very structure of his mind. This is interesting and it is significant. John was living in a time when to be a Christian was an agonizing thing. He himself knew banishment and imprisonment and hard labour; and there were many who knew death in its most cruel forms. And the best way to maintain courage and hope in such a situation was to remember the past. The best way to be certain that God would not fail in the present was to remember that God had not failed in the past. John strengthened his soul for

present trial by continuously remembering the greatness
and the goodness of God in the past. God was not, so to
speak, an untried God. Hitherto the Lord had helped, and
God's arm was not shortened and His power was not grown
less.

Here in this passage John sets down the motto and the
text of his whole book. He sets down his confidence in the
triumphant return of Christ, a return which would rescue
Christians in distress from the cruelty of their enemies.
It was John's conviction that soon or late the enemies of
God must perish, and the friends of God must enter into
glory.

(i) To some, to the Christians, the return of Christ is a
promise on which to feed the soul. John takes as his picture
of that return a vision in *Daniel*. Daniel has a vision of
the four bestial powers who have held the world in their
grip. The picture is in *Daniel* 7.1-14. There was Babylon,
the power that was like a lion with eagle's wings (7.4).
There was Persia, the power that was like a savage bear
(7.5). There was Greece, the power that was like a winged
leopard (7.6). There was Rome, a beast with iron teeth,
beyond description (7.7). But the day of these bestial and
savage and inhuman empires was over, and the dominion
was to be given to a humane and gentle power like a son
of man; to that kindly and gentle power God, the Ancient
of Days, would give dominion. " I saw in the night visions,
and, behold, one like a son of man, came with the clouds
of heaven, and came to the Ancient of Days, and they
brought him near before Him, and there was given him
dominion, and glory, and a kingdom that all people,
nations and languages should serve him " (7.13, 14). It is
from that passage in *Daniel* that there emerges the ever-
recurring picture of the Son of Man coming on the clouds
(*Mark* 13.26; 14.62; *Matthew* 24.30; 26.64). When we
strip away from this the purely temporary imagery—we, for
instance, no longer think of heaven as a localized place
above the sky—we are left with the eternal and unchanging

truth that the day comes when Jesus Christ will be Lord of all; and in that hope there has ever been the strength and the comfort of Christians for whom life was difficult and for whom Christianity was death.

(ii) To some, to the enemies of Christ, *the return of Christ is a threat*. To make this point John again quotes the Old Testament. This time he quotes from *Zechariah* 12.10 which contains the words: " When they look on him whom they have pierced, they shall mourn for him, as one mourns for an only child, and weep bitterly over him, as one weeps over a first-born." (Note that the Authorized Version has " They shall look on *me* whom they have pierced." The correct reading, as the American Revised Standard Version shows, and as John knew, is *him*). The story behind the *Zechariah* saying is this. God gave His people a good shepherd; but the people in their disobedient folly killed the good shepherd, and took to themselves evil and self-seeking shepherds. But the day will come when in the grace of God they will bitterly and sorrowfully repent, and in that day they will look on the good shepherd whom they pierced, and they will sorrowfully lament for him and for what they have done. John takes that picture and applies it to Jesus. Men crucified Jesus, but the day will come when they will look on Him again; and this time, He will not be a broken figure on a cross, subject to the hate of man; He will be a regal figure of glory and splendour to whom the universal dominion has been given. We can think of the sorrow and the terror in the hearts of those who see in His majestic glory the Christ whom they crucified. For such the coming again of Jesus Christ is a terror and a threat.

It is, of course, true that the first reference of these words is to the Jews and the Romans who actually crucified Jesus. But in every age all who sin and disregard Jesus Christ crucify Him again. The day will come when those who disregarded Jesus Christ, and when those who opposed Jesus Christ, will find Him who, as they thought, did not matter, the Lord of the universe and the judge of their souls.

The passage closes with the two exclamations—" Yea! Amen! " In the Greek the two words are *vai* and *amēn*. The point is that *nai* is the Greek and *amēn* is the Hebrew, for a solemn affirmation—" Yes, indeed! So let it be! " And by using the expression both in Greek and Hebrew John specially stresses it, and specially underlines its awful solemnity.

THE GOD IN WHOM WE TRUST

Revelation 1.8

> I am alpha and omega, says the Lord God, He who is, and who was, and who is to come, the Almighty.

HEREIN is a tremendous description of the God in whom we trust and the God whom we adore.

(i) God is alpha and omega. *Alpha* is the first letter and *omega* is the last letter of the Greek alphabet, and the phrase *alpha to omega* indicates absolute completeness. The first letter of the Hebrew letter is *aleph* and the last letter is *tau*; and the Jews used the same kind of expression. The Rabbis said that Adam transgressed the Law, and Abraham kept the Law from *aleph* to *tau*. They said that God has blessed Israel from *aleph* to *tau*. So, then, this expression indicates completeness from which nothing is lacking. God is absolutely complete; in Him there is nothing lacking. He has in Himself what H. B. Swete called " the boundless life which embraces all and transcends all." The God in whom we trust is the God in whom all things have their being, and in whom there is nothing lacking.

(ii) God is He who is, and who was, and who is to come. That is to say, God is the Eternal. He was before time began; He is now; and He will be when time ends. He has been the God of all who have trusted in Him; He is the God in whom at this present moment we can put our trust; and

there can be no event and no time in the future which can
separate us from God.

> Nor death nor life, nor earth nor hell,
>   nor time's destroying sway,
> Can e'er efface us from His heart,
>   or make His love decay.

> Each future period that will bless,
>   as it has blessed the past;
> He lov'd us from the first of time,
>   He loves us to the last.

(iii) God is the Almighty. The word for *Almighty* is
pantokratōr, which describes God as the one who has
dominion over all things, the one who controls all things,
the one who holds all things in His grasp.

The suggestive fact is that this word occurs in the New
Testament seven times. Once it occurs in 2 *Corinthians* 6.18
in a quotation from the Old Testament, and all the six
other instances of it are in the *Revelation*. This is a word
which is distinctive of John. Think of the circumstances
in which John was writing. The embattled might of Rome
had risen up to crush the Christian Church. No empire
had ever been able to withstand Rome; Rome was the
all-conquering and the all-powerful. What possible chance
had the Christian Church, small, mainly composed of slaves,
without influence and power, against Rome? What chance
against Rome had " the panting, huddled flock whose crime
was Christ "? Humanly speaking the Christian Church had
no chance. All it could look for was annihilation. But if
men thought that, they had left the most important factor
of all out of the reckoning—they had left out God the
pantokratōr, the Almighty, the one in the grip of whose
hand are all things.

It is this word which in the Greek Old Testament describes
the Lord of Sabaoth, the Lord of hosts (*Amos* 9.5; *Hosea*
12.5). It is this word which John uses in the tremendous
text: " The Lord God *omnipotent* reigneth " (*Revelation*
19.6). If men are in the hands of God like that, nothing

can pluck them from the hand of God. If behind the Christian Church there is a God like that, then, so long as the Church is true to her Lord, nothing can destroy her. Rome might rise up to crush the Church, but Rome too was in the hands of the *pantokratōr*.

> My times are in Thy hand:
> I'll always trust in Thee;
> And, after death, at Thy right hand
> I shall for ever be.

THROUGH TRIBULATION TO THE KINGDOM

Revelation I.9

> I, John, your brother and partner in tribulation, in the kingdom, and in that steadfast endurance which life in Christ alone can give, was in the island which is called Patmos, for the sake of the word given by God and confirmed by Jesus Christ.

HERE John introduces himself. He does not introduce himself by any official title; he calls himself *your brother and partner in tribulation*. His right to speak was that he had come through all that those to whom he was writing were going through. His right to speak came not from ecclesiastical appointment, but from experience. Ezekiel writes in his book: " Then I came to them of the captivity at Tel-abib, that dwelt by the river of Chebar, and I sat where they sat " (*Ezekiel* 3.15). Men will never listen to the man who preaches the virtue of endurance from the comfort of an easy chair; men will never listen to the man who preaches heroic courage to others while he himself has sought a prudent safety. It is the man who has gone through it who can help others who are going through it. The academic distinctions of the preacher are useless until he has graduated in the university of human experience. As the Indians have it: " No man can criticize another man until he has walked for a day in his mocassins." John and Ezekiel could speak because they had sat where their people were sitting.

John puts three words together—tribulation, kingdom, steadfast endurance. *Tribulation* is *thlipsis*. Originally *thlipsis* meant simply *pressure*, and could, for instance, describe the pressure of a great stone on a man's body. At first it was used quite literally, but in the New Testament it has come to describe that pressure of events which is persecution. *Steadfast endurance* is *hupomonē*. *Hupomonē* does not describe the patience which sits down with folded hands and bowed head and simply passively submits to the tide of events; *hupomonē* describes the spirit of courage and conquest which begets gallantry and transmutes even suffering into glory. Now the situation of the Christians was this. They were in *thlipsis*; they were in the midst of persecution, and, as John saw it, of the terrible world-shaking and soul-shattering events which preceded the end of the world. They were looking towards *basileia*, the kingdom; into the kingdom they desired to enter, and on the kingdom they set their hearts. In such a position there was only one way from *thlipsis* to *basileia*, from affliction to glory, and that was *via hupomonē*, gallant and courageous and conquering endurance. As R. H. Charles put it, *hupomonē* is the spiritual alchemy which can change *thlipsis* into *basileia*. This all-conquering endurance is the one thing which can turn affliction into glory. Jesus said: " He that shall endure unto the end, the same shall be saved " (*Matthew* 24.13). Paul told his people: " We must through much tribulation enter into the kingdom of God " (*Acts* 14.22). In 2 *Timothy* we read: " If we endure, we shall also reign with Him " (2 *Timothy* 2.12).

The way to the kingdom is the way of courage and endurance. No lover of ease and comfort, no craven and coward creature, no one flabby in body and in mind, ever achieved one of the great journeys of the world. The journey to the kingdom is the greatest journey of all, and it requires the greatest endurance of all.

But before we leave this passage we must note one thing. That endurance is to be found in Christ. He Himself endured to the end, and He is able to enable those who walk with Him to achieve the same endurance, and to reach the same goal.

THE ISLAND OF BANISHMENT

Revelation 1.9 (*continued*)

JOHN tells us that, when the visions of the *Revelation* came to him, he was in the island that is called Patmos. It was the unanimous tradition of the early Church that John was banished to the island of Patmos in the reign of Domitian. Tertullian says: " The apostle John was banished to the island " (*On the Prescription of Heretics*, 36). Origen says: " The Roman Emperor, as tradition tells us, condemned John to the island of Patmos for witnessing to the word of truth " (*Homilies on Matthew*). Clement of Alexandria tells us: " On the death of the tyrant John returned to Ephesus from the island of Patmos " (*The Rich Man's Salvation*, 42). Jerome says that John was banished in the fourteenth year after Nero and liberated on the death of Domitian (*Concerning Illustrious Men*, 9). This would mean that John was banished to Patmos about A.D. 94 and that he was liberated about A.D. 96.

Patmos is a barren rocky little island belonging to a group of islands called the Sporades. It is ten miles long by five miles wide. It is crescent-shaped, with the horns of the crescent pointing to the east. Its shape makes it a good natural harbour. It lies forty miles off the coast of Asia Minor, and it was important because it was the last haven on the voyage from Rome to Ephesus, and the first on the voyage in the reverse direction.

Banishment to a remote island was a common form of Roman punishment. It was usually meted out in the case of political prisoners, and, as far as they were concerned, there could be worse punishments. Such banishment involved the loss of civil rights and of all property, except a pittance enough for a bare existence. People so banished

THE REVELATION OF JOHN

were not personally ill-treated and were not confined in prison on their island, but were free to move within its narrow limits. Such would be banishment for a political prisoner; but it would be very different for John. John was a leader of the Christians, and the Christians were criminals. The wonder is that he was not executed straight away. Banishment for John would involve hard labour in the quarries. Sir William Ramsay describes the kind of banishment which John would undergo. It would be "preceded by scourging, marked by perpetual fetters, scanty clothing, insufficient food, sleep on the bare ground, a dark prison, work under the lash of the military overseer." In Patmos the circumstances of John's life would be hard indeed.

Patmos left its mark on John's writing. To this day they show visitors on Patmos a cave in a cliff in Patmos overlooking the sea, where, they say, the *Revelation* was written. There are magnificent views of the sea from Patmos, and, as Strahan says, the *Revelation* is full of "the sights and the sounds of the infinite sea." The word *thalassa*, the sea, occurs in the *Revelation* no fewer than twenty-five times. Strahan writes: "Nowhere is 'the voice of many waters' more musical than in Patmos; nowhere does the rising and setting sun make a more splendid 'sea of glass mingled with fire'; yet nowhere is the longing more natural that the separating sea should be no more."

It was to all the hardships and pain and weariness of banishment and hard labour of Patmos that John went *for the sake of the word given by God*. So far as the Greek goes, that phrase is capable of three interpretations. It could mean that John went to Patmos to *preach* the word of God. It could mean that John, as it were, withdrew to the loneliness of Patmos to *receive* the word of God and the visions of the *Revelation*. But it is quite certain that what it means is that it was John's unshakable loyalty to the word of God, and his insistence on preaching the

message of Jesus Christ which brought him to the loneliness
and the pain of banishment in Patmos.

IN THE SPIRIT ON THE LORD'S DAY

Revelation 1.10, 11

> I was in the Spirit on the Lord's Day, and I heard
> behind me a great voice, like the sound of a trumpet,
> saying: " Write what you see in a book, and send it to
> the seven Churches, to Ephesus and to Smyrna, and to
> Pergamos and to Thyatira and to Sardis and to
> Philadelphia and to Laodicea."

HISTORICALLY this is an extremely interesting passage,
for this is the first reference in literature to the Lord's Day.

We have often spoken of the Day of the Lord, that
day of wrath and judgment which was to be the day when
God descended on the earth, and when this present age with
all its evil was to be shatteringly changed into the age to
come. There are some few who think that what John is
saying is that he was transported in a vision to that Day
of the Lord, and that he saw in advance all the astonishing
things which were to happen then, when this world ended
and the new world began. Those who hold that view are
very few, and it is not a natural meaning for the words.

It is quite certain that when John uses the expression
the Lord's Day he is using it as we use it, and, as we have
said, this is the first passage in literature where there is any
mention of the Lord's Day.

How, then, did the Christian Church cease to observe
the Sabbath and come to observe the Lord's Day? The
Sabbath is our Saturday, the last day of the week. The
Lord's Day is Sunday, the first day of the week. The
Sabbath commemorated the rest of God after the creation
of the world. The Lord's Day commemorates the rising
of Jesus from the dead. But how did the change from one

to the other in the Christian Church take place? The three earliest references to the Lord's Day may well be the following. *The Didachē, The Teaching of the Twelve Apostles*, which is the first manual of Christian worship and instruction, says of the Christian Church: " On the Lord's Day we meet and break bread " (*Didachē* 14.1). Ignatius of Antioch, writing to the Magnesians, describes the Christians as " no longer living for the Sabbath, but for the Lord's Day " (Ignatius, *To the Magnesians*, 9.1). Melito of Sardis wrote a treatise *Concerning the Lord's Day*. We know that by early in the second century the Sabbath had been abandoned and the Lord's Day was the accepted Christian day.

One thing seems certain. All these early references come from Asia Minor, and it was there that the observance of the Lord's Day first came into force. But what was it that suggested to the Christians a *weekly* observance of the first day of the week? Easter is the *yearly* commemoration of the rising again of Jesus, but what moved the Christian Church to a weekly commemoration? In the east there was a day of the month and a day of the week which were called *Sebastē*, which means *The Emperor's Day*. The pagans had a weekly and a monthly day dedicated to the Roman Emperor; it was no doubt this which made the Christians decide that the first day of the week must be dedicated to their Lord. Just as the pagans celebrated The Emperor's Day each week so the Christians determined each week to celebrate The Lord's Day.

John was *in the Spirit*. This phrase means that John was in an ecstasy in which he was lifted beyond the things of space and time, into the world of eternity and of God. " The Spirit took me up," said Ezekiel (*Ezekiel* 3.12), " and I heard behind me a voice of a great rushing." For John the voice was like the sound of a trumpet. The sound of the trumpet is woven into the language of the New Testament (*Matthew* 24.31; I *Corinthians* 15.42; I *Thessalonians* 4.16). There is no doubt that in the mind of John there is here another Old Testament picture. In the account of the giving of the Law it is said: "There were thunders and lightnings, and a thick cloud upon the mount, and the voice of the trumpet exceeding loud" (*Exodus* 19.16). The idea is the commanding and piercing clarity of the trumpet. The voice of God sounds with the commanding, unmistakable clarity of a trumpet call.

John is told to write the vision which he sees. It is his duty to share the message which God gives to him. A man must first hear and then transmit. A vision and a message are not something to be received selfishly for one's own edification; they are something to be transmitted to men, even if the price of the transmission is costly indeed. It may be that a man must withdraw to see his vision, but he must also go forth to tell his vision.

Two phrases go together. John was *in Patmos*; and John was *in the Spirit*. We have seen what Patmos was like, and we have seen the pain and the hardship that John was undergoing. No matter where a man is, no matter how hard his life, no matter what a man is passing through, he may still be in the Spirit. And, if he is in the Spirit, even on Patmos, the glory and the message of God will come to him. There is no situation in life in which the Spirit cannot speak to us, and, when the Spirit does speak, we know the glory of God, even on Patmos.

THE DIVINE MESSENGER

Revelation 1.12, 13

> And I turned to see the voice that was speaking to me; and, when I had turned, I saw seven golden lampstands, and, in the midst of the lampstands, one like a son of man, clothed in a robe that reached to his feet, and girt about the breasts with a golden girdle.

WE now begin on the first of John's visions; and we shall see that his mind is to saturated with Scripture that element after element in the picture has an Old Testament background and counterpart.

John says that he turned *to see the voice*. We do not *see* a voice, but here John is identifying the voice and the speaker. We would say: " I turned to see whose was the voice which was speaking to me."

When he turned, he saw *seven golden lampstands*. Now John does not only quote and allude to the Old Testament; he takes items from many places in the Old Testament and out of them he forms a composite picture. The picture of the seven golden lampstands has three sources and origins.

(a) It comes from the picture of the candlestick of pure gold in the Tabernacle. It was to have six branches, three on one side and three on the other; and it was to have seven lamps to give light (*Exodus* 25.31-37). Part of the vision comes from the Tabernacle in the wilderness where God met with His people.

(b) It comes from the picture of Solomon's Temple. In it there were to be five candlesticks of pure gold on the right hand and five on the left (I *Kings* 7.49).

(c) It comes from the vision of Zechariah. Zechariah in his vision saw " a candlestick all of gold, with a bowl upon the top of it, and his seven lamps thereon " (*Zechariah* 4.2).

When John sees a vision, he sees it in terms of scenes and pictures from the Old Testament places and occasions when God had already revealed Himself and His truth to His people. Surely there is a lesson here. The best way to prepare oneself for new revelation of truth is to study, and feed the heart on, the revelation which God has already given in His own word.

In the midst of the lampstands he saw one *like a son of man*. Here we are back to the picture of *Daniel* 7.13, in which the kingdom and the power and the dominion are given by the Ancient of Days to one like a son of man. As we well know from Jesus' use of it, this title Son of Man became nothing less than the title of the Messiah; and by using it here John makes it plain that the revelation which he is to receive is coming to him from no other source than from Jesus Christ Himself. The *Revelation* is the direct message of the risen and glorified Christ.

This figure was clothed with *a robe which reached down to his feet,* and he was *girt about the breasts with a golden girdle.* Here again we have three pictures.

(a) The word which describes the robe is *podērēs,* which means *reaching down to the feet.* This is the word which the Greek Old Testament uses to describe the robe of the High Priest (*Exodus* 28.4; 29.5; *Leviticus* 16.4). Josephus also describes carefully the garments which the priests and the High Priest wore when they were serving in the Temple. They wore " a long robe reaching to the feet," and around the breast, " higher than the elbows," they wore a girdle which was loosely wound round and round the body. The girdle was embroidered with colours and flowers, with a mixture of gold interwoven (Josephus, *The Antiquities of the Jews,* 3.7.2, 4). All this means that the description of the robe and the girdle of the glorified Christ is almost exactly the description of the dress of the priests and of the High Priest. Here, then, is the symbol of the high priestly character of the work of the Risen Lord. A priest, as the Jews saw it, is a man who himself has access to God, and who opens the way for others to come to God. Even in the heavenly places Jesus, the great High Priest, is still carrying on His priestly work, and opening the way for us and for all men to the presence of God.

(b) But other people besides priests wore the long robe reaching to the feet, and the high girdle. Such a robe was the dress of great ones, of princes, and of kings. *Podērēs, reaching down to the feet,* is the description of the robe of Jonathan (I *Samuel* 18.24); of Saul (I *Samuel* 24.5, 12); of the princes of the sea (*Ezekiel* 26.16). The robe that the Risen Christ was wearing was the robe of royalty. No longer was He a criminal on a cross; He was dressed gloriously and majestically like a king. So here we are shown the royalty of Christ. Christ is Priest and Christ is King.

(iii) There is still another part of this picture. In the vision of Daniel, the divine figure who came to tell Daniel the truth of God was clothed in fine linen (the Greek Old Testament calls his garment *podērēs*) and girt with fine gold (*Daniel* 10.5). This, then, is the dress of the messenger of God. Now the great messenger of God is the prophet; the prophet is God's messenger *par excellence*. So this gives us the picture of Jesus Christ as the divine and supreme messenger of God.

Here, indeed, is a tremendous picture. When we trace back the origins of the thought and the pictures of John, we see that by the very dress of the Risen Lord, he is showing Him to us in His threefold eternal office of Prophet, Priest and King, the one who brings the truth of God, the one who enables others to enter into the presence of God, the one to whom God has given the power and the dominion and the throne for ever.

THE PICTURE OF THE RISEN CHRIST

Revelation 1.14-18

> His head and his hair were white, as white as wool, like snow; and his eyes were as a flame of fire; and his feet were like beaten brass, as if it had been refined in a furnace; and his voice was as the voice of many waters; he had seven stars in his right hand; and out of his mouth there was coming a sharp two-edged sword; and his face was as the sun shining in its strength. And when I saw him, I fell at his feet like a dead man. And he put his right hand on me and said: " Stop being afraid. I am the first and the last; I am the living one although I was dead, and, behold, I am alive for ever and ever; and I have the keys of death and of Hades."

BEFORE we begin to look at this passage in detail, there are two general facts which we must note.

(i) It is easy to miss seeing how carefully wrought a work of literature the *Revelation* is. It is not a book which was flung together in a hurry; it is a closely integrated and artistic literary whole. In this passage we have a whole series of descriptions of the Risen Christ; and the interesting thing is that each of the letters to the seven Churches, which follow in the next two chapters, with the exception of the letter to Laodicea, opens with a description of the Risen Christ taken from this chapter. It is as if this chapter sounded a series of themes which are later to become the texts for the letters to the Churches. Let us set down the beginning of each of the first six letters, and let us see how they correspond to the description of the Risen Christ in this passage.

> Unto the angel of the Church of Ephesus, write: These things says he *who holds the seven stars in his hand* (2.1).

> Unto the angel of the Church of Smyrna, write: These things says *the first and the last, who was dead and is alive* (2.8).

> Unto the angel of the Church in Pergamum write: These things says he *who has the sharp two-edged sword* (2.12).

> Unto the angel of the Church of Thyatira, write: These things says the Son of God, *who has his eyes like a flaming fire, and his feet like brass* (2.18).

> Unto the angel of the Church of Sardis write: These things says he *who has* the seven spirits and *the seven stars* (3.1).

> Unto the angel of the Church in Philadelphia, write: These things says he that is holy, he that is true, *he that hath the key of David*, he that opens and no man shuts; and shuts and no man opens (3.7).

This is literary care and craftsmanship of a very high standard. There is a pattern in the *Revelation* which is the product of John's loving skill in words.

(ii) The second important thing to note is this. In

this passage John takes titles which in the Old Testament
are descriptions of God and applies them to the Risen
Christ. He takes things which are the prerogative of God
Himself, and gives them to Jesus Christ.

His head and his hair were white, as white wool, like
snow.

In *Daniel* 7.9 that is a description of the Ancient of Days
who is none other than God Himself.

His voice was as the sound of many waters.

In *Ezekiel* 43.2 that is a description of God's own voice.

He had the seven stars in his hand.

In the Old Testament it is God Himself who controls the
stars. In *Job* it is God's question to Job: "Canst thou
bind the sweet influence of the Pleiades, or loose the bands
of Arcturus?" (*Job* 38.31). The control of the stars is God's

I am the first and the last.

In *Isaiah* the prophet hears the voice of God saying:
"I am the first and I am the last, and beside me there is
no God" (*Isaiah* 44.6; cp. 48.12).

I am the living one.

In the Old Testament it is God who is pre-eminently and
characteristically "the living God" (*Joshua* 3.10; *Psalm*
42.2; *Hosea* 1.10).

I have the keys of death and of Hades.

The Rabbis had a saying that there were three keys which
belonged to God, and which God would share with no other
—the keys of birth, of rain, and of raising the dead.

Nothing could better show the reverence in which John
holds Jesus Christ. He holds Jesus Christ so high that he
can give Him nothing less than the titles and the prerogatives which in the Old Testament belong to God.

> The highest place that heaven affords
>   Is His, is His by right,
> The King of kings, and Lord of lords,
>   And heaven's eternal Light.

THE REVELATION OF JOHN

THE TITLES OF THE RISEN LORD—I

Revelation 1.14-18 *(continued)*

LET us look very briefly at each of the titles by which the
Risen Lord is here called, and at each of the descriptions
of Him.

> His head and His hair were white, as white wool,
> like snow.

This, as we have seen, is taken from the description of the
Ancient of Days in *Daniel* 7.9. It is symbolic of two things.
(a) It stands for great age; and it speaks to us of the
eternal existence of Jesus Christ, the Son. It takes Him
back into the heavenly places to all eternity. (b) It speaks
to us of divine purity. The snow and the white wool are the
emblems of sinless and stainless purity. " Though your
sins be as scarlet," said Isaiah, " they shall be as white as
snow; though they be red like crimson, they shall be as
wool " (*Isaiah* 1.18). Here, then, we have the symbols of
the pre-existence and the sinlessness of Christ.

> His eyes were as a flame of fire.

Daniel is always in John's mind, and this is part of the
description of the divine figure who brought the vision to
Daniel. " His eyes were as lamps of fire " (*Daniel* 10.6).
When we read the gospel story, we get the impression that
he who had once seen the eyes of Jesus could never forget
them. Again and again we have the vivid picture of the
eyes of Jesus sweeping round the circle of people in the
midst of whom He was (*Mark* 3.34; 10.23; 11.11); sometimes His eyes swept round in anger (*Mark* 3.5); sometimes
they fastened on someone in love (*Mark* 10.21); and
sometimes they had in them all the sorrow of one whose
friends had wounded him to the quick (*Luke* 22.61). Simply
to read the gospel story is to see that he who had seen the
eyes of Jesus could never forget them.

His feet were like beaten brass, as if it had been refined by fire in a furnace.

The word which is translated *beaten brass* is *chalkolibanos*. No one really knows what the metal is. Perhaps it was that fabulous compound called *electrum*, which the ancients believed to be an alloy of gold and silver, and more precious than either. Here again it is the Old Testament which gives John his vision. In *Daniel* it is said of the divine messenger that "his feet were like in colour to polished brass" (*Daniel* 10.6); in *Ezekiel* it is said of the angelic beings that "their feet sparkled like the colour of burnished brass" (*Ezekiel* 1.7). It may be that we are to see two things in the picture. The brass itself stands for *strength*, for the immovable steadfastness of God; and the shining, glittering rays stand for *speed*, for the swiftness of the feet of God to help His own or to punish sin.

His voice was as the sound of many waters.

This is the description of the voice of God in *Ezekiel* 43.2. But it may be that we can catch here an echo of the little island of Patmos. As H. B. Swete has it: "The roar of the Aegean was in the ears of the seer." It may be that as John listened to the surge of the sea, it gave him a simile for the voice of God. H. B. Swete has a very lovely thought here. The voice of God is not confined to one note. Here it is like the terrifying surge and thunder of the sea. But that same voice of God can be like a still small voice (I *Kings* 19.12), or, as the Greek version of the Old Testament has it, like a gentle breeze. The voice of God can thunder its terrifying and majestic rebuke; and the voice of God can croon with the soothing comfort of a mother over her hurt child.

He had seven stars in His right hand.

Here again, as we have seen, we have something which was the right and the prerogative of God alone. But there is again something lovely here. When the seer fell in awed terror before the vision of the Risen Christ, the

Christ stretched out his right hand and placed it on him and bade him not to be afraid. That very same hand which holds the stars is placed in soothing comfort on the head and the shoulder of the frightened child. The hand of Christ is strong enough to uphold the heavens and gentle enough to wipe away our tears.

THE TITLES OF THE RISEN LORD—2

Revelation 1.14-18 (continued)

There was coming forth from his mouth a sharp, two-edged sword.

THE sword which is referred to is not a long, narrow sword like a fencer's blade; it was a short, actually tongue-shaped sword for close fighting. Here again the seer has gone here and there in the Old Testament for his picture. Isaiah says of God: " He shall smite the earth with the rod of His mouth " (*Isaiah* 11.4). Isaiah says of himself: " He hath made my mouth like a sharp sword " (*Isaiah* 49.2). The symbolism tells us of the penetrating quality of the word of God. The word of God, if we listen to it, is such that no shield of self-deception can withstand it; it strips away our disguises and our self-deludings, and lays bare our sin, and then leads to pardon. " The word of God is quick and powerful and sharper than any two-edged sword " (*Hebrews* 4.12). " The Lord will consume the wicked with the breath of His mouth " (2 *Thessalonians* 2.8).

His face was as the sun shining in its strength.
In *Judges* there is a great picture which may well have been in John's mind. The enemies of God shall perish, " but let them that love Him be as the sun when he goeth forth in his might " (*Judges* 5.4). If that is true of them that love God, how much truer it must be of God's beloved Son. But Swete sees something even lovelier here. He sees nothing less than a memory of the Transfiguration. On that occasion Jesus was transfigured before Peter, James

and John, " and His face did shine as the sun " (*Matthew* 17.2). No one who had seen that sight could ever forget the glow of the glory; and it may be that if the writer of this book is that same John he saw again on the face of the Risen Christ the glory he had glimpsed on the Mount of Transfiguration.

When I saw Him, I fell at His feet like a dead man. This was the experience of Ezekiel when God spoke to him (*Ezekiel* 1.28; 3.23; 43.3). But surely we can find here again a memory of the Gospel story. On that day in Galilee when there was the wondrous catch of fishes, and when Peter glimpsed who Jesus was, Peter fell down at Jesus' knees, conscious only that he was a sinful man (*Luke* 5.1-11). To the end of the day there can be nothing but reverence in the presence of the holiness and the glory of the Risen Christ.

Stop being afraid. Surely here, too, we have another reminiscence of the Gospel story, for these were words which the disciples had heard more than once from the lips of Jesus in the days of His flesh. It was thus He spoke to them when He came to them across the water (*Matthew* 14.27; *Mark* 6.50); and it was thus above all that He spoke to them on the Mount of Transfiguration, when they were awed and terrified at the sound of the divine voice (*Matthew* 17.7). Even in heaven, when we approach the unapproachable glory, Jesus is saying: " I am here; do not be afraid."

I am the first and the last. As we have seen, in the Old Testament this is nothing other than the self-description of God Himself (*Isaiah* 44.6; 48.12). It is the promise of Jesus that He is there at the beginning and the end. He is there in the moment of birth and at the time of death. He is there when we set out upon the Christian way, and He is there when we finish our course. He is there when we lay our hands to any task for Him, or for men, and He is there when we complete it. As F. W. H. Myers makes Paul say in his poem:

> Yea thro' life, death, thro' sorrow and thro' sinning
>   He shall suffice me, for He hath sufficed:
> Christ is the end, for Christ was the beginning,
>   Christ the beginning, for the end is Christ.

> I am the living one, although I was dead and I am alive
> for ever and for ever.

Here is at once the claim and the promise of Christ. Here is the claim of the Resurrection, the claim of one who conquered death, and here is the promise of one who is alive for evermore to be with His people.

> I have the keys of death and Hades.

Death has its gates (*Psalm* 9.13; 107.18; *Isaiah* 38.10); and Christ has the keys of these gates. There were those who took this claim—and there still are those who do so—as a reference to the descent into hell (1 *Peter* 3.18-20). There was a conception in the ancient Church that when Jesus descended into Hades, the region of the dead, He unlocked the doors and brought out from thence Abraham and all God's faithful people who had lived and died in the generations before. But we may take it in an even wider sense than that; for we who are Christians believe that Jesus Christ has authority over death, that He has abolished death and that He has brought life and immortality to light through His glorious gospel (2 *Timothy* 1.10), that because He lives we shall live also (*John* 14.19), and that, therefore, for us and for those whom we love the bitterness of death is for ever past.

THE CHURCHES AND THEIR ANGELS

Revelation 1.20

> Here is the secret meaning of the seven stars which you saw in my right hand, and the seven golden lampstands. The seven stars are the angels of the seven Churches, and the seven lampstands are the seven Churches.

THIS passage begins with a word which throughout the

New Testament is used in a very special sense. The Authorized Version speaks of the *mystery* of the seven stars and of the seven golden candlesticks. In Greek the word *mystery* is *mustērion*; it does not mean a *mystery* in our sense of the term. It means something which is meaningless to the outsider who does not possess the key, but meaningful to the initiate who does possess the key. A mystery is something which has an inner meaning which is plain to those who have been granted the knowledge to see it. So here the Risen Christ goes on to give the inner meaning of the seven stars and the seven lampstands.

The seven lampstands stand for the seven Churches. One of the great titles of the Christian is that the Christian is the light of the world (*Matthew* 5.14; *Philippians* 2.15). But one of the old Greek commentators has a wise and penetrating comment on this. He says that the Churches are called, not the light itself, but the lampstand on which the light is set; because it is not the Churches themselves which produce the light; the giver of light is Jesus Christ; and the Church is only the vessel within which the light shines, and within which the light is contained. The Christian's light is, indeed, always a borrowed light, for he shines, not with his own light, but with the reflection of the light of Jesus Christ.

One of the great problems of the *Revelation* is to decide what John means by the *angels of the Churches*. Each of the letters to the seven Churches is addressed to the *angel* of the Church. Who were these angels? More than one explanation has been offered.

(i) The word *aggelos*—gg in Greek is pronounced *ng*— has two meanings. It means an *angel*; but far oftener it means a *messenger*, for which it is the normal Greek word. It is suggested that messengers of all the Churches have assembled to receive a message from John, and to take that message back to their congregations. If that is so, each letter will begin: " To the messenger of the Church of. . . . " As far as the Greek goes this is theoretically perfectly possible; and it gives good sense; but the difficulty is that the word *aggelos* is used in the *Revelation* about fifty times apart from its use here and in the letters to the seven Churches, and without exception it means *angel*. When John uses the word *aggelos* he does not use it in the sense of *messenger*; he uses it in the sense of *angel*.

(ii) It is suggested that the word *aggelos* means the bishops of the Churches. It is suggested, either that the bishops of the Churches have gathered to meet John, or that he is directing these letters to them. In favour of this theory there is quoted the words of Malachi: " The priest's lips should keep knowledge, and they should seek the law at his mouth; for he is the *messenger* of the Lord of hosts " (*Malachi* 2.7). Now, of course, in the Greek Old Testament, the word *messenger* is *aggelos*; here the priest is being described as the *aggelos* of the Lord; and it is suggested that that title could very easily be transferred to the bishops and the leaders of the Churches. They are the *aggeloi*, the messengers of the Lord to their Churches, and to them John speaks. Again this explanation gives good sense; but it suffers from the same objection as the first explanation; it attaches the word *aggelos* to a human person, and that John never elsewhere does.

(iii) It is suggested that this has got to do with the idea of guardian angels. In Hebrew thought every nation had its presiding angel (cp. *Daniel* 10.13, 20, 21). Michael, for instance, was held to be the guardian angel of Israel (*Daniel* 13.1). People, too, had their guardian angels. When Rhoda came with the news that Peter had escaped from prison, they would not believe her, and said that it was his angel (*Acts* 12.15). Jesus Himself spoke of the angels who guard a little child (*Matthew* 18.10). If that be so, the angels are the guardian angels of the Churches. This produces the difficulty that it would then be the guardian angels of the Churches who are being warned and rebuked for the sins of the Churches. In point of fact, Origen believed that this was the case. He said that the guardian angel of a Church was like the tutor of a child. If a child goes wrong, the tutor is blamed; and if a Church goes wrong, God in His mercy blames the angel of the Church. The difficulty about that is that, though the angel of the Church is mentioned in the address of each letter, yet undoubtedly it is the members of the Church who are being addressed.

(iv) Both Greeks and Jews believed that every earthly thing had, as it were, a heavenly counterpart; and it is suggested that the angel is the heavenly counterpart of the Church; that, to put it in a modern way, the angel is the ideal of the Church; and that the Churches are being addressed as their ideal selves to bring them back to the right way.

None of the explanations is fully satisfactory; but maybe the last is the best, for there is no doubt that in the letters the angel and the Church are identified and are one and the same.

We now go on to study the letters to the Seven Churches. In the case of these letters we shall adopt a slightly different method of study. In each case we shall give an outline of the history and the contemporary background of the city in which the Church was, before we read and study the text of the letter sent to it. The reason for that is that the letters will become much more meaningful and vivid when we read them in the light of the history and conditions of the cities to which they were sent; and once we have studied the general background then we will go on to study each letter in detail.

THE LETTER TO EPHESUS

Revelation 2.1-7

To the angel of the Church in Ephesus, write:

These things says He who holds the seven stars in His right hand, and who walks in the midst of the seven golden lampstands.

I know your works—I mean your toil, and your steadfast endurance, and I know that you cannot bear evil men, and that you have put to the test those who call themselves apostles, and who are not, and have proved them liars. I know that you possess steadfast endurance. I know all that you have borne for my name's sake, and I know that you have not been worn out by your efforts. All the same I have this against you—that you have left your first love. Remember, then, whence you have fallen, and repent, and make your conduct such as it was at first. If you do not, I am coming to you, and I will remove your lampstand from its place, if you do not repent.

But you do possess this virtue—you hate the works of the Nicolaitans, which I too hate.

Let him who has an ear hear what the Spirit is saying to the Churches. I will give to him who overcomes to eat of the tree of life, which is in the Paradise of God.

EPHESUS,
FIRST AND GREATEST

Revelation 2.1-7

WHEN we know something of the history of Ephesus, and when we learn something of conditions there when John wrote his letter to Ephesus, it is easy to see why Ephesus comes first in the list of the seven Churches.

It is true that Pergamum was the official capital of the province of Asia, but in actual fact Ephesus was by far the greatest city in the province. It claimed as its proud title " The first and the greatest metropolis of Asia." A Roman writer called it *Lumen Asiae*, The Light of Asia. Ephesus, as it was said, was Asia. Let us see, then, the factors which gave Ephesus its pre-eminent greatness.

(i) In the time of John, Ephesus was the greatest harbour in Asia. All the roads of the Cayster Valley— the Cayster was the river on which it stood—converged upon it. But the roads came from further afield than that. It was at Ephesus that the road from the far-off Euphrates and from Mesopotamia reached the Mediterranean, having come by way of Colossae and Laodicea. It was at Ephesus that the road from Galatia reached the sea, having come by way of Sardis. And from the south there come up the road from the rich Maeander Valley. Strabo, the ancient geographer, called Ephesus " The Market of Asia," and it may well be that in *Revelation* 18.12, 13 John was setting down nothing other than a description of the varied riches of the market-place of Ephesus.

For people entering Asia, Ephesus was inevitably the Gateway of Asia. One of its distinctions, laid down by statute, was that when the Roman proconsul came to take up office as governor of Asia, he must disembark at Ephesus, and enter his province there. For all the travellers and the trade, flowing into Ephesus, from the Cayster and the Maeander Valleys, from Galatia, from the Euphrates and from Mesopotamia, Ephesus was the Highway to Rome.

In later times, when the martyrs were brought from Asia to be flung to the lions in the arena in Rome, Ignatius called Ephesus the Highway of the Martyrs.

Its position made Ephesus the wealthiest and the greatest city in all Asia. Into it and out of it there poured an unceasing stream of men and merchandise, so that it has been aptly called The Vanity Fair of the Ancient World.

(ii) Ephesus had certain very important political distinctions. It was a *free city*. There were in the Roman Empire certain cities which were free cities; they had had that honour conferred upon them because of their fidelity and their services to the Empire. A free city was within its own limits self-governing; and it was exempted from ever having Roman troops garrisoned or stationed there. It was an *assize town*. The Roman provincial governors made periodical tours of their provinces; and at certain specially chosen cities and towns courts were held, where the governor, when he came, tried the most important cases and dispensed Roman justice. Assize towns had at certain times of the year all the pomp and panoply and colour of the arrival of the governor in all his state. Still further, Ephesus held yearly the most famous games in Asia, and at the time of the games from all over the province people poured into Ephesus.

(iii) Ephesus was the centre of the worship of Artemis or, as the Authorized Version calls her, Diana of the Ephesians. The Temple of Artemis was one of the seven wonders of the ancient world. It was four hundred and twenty-five feet long by two hundred and twenty feet wide; it had one hundred and twenty columns, each sixty feet high, each the gift of a king, and thirty-six of them were richly gilded and inlaid. Ancient temples consisted mostly of colonnades with only the centre portion roofed over. The centre portion of the Temple of Artemis was roofed over with cypress wood. The image of Artemis was one of the most sacred images in the ancient world. It was by no means beautiful; it was a squat, black, many-breasted figure, but it was so ancient that none knew its origin. We have only to read *Acts* 19 to see how precious Artemis and her temple were to Ephesus. Not only was Ephesus famed for the worship of Artemis; in the time of John it had also famous temples to the godhead of the Roman Emperors, Claudius and Nero, and in the after days it was to add temples of Hadrian and Severus. In Ephesus pagan religion was at its strongest.

(iv) Ephesus was a notorious centre of pagan superstition. It was famous for the *Ephesian Letters*. Ephesian letters were amulets and charms. They were supposed to be infallible remedies for sickness; to bring children to those who were childless; to ensure success in any contest or journey or undertaking; and people came from all over the world to buy them.

(v) The population of Ephesus was very mixed. Its citizens were divided into tribes. There were six tribes. One consisted of those who were descendants of the original natives of the country before the Greeks came; one consisted of those who were direct descendants of the original colonists from Athens; three consisted of other Greeks; and one, it is probable, consisted of Jews. Besides being a centre of religion the Temple of Artemis was also a centre of crime and of immorality. The Temple area possessed the right of asylum; any criminal who had committed any crime was safe, if he could reach it. The temple possessed hundreds of priestesses who were sacred prostitutes attached to the temple. The mixed nature of the population, the influx of the criminal classes, the immorality of the temple worship combined to make Ephesus a notoriously evil place. Heraclitus was one of the most famous of ancient philosophers; he was known as " the weeping philosopher." His explanation of his own tears was that no one could live in Ephesus without weeping at the immorality which he must see on every side.

Such was Ephesus; a more unpromising soil for the sowing of the seed of Christianity can scarcely be imagined;

and yet it was there that Christianity had some of its greatest triumphs. R. C. Trench writes: "Nowhere did the word of God find a kindlier soil, strike root more deeply, or bear fairer fruits of faith and love."

Paul stayed longer in Ephesus than in any other city (*Acts* 20.31). It was with Ephesus that Timothy was connected so that he is called its first bishop (I *Timothy* 1.3). It is in Ephesus that we find Aquila, Priscilla and Apollos (*Acts* 18.19, 24, 26). Surely to no one was Paul ever more close than he was to the Ephesian elders, as his farewell address to them so beautifully shows (*Acts* 20.17-38). In the later days John was the leading figure of Ephesus. Legend and tradition have it that he brought Mary the mother of Jesus to Ephesus, and that she was buried there. When Ignatius of Antioch wrote his letter to Ephesus, on his way to being martyred in Rome, he could write: "You were ever of one mind with the apostles in the power of Jesus Christ."

There can be few places which better prove the conquering power of the Christian faith.

Before we leave this general description of Ephesus, we may note one more thing. We have spoken of Ephesus as the greatest harbour of Asia. Today there is little left in Ephesus but ruins; and today Ephesus is no less than six miles from the sea. The coast is now " a harbourless line of sandy beach, unapproachable by a ship." What was once the Gulf of Ephesus and the harbour of Ephesus is now " a marsh dense with reeds." It was ever a fight to keep the harbour of Ephesus open, because of the silt which the Cayster brings down. The fight was lost, and Ephesus vanished from the scene. Its crowded harbour is now a marsh six miles from the sea, and its once thronging streets are now a waste and a desolation.

EPHESUS
CHRIST AND HIS CHURCH

Revelation 2.1-7 (continued)

JOHN begins the letter to Ephesus with two descriptions of the Risen Christ.

(i) He is He who holds the seven stars in His right hand. We have already seen that the seven stars stand for the Churches. Christ holds the Churches in His hand. The word for *to hold* is *kratein*, and it is a strong word. It means that Jesus Christ has complete control over the Church. It means that, if the Church submits to that control of Christ, it will never go wrong. And more than that—our safety and our security lie in the fact that we are in the hand of Christ. As John gives us the words of Jesus about His own: " They shall never perish, neither shall any man pluck them out of my hand " (*John* 10.28). When the Church submits to the control of Christ, her doctrine and her existence are for ever safe.

But there is another point here—a point which emerges only in the Greek. The verb *kratein, to hold,* normally takes a genitive case after it; the genitive case is the case which in English we express by the word *of. Kratein* takes the genitive because, when we take hold of a thing, we seldom take hold of *the whole of it.* The thing is so big that we can only take hold of *part of it.* We cannot grasp a whole table, or a whole large parcel in our hands; we can only take a grip of part of it. When *kratein* does take a direct accusative after it, it means that the whole object is gripped and grasped within the hand. For instance, we can grasp the whole of a nut, or the whole of a scrap of pencil in our hand. Here, as we have seen *kratein* takes the accusative after it. And that means that Christ clasps the whole of the seven stars in His hand; and that means that Christ clasps *the whole of the Church* in His hand. We would do well to remember that. It is not only *our* Church which is in the hand of Christ; the *whole* Church is in the hand of Christ. Christ is not the Christ of any sect or communion or denomination, still less of any congregation. He is the Christ of the whole Church. When men put up barriers between Church and Church, they do what Jesus Christ never does and never will do.

(ii) He is He who walks in the midst of the seven golden lampstands. The lampstands are the Churches. This expression tells us of Christ's unwearied activity in the midst of His Churches. He is not confined to any one of them; He is in all of them. There is no Church from which His presence is absent. Wherever men are met to worship in His name, Christ is there.

John goes on to say certain things about the people of the Church of Ephesus.

(i) The Risen Christ praises their *toil*. The word is *kopos* and it is a favourite New Testament word. Tryphena, Tryphosa and Persis all *labour* in the Lord (Romans 16.12). The one thing that Paul claims is that he has *laboured* more than all (I Corinthians 15.10). He fears lest the Galatians slip back, and his *labour* is in vain (Galatians 4.11). In each case—and there are many others—the word is either the noun *kopos*, or the verb *kopian*. The special characteristic of these words is that they describe labour to the point of sweat; labour to the point of exhaustion; the kind of toil which takes everything of mind and sinew that a man can put into it. The Christian way is not for the dilettante and for the man who fears to break sweat. The Christian must spend his life going all out for Christ and for his fellow-men. The Christian is the toiler for Christ, and, even if physical toil is forbidden to him and impossible for him, he can still toil in prayer.

(ii) The Risen Christ praises their *steadfast endurance*. Here is the word *hupomonē* which we have come upon again and again. *Hupomonē* is not the grim patience which resignedly accepts things, and which bows its head when troubles flow over it. *Hupomonē* is the courageous gallantry which accepts suffering and hardship and loss and turns them into grace and glory. It is often said that suffering colours life; but when we meet life with the *hupomonē*, which Christ can give, the colour of life is never grey or black, for life is always tinged with radiance and with glory.

EPHESUS
WHEN ORTHODOXY COSTS TOO MUCH

Revelation 2.1-7 (continued)

THE Risen Christ goes on to praise the Christians of Ephesus, because they have tested evil men and have proved them liars.

Many an evil man came into the little congregations of the early Church. Jesus had warned of the false prophets who are wolves in sheep's clothing (*Matthew* 7.15). In his farewell speech to the elders of this very Church at Ephesus, Paul had warned them that grievous wolves would invade the flock (*Acts* 20.9). These evil men were of many kinds. There were emissaries of the Jews who sought to entangle Christians again in the Law, and who followed Paul everywhere, trying to undo his work. There were those who, as we shall see, tried to turn liberty into licence, and to pervert Christianity into a justification for immorality. There were professional beggars and hangers on who preyed on the charity of the Christian congregations, and who lived a comfortable enough life by moving from Church to Church. The Church at Ephesus was even more open to these itinerant menaces and frauds than any other Church. It was on the highway to Rome and the highway to the east, and what R. C. Trench called " the whole rabble of evil-doers " was liable to descend upon it.

More than once the New Testament insists on the necessity of testing. John in his First Letter insists that the spirits who claim to come from God should be tested; his test was that every true evangelist believes and preaches that Jesus Christ is come in the flesh, that is to say, that he

accepts the Incarnation in all its fulness (I *John* 4.1-3).
Paul insists that the Thessalonians should test all things,
and then hold on to that which is good (I *Thessalonians*
5.20). He insists that, when the prophets preach, they are
subject to the testing of the other prophets (I *Corinthians*
14.29). A man cannot proclaim his private views in the
assembly of God's people; he must abide in the tradition
of the Church. Jesus demanded the hardest test of all:
" By their fruits ye shall know them " (*Matthew* 7.15-20).

The Church at Ephesus had faithfully applied its tests,
and had weeded out and debarred from its fellowship all
evil and misguided men; but the trouble was that something had gone lost in the process. " I have this against
you," says the Risen Christ, " that you have lost your first
love." That phrase may have two meanings.

(*a*) It can mean that the first enthusiasm is gone.
Jeremiah speaks of the devotion of Israel to God in the early
days. God says to the nation that He remembers, " the
kindness of thy youth, the love of thine espousals " (*Jeremiah* 2.2). There had been a honeymoon period, but the
first flush of enthusiasm was past. It may be that the
Risen Christ is saying that all the enthusiasm and the thrill
has gone out of the religion of the Church of Ephesus.

(*b*) But much more likely what this means is that the
first fine rapture of Christian fellowship and love for the
brotherhood is gone. In the first days the members of the
Church at Ephesus had really loved each other; they had
been a band of brothers; dissension had never reared its
head; the heart was ready to kindle and the hand was
ready to help. But something had gone wrong. It may well
be that heresy-hunting had killed love; it may well be that
the eagerness to root out all mistaken men had ended in a
sour and rigid orthodoxy. It may be that orthodoxy had
been achieved, but at the price of fellowship. When that
happens, orthodoxy has cost too much. It is so often true
that when a minister is first settled in his parish and in
his charge there is a warmth of fellowship and a wealth of

good will; and then something goes wrong; and the fellow-ship is exchanged for bickering; and the comradeship becomes suspicion; and the first love is gone. All the orthodoxy in the world will never take the place of love.

EPHESUS
THE STEPS ON THE RETURN JOURNEY

Revelation 2.1-7 (continued)

So in Ephesus something had gone wrong. The earnest toil was there; the gallant endurance was there; the unimpeachable orthodoxy was there; but the love was gone. So the Risen Christ makes His appeal, and His appeal is for the three steps of the return journey.

(i) First, he says *Remember*. It must be noted that the Risen Christ is not here speaking to someone who has never been inside the Church; He is speaking to those who are inside the Church, but who have somehow lost the way. Memory can often be the first step on the way back. In the far country the prodigal son suddenly remembered his home (*Luke* 15.17). That for him was the first step on the road back. O. Henry has a short story. There was a lad who had been brought up in a village; and in the village school he had sat beside a village girl, clean and fresh and innocent and sweet. The lad found his way to the city; fell into bad company; became an expert pick-pocket and sneak thief. He was on the street one day; he had just picked a pocket—a neat job, well done—and he was pleased with himself. Suddenly he saw someone coming down the street; it was the girl he had used to sit beside at school. She was still the same, fresh, innocent, sweet. She did not see him; he took care of that. But suddenly he remembered, remembered what he had been, and realized what he was. He leaned his burning head against the cool iron of a lamp post. " God," he said,

THE REVELATION OF JOHN

" how I hate myself." Memory was offering him the way
back. William Cowper wrote:

> Where is the blessedness I knew
> When first I saw the Lord?
> Where is the soul-refreshing view
> Of Jesus and His word?

A verse like that may sound like nothing but tragedy and
sorrow, but in point of fact it can be the first step of the
way back; for the first essential step to betterment and
to amendment is to realize that something has gone wrong.

(ii) Second, He says *Repent*. When we discover that
something has gone wrong, and when we remember whence
we have fallen, there is more than one possible reaction.
We may hopelessly feel that no fine thing can last with its
first lustre and its first bloom, and we can, as we would say,
accept the inevitable. We may be filled with a feeling of
resentment, and we may blame life instead of facing
ourselves. We may become angry and embittered people
with a grievance against things in general, blaming the
shortcomings of others rather than seeking the fault
which is our own. We may decide that the old thrill is to
be found along forbidden pathways, and we may try to
find a spice for life in sin. But the Risen Christ says,
" Repent! " Repentance is the admission that the fault is
ours, and the experience of godly sorrow that it is so. The
prodigal's reaction is: " I will arise and go unto my father
and say I have sinned." No excuses, no blaming others—
but " I have sinned " (*Luke* 15.18). It is Saul's cry of the
heart when he realizes his own folly: " I have played the
fool and I have erred exceedingly " (I *Samuel* 26.21). The
hardest thing about repentance is the acceptance of personal
responsibility for our failure and our fall, for once the
responsibility is accepted the godly sorrow will surely
follow.

(iii) Third, He says *Do*. The sorrow of repentance is
not meant to drive a man to despair; it is meant to drive
him to two things. First, it is meant to drive him to fling

79

himself on the grace of God, saying only: " God, be merciful to me a sinner." Second, it is meant to drive him to action that he may bring forth fruits meet for repentance. No man has truly repented when he goes and does the same things again. Fosdick said that the great truth of Christianity is that " no man need stay the way he is." The proof and the fruit of repentance is a changed life, a life changed by our effort in co-operation with the grace of God.

The three steps on the way back are memory, repentance, and action.

EPHESUS
A RUINOUS HERESY
Revelation 2.1-7 (continued)

WE meet here a heresy which the Risen Christ says that He hates, and which He praises Ephesus for also hating. It may seem strange to attribute hatred to the Risen Christ; but two things are to be remembered. First, if we love anyone with passionate devotion and intensity, then we will necessarily hate anything which threatens to ruin that person in body and in soul. Second, it must always be remembered that it is necessary to hate the sin, but to love the sinner. God's holy anger is kindled against sin, but God's love for the sinner never wearies and never grows cold.

The heretics whom we meet here are the Nicolaitans. Here they are only named, but not defined. But we meet them again in Pergamum (verse 15). There they are very closely connected with those " who hold the teaching of Balaam," and that is connected with eating things offered to idols and with fornication (verse 14). And we meet precisely the same problem at Thyatira where the wicked Jezebel is said to cause Christians to commit fornication and to eat things offered to idols.

We may first note that this danger is not coming from outside the Church, but from inside. These heretics are the enemy within the gates. Their claim was, not that they were destroying Christianity, but that they were presenting an improved and modernized version of it.

We may, second, note that in the letter to Pergamum the Nicolaitans and those who hold the teaching of Balaam are closely connected. They were, in fact, one and the same. There is a play on words here. The name *Nicolaus*, the founder of the Nicolaitans, could be derived from two Greek words, *nikan*, which means *to conquer*, and *laos*, which means *the people*. *Balaam* can be derived from two Hebrew words, *bela* which means to *conquer* and *ha'am*, which means *the people*. The two names, then, are the same name, Nicolaus being the Greek form of it, and Balaam the Hebrew form of it; and both names can describe an evil, but influential, teacher, who has won an evil victory over the people, and subjugated them to poisonous heresy.

What, then, is the story of Balaam? In *Numbers* 25.1-5 we find a strange story in which the Israelites were seduced into illegal and sacrilegious unions with Moabite women, and into the worship of Baal-peor, a seduction which, if it had not been sternly checked, might have ruined the whole religion of Israel and destroyed her as a nation. When we go on to *Numbers* 31.16 we find that seduction definitely attributed to the evil influence of Balaam. Balaam, then, in Hebrew history and tradition stood for an evil man who seduced the people into immorality and sin.

Let us now go on to see what the early Church historians have to tell us about these Nicolaitans. The majority of them identify these Nicolaitans with the followers of Nicolaus, the proselyte of Antioch, who was one of the seven commonly called deacons (*Acts* 6.5). The idea is that Nicolaus went wrong and became a heretic. Irenaeus says of the Nicolaitans that " they lived lives of unrestrained indulgence " (*Against Heresies*, 1.26.3). Hippolytus says that Nicolaus was one of the seven and that " he departed from correct doctrine, and was in the habit of inculcating indifference of food and life " (*Refutation of Heresies*, 7.24).

The Apostolic Constitutions (6.8) describe the Nicolaitans as " shameless in uncleanness." Clement of Alexandria says that the Nicolaitans " abandon themselves to pleasure like goats . . . leading a life of self-indulgence." But he acquits Nicolaus of all blame and says that they perverted the saying of Nicolaus " that the flesh must be abused." By this Nicolaus meant that the body must be kept under; the heretics perverted it into meaning that the flesh can be used as shamelessly as a man wishes (*The Miscellanies* 2.20). So, then, the Nicolaitans obviously taught immorality and loose living.

Let us see if we can identify their point of view and their teaching a little more definitely. The letter to Pergamum tells us that they seduced people into eating meat offered to idols and into fornication. Now, when we turn to the decree of the Council of Jerusalem, we find that two of the conditions on which the Gentiles were to be admitted to the Church were that they were to abstain from things offered to idols and from fornication (*Acts* 15.28, 29). These are the very conditions that the Nicolaitans broke.

The Nicolaitans were almost certainly people who argued on these lines. (*a*) The Law is ended; therefore, there are no laws and no rules and no regulations, and we are entitled to do what we like. They confused Christian liberty with unchristian licence. They were the very kind of people whom Paul urged not to use their liberty as an occasion for the flesh (*Galatians* 5.13). (*b*) They probably argued that the body is evil anyway, and that the spirit alone is good, and that, therefore, a man could do what he liked with his body, because the body did not matter. Since the body was so unimportant, it was of no importance if the lusts of the body were sated and glutted. (*c*) They probably argued that the Christian was so defended by grace that he could go anywhere and do anything and take no harm. Grace would protect him, and grace would win him forgiveness no matter what he did.

It is clear that the Nicolaitans were exceedingly dangerous, for they took the greatest Christian truths and perverted them for their own ends.

What lay behind this Nicolaitan perversion of the truth? The trouble was the necessary difference between the Christian and the pagan society in which he moved. The heathen had no hesitation in eating meat offered to idols; it was set before him at every social feast and occasion. Could a Christian attend such a feast? The heathen had no idea of chastity; relations before marriage and outside marriage were accepted as completely normal and brought no shame and no rebuke. Must a Christian be so very different? Must he divorce himself from the standards and practices of the world in which he lived? Must he isolate himself like that? The Nicolaitans were suggesting that there was no reason at all why a Christian should not come to terms with the world. Sir William Ramsay describes their teaching thus: " It was an attempt to effect a reasonable compromise with the established usages of the Graeco-Roman society, and to retain as many as possible of those usages in the Christian system of life." This teaching naturally affected most the cultured and the well-to-do and the upper classes because they had most to lose, if they went all the way with the Christian demand. To John the Nicolaitans were worse than pagans, for they were the enemy within the gates.

The Nicolaitans were those who wished to compromise with the world; they were not prepared to be different; they were not prepared to make the great decision; they wished to have the best of both worlds. They were the most dangerous of all heretics from a practical point of view, for, if their teaching had been successful, the result would have been that the world would have changed Christianity, and not Christianity the world.

EPHESUS
THE GREAT REWARD

Revelation 2.1-7 (continued)

FINALLY, the Risen Christ makes his great promise to those who overcome. In that picture there are two very beautiful conceptions.

(i) There is the conception of *the tree of life*. The tree of life is part of the story of the Garden of Eden; in the midst of the garden there was the tree of life (*Genesis* 2.9); it was the tree of which Adam was forbidden to eat (*Genesis* 2.16, 17); the tree whose fruit would make a man like God, and for eating which Adam and Eve were driven from Eden (*Genesis* 3.22-24).

In later Jewish thought the tree of life came to stand for that which gave man life which was life indeed. Wisdom is a tree of life to them that lay hold upon her (*Proverbs* 3.18); the fruit of the righteous is a tree of life (*Proverbs* 11.30); hope fulfilled is a tree of life (*Proverbs* 13.12); a wholesome tongue is a tree of life (*Proverbs* 15.4). The tree of life came to describe anything which was the source of the kind of life that a man ought to live.

To this there is to be added another picture. In the Garden of Eden story Adam was first forbidden to eat of the tree of life, and then he was barred from the garden so that the tree of life was lost for ever. But it was a regular Jewish conception that, when the Messiah came, and the new age dawned, the tree of life would be in the midst of men, and those who had been faithful would eat of it. The wise man said: " They that do the things that please Thee shall receive the fruit of the tree of immortality " *Ecclesiasticus* 19.19). The rabbis had a picture of the tree of life in paradise. Its boughs overshadowed the whole of paradise; it had five hundred thousand fragrant perfumes, and its fruit as many pleasant tastes, and every one of them different. The idea was that what Adam had lost the Messiah would restore. To eat of the tree of life means to enter into the blessedness of the righteous in the Kingdom of Christ; it means to have all the joys that the faithful conquerors will have when Christ reigns supreme.

(ii) There is the conception of *paradise*, and the very sound of the word *paradise* is a lovely sound. We use this word often, but it may be that we do not attach any very definite meaning to it. When we study the history of the word, and when we see how the great thinkers of the Church used it, we come upon some of the most adventurous thinking that the world has ever known.

(*a*) Originally paradise was a Persian word. Xenophon wrote much about the Persians, and it was he who introduced the word into the Greek language. Originally paradise meant a pleasure garden, full of pleasant parks and meadows, with stately trees and flower gardens, and often with wild animals roving in semi-captivity. When Xenophon is describing the state in which the Persian king lived, he says that the great king takes care that, wherever he resides, there are *paradises*, as they call them, full of all the good and beautiful things the soil can produce (Xenophon, *Oeconomicus*, 4.13). Paradise is a lovely word to describe a thing of serene beauty.

(*b*) In the Septuagint, the Greek translation of the Old Testament the word paradise has two uses. First, it is regularly used for the *Garden* of Eden (*Genesis* 2.8; 3.1). Paradise means a garden and Eden was the fairest garden of all. Second, it is regularly used of any stately garden. When Isaiah speaks of a *garden* that has no water, it is the word *paradise* that is used (*Isaiah* 1.30). It is the word used when Jeremiah says: " Plant *gardens* and eat the fruit of them " (*Jeremiah* 29.5). It is the word used when the preacher says: " I made me *gardens* and orchards, and I planted trees in them of all kinds of fruits " (*Ecclesiastes* 2.5).

So the picture of the word paradise emerges, and it is the picture of a garden beautiful beyond compare.

(iii) In early Christian thought the word has a special meaning. In Jewish thought after death the souls of all alike went to Hades, which was a grey, shadowy, strengthless, ghostly place, a place of the shades. Now early Christian thought conceived quite definitely of an intermediate state between earth and heaven. There was, so they believed, an intermediate state to which all men went, and in which they remained until the final judgment of all things should come. This place was conceived of by Tertullian as a vast subterranean cavern beneath the earth. But there was a special part of it in which the patriarchs and the prophets lived, and that part was paradise. Philo describes it as a place " vexed by neither rain, nor snow, nor waves, but which the gentle Zephyr refreshes, breathing ever on it from the ocean." As Tertullian saw it, only one kind of person went straight to this paradise, and that was the martyr. " The sole key," he said, " to unlock paradise is your own life's blood " (Tertullian, *Concerning the Soul*, 55).

Origen was one of the most adventurous thinkers the Church ever produced. He writes like this: " I think that all the saints (he is using the word *saints* as Paul used it in the addresses of his letters, and means *Christians*) who depart from this life will remain in some place situated on the earth, which holy Scripture calls paradise, as in some place of instruction, and, so to speak, class-room or school of souls. . . . If anyone indeed be pure in heart and holy in mind, and more practised in perception, he will by making more rapid progress, quickly ascend to a place in the air, and reach the kingdom of heaven, through these mansions (he uses the word in the sense of *stages*) which the Greeks called *spheres*, and which holy Scripture calls *heavens*. . . . He will in the end follow Him who has passed into the heavens, Jesus the Son of God, who said: ' I will that where I am, these may be also.' It is of this diversity of places He speaks, when He said: ' In my Father's house are many mansions ' " (Origen, *De Principiis*, 2.6).

The great early thinkers did not identify paradise and heaven; paradise was the intermediate stage, the training ground, where the souls of the righteous were fitted to enter into the presence of God. There is something very lovely here. Who has not felt that the leap from earth to heaven is too great for one step, and who has not felt the need of a gradual entering nearer and nearer into the presence of God? May it have been of this that Charles Wesley was thinking, when he sang:

> *Changed from glory into glory,*
>   Till in heaven we take our place,
> Till we cast our crowns before Thee,
>   Lost in wonder, love, and praise.

(iv) I do not think that in the end in Christian thought the word paradise retained this idea of an intermediate state. It came to be equivalent to heaven, the immediate presence and glory of God. Whenever we think of the word paradise, our minds must turn to the words of Jesus to the dying and penitent thief: " Today shalt thou be with me in paradise " (*Luke* 23.43). Here we are in the presence of mysteries about which it would be irreverent and blasphemous to dogmatize; but is there any better definition of paradise, and of heaven, than to say that they are life for ever in the presence and in the company of our Lord? If we in simplicity accept the words of Jesus, paradise is life with Christ.

> When death these mortal eyes shall seal,
>   And still this throbbing heart,
> The rending veil shall Thee reveal
>   All glorious as Thou art—

and that is paradise.

THE LETTER TO SMYRNA

Revelation 2.8-11

And to the angel of the Church in Smyrna, write:

> These things says the first and the last, who passed through death, and who came to life again.

> I know the affliction and the poverty you endure—you are rich in spite of it—and I know the slanders which proceed from those who call themselves Jews and who are not, but who are a synagogue of Satan. Have no fear of what you will have to go through. Behold! the devil is going to throw some of you into prison, in order to test you, and you will have a time of affliction which will last for ten days. Show yourselves loyal to death, and I will give you the crown of life.

> Let him who has an ear hear what the Spirit is saying to the Churches. He who overcomes will not be hurt by the second death.

SMYRNA
THE CROWN OF ASIA

Revelation 2.8-11

IF it was inevitable that Ephesus should come first in the list of the seven Churches, it was but natural that Smyrna its great rival should come second. Of all the cities of Asia, Smyrna was the loveliest. Men called it the ornament of Asia, the crown of Asia, and the flower of Asia. Lucian said that it was " the fairest of the cities of Ionia." Aristides, the orator, who sang the praise of Smyrna with such splendour, spoke of " the grace which extends over every part like a rainbow . . . the brightness which pervades every part, and reaches up to the heavens, like the glitter of the bronze of armour in Homer." On the score of loveliness no city could challenge Smyrna. It added to the charm of Smyrna that the west wind, the gentle zephyr ever blew through its streets. " The wind," said Aristides, " blows through every part of the city, and make it as fresh as a grove of trees." The constant west wind had only one disadvantage. The sewage of the city drained into the gulf on which the city stood, and the west wind tended to blow it back upon the city rather than out to the sea.

Smyrna was magnificently situated. It stood at the end of the road which crossed Lydia and Phrygia and travelled out to the far east, and it commanded the trade of the rich Hermus valley. Inevitably Smyrna was a great trading city. The city itself stood at the end of a long arm of the sea, which ended in a small land-locked harbour in the very heart of the city. It was the safest of all harbours, and the most convenient; and it had the added advantage that in time of war the small compact harbour could be easily closed by a chain across the mouth of it. It was fitting that on the coins of Smyrna there should be an inscription of a merchant ship ready for the sea.

The setting of the city was equally beautiful. It began at the harbour; it traversed the narrow foothills; and then behind the city there rose the Pagos, a hill covered with temples and noble buildings. These noble buildings encircled Smyrna's hill, and they were spoken of as " The Crown of Smyrna." Smyrna knew all about crowns (verse 10), for that was the very name by which men called the buildings on her hill. A modern traveller describes it as " a queenly city crowned with towers." Aristides likened it to a great statue with the feet in the sea; the middle parts in the plain and the foothills; and the head, crowned with great buildings, on the Pagos behind. Aristides called Smyrna " a flower of beauty such as earth and sun had never showed to mankind."

Its history had not a little to do with the beauty of Smyrna, for Smyrna was one of the very few planned cities in the world. It had been founded as a Greek colony as far back as 1000 B.C. Round about 600 B.C. disaster had befallen it, for then the Lydians had broken in from the east and had destroyed it. For four hundred years Smyrna had been no city, but a collection of little villages; then round about 200 B.C. Lysimachus had rebuilt it, and had rebuilt it as a planned and unified whole. It was built with great, straight, broad, sweeping streets. Strabo speaks of the handsomeness of the streets, the excellence of the paving, and the great rectangular blocks in which it was built. Most famous of all the streets was the Street of Gold, which began with the Temple of Zeus and ended with the Temple of Cybele. It ran, as it were, cross-wise across the foothills of the Pagos; and, if the buildings which encircled the Pagos were the crown of Smyrna, the Street of Gold was the necklace round the hill.

Here we have an interesting and a significant thing, and a thing which shows the care and knowledge with which John set down his letters from the Risen Christ. The Risen Christ is called, " He who was dead and is alive again." That was nothing other than an echo of the experience of Smyrna itself. It had lived; for four hundred years as a city it had been dead; and with Lysimachus it had sprung to life again.

But Smyrna had other claims to greatness besides the beauty of the city. Smyrna was a free city. Smyrna well knew what loyalty and fidelity were. Of all the eastern cities Smyrna had been most notably loyal to Rome. Long before Rome was the undisputed mistress of the world, Smyrna had cast in its lot with Rome, never to waver in its fidelity. Cicero called Smyrna " one of our most faithful and our most ancient allies." In the campaign against Mithradates in the far east things had gone badly with Rome. And when the soldiers of Rome were suffering from hunger and from cold, the people of Smyrna had stripped off their own clothes to send them to the Roman soldiers in their trouble.

Such was the reverence of Smyrna for Rome that as far back as 195 B.C. it was the first city in the world to erect a temple to the goddess Roma and to the spirit of Rome. And in A.D. 26, when the cities of Asia Minor were competing for the privilege of erecting a temple to the godhead of Tiberius, Smyrna was picked out from them all for that honour, overcoming even Ephesus in the contest for it. The fidelity of Smyrna to Rome was famous in the ancient world.

But not only was Smyrna great in trade, in beauty, in political and in religious eminence; it was also a city where culture flourished and where knowledge and the arts were held in the highest esteem. Apollonius of Tyana had urged upon Smyrna the truth that only men can make a city great. He said: " Though Smyrna is the most beautiful of all cities under the sun, and makes the sea its own, and holds the fountains of the zephyr, yet it is a greater charm to wear a crown of men than a crown of porticoes and pictures and gold beyond the standard of mankind: for buildings are seen only in their own place, but men are seen everywhere and spoken about everywhere and make their city as vast as the range of countries which they can visit." So Smyrna had a stadium in which famous games were yearly held; a magnificent public library; an Odeion which was the home of music; a theatre which was one of the largest in Asia Minor. In particular, Smyrna was one of the cities which laid claim to being the birthplace of Homer; it had a memorial building called the Homereion; it put Homer's head on its coinage. This was, indeed, a disputed claim. Thomas Heywood, the seventeenth century poet, wrote the famous epigram:

> Seven cities warr'd for Homer, being dead,
> Who, living, had no roof to shroud his head.

In such a city we would expect magnificent architecture, and in Smyrna there was a host of temples, to Cybele, to Zeus, to Apollo, to the Nemeseis, to Aphrodite, and to Asclepios. In Smyrna there dwelt the splendour of heathen culture at its highest and pagan religion at its most magnificent.

Smyrna had rather more than its share of a characteristic which was common to all Greek cities. Mommsen said that Asia Minor was " a paradise of municipal vanity," and Smyrna of all cities was noted for " its municipal rivalry and its local pride." Everyone in it wished to exalt Smyrna, and everyone in it wished himself to climb to the top of the municipal tree. It is not without point that in the address of the letter the Risen Christ is called " the first and the last." In comparison with His glory all earthly distinctions are empty and worthless. Strife for the first place in worldly things pales into unimportance when it is seen in the light of the eternal glories.

There remains one feature of Smyrna which stands out in the letter, and which had very serious consequences for the Christians there. In Smyrna the Jews were specially numerous and specially influential (verse 9). We find them, for instance, contributing 10,000 *denarii* for the beautification of the city. It is clear that in Smyrna they were specially hostile to the Christian Church, no doubt because it was from them, and from those interested in Judaism that Christianity drew many of its converts. The Jews did everything they could to damage the Church, and to persuade the Roman authorities to active persecution. So, then, we may well end this study of Smyrna with the story of the most famous Christian martyrdom which happened there.

Polycarp was Bishop of Smyrna, and he was martyred on Saturday, 23rd February, A.D. 155. It was the time of the public games; the city was crowded; and the crowds were excited. Suddenly the shout went up: " Away with the atheists; let Polycarp be searched for." No doubt Polycarp could have escaped; but already he had had a dream vision in which he saw the pillow under his head burning with fire, and he had awakened to tell his disciples: " I must be burnt alive."

His whereabouts was betrayed to the persecutors by a little slave who collapsed under torture. They came to arrest him. He ordered that those who had come for him should be given a meal, and provided with all they wished, while he asked for himself the privilege of one last hour in prayer. Not even the police captain wished to see Polycarp die. On the brief journey to the city, he pled with the old man: " What harm is it to say, ' Caesar is Lord ' and to offer sacrifice and to be saved? " But Polycarp was adamant that for him only Jesus Christ was Lord.

When he entered the arena there came a voice from heaven saying: " Be strong, Polycarp, and play the man." The proconsul gave him the choice of cursing the name of Christ and making sacrifice to Caesar or death. " Eighty and six years have I served Him," said Polycarp, " and He has done me no wrong. How can I blaspheme my King who saved me? " The proconsul threatened him with burning, and Polycarp replied: " You threaten me with the fire that burns for a time, and is quickly quenched, for you do not know the fire which awaits the wicked in the judgment to come and in everlasting punishment.

Why are you waiting? Come, do what you will." In spite of the appeals of even the persecutors Polycarp remained immovable.

So the crowds came flocking with faggots from the workshops and from the baths, and the Jews, even although it was the Sabbath, and even although they were breaking the Sabbath law by carrying such burdens, were foremost in the clamour and foremost in bringing wood for the fire. They were going to bind him to the stake. " Leave me as I am," he said, " for He who gives me power to endure the fire, will grant me to remain in the flames unmoved even without the security you will give by the nails." So they left him loosely bound in the flames, and Polycarp prayed his great prayer:

> O Lord God Almighty, Father of Thy beloved and blessed Child, Jesus Christ, through whom we have received full knowledge of Thee, God of angels and powers, and of all creation, and of the whole family of the righteous, who live before Thee, I bless Thee that Thou hast granted unto me this day and hour, that I may share, among the number of the martyrs, in the cup of Thy Christ, for the resurrection to eternal life, both of soul and body in the immortality of the Holy Spirit. And may I today be received among them before Thee, as a rich and acceptable sacrifice, as Thou, the God without falsehood and of truth, hast prepared beforehand and shown forth and fulfilled. For this reason I also praise Thee for all things. I bless Thee, I glorify Thee through the eternal and heavenly High Priest, Jesus Christ, Thy beloved Child, through whom be glory to Thee with Him and the Holy Spirit, both now and for the ages that are to come. Amen.

So much is plain fact, but then the story drifts into legend, for it goes on to tell that the flames made a kind of room or tent around Polycarp and left him untouched. At length the executioner stabbed him to death to achieve what the flames could not do. " And when he did this there came out a dove, and much blood, so that the fire was quenched, and all the crowd marvelled that there was

such a difference between the unbelievers and the elect."
So Polycarp died at Smyrna, a martyr for the faith, faithful
unto death.

It can have been no easy engagement to be a Christian
at Smyrna, and yet the letter to Smyrna is one of the two
letters in which there is nothing but undiluted praise.

SMYRNA
UNDER TRIAL

Revelation 2.8-11 (continued)

THE Church of Smyrna was in trouble and further trial
was imminent.

There are three things that the letter says about this
trial.

(i) It is *thlipsis, affliction.* We have already seen that
the word *thlipsis* originally meant literal pressure, literal
crushing beneath a weight. The pressure of events is on the
Church at Smyrna, and the force of circumstances is trying
to crush the Christianity out of them.

(ii) It is *poverty.* In the New Testament poverty and
Christianity are closely connected. " Blessed be ye poor,"
said Jesus, as Luke has it (*Luke* 6.20). Paul described the
Christians at Corinth as being poor yet making many rich
(2 *Corinthians* 6.10). James speaks of God choosing the poor
in this world to be rich in faith (*James* 2.5).

We must note the word that is used; it is the word
ptōcheia. In Greek there are two words for *poverty.* There is
penia, which describes the state of the man who is not
wealthy, and who, as the Greeks defined it, must satisfy
his own needs with his own hands. And there is *ptōcheia,*
which describes absolute poverty and complete destitution.
It has been put this way—*penia* describes the state of the
man who has nothing superfluous; *ptōcheia* describes the
state of the man who has nothing at all.

The poverty of the Christian was due to two things. It
was due to the fact that most of them belonged to the

lower classes of society, and many of them were slaves. The gulf between the top and the bottom of the social scale is no new thing. In the ancient world it was even wider than it is now. These letters are written to cities in Asia, but we know that in Rome the poorer classes literally starved, because contrary winds delayed the corn ships from Alexandria, and the corn dole could not be distributed. The early Christians knew what grinding poverty was.

But there was another reason for the poverty of the Christians. Sometimes they suffered from the spoiling of their goods (*Hebrews* 10.4). There were times when the heathen mob would suddenly attack the Christians and wreck their homes and deliberately smash and steal such possessions as they had. Life was not easy for a Christian in Smyrna, or anywhere else in the ancient world.

(iii) There is *imprisonment*. John forecasts an imprisonment of *ten days*. That is not to be taken literally. In ancient custom *ten days* was an expression for a short time which was soon to come to an end. So this prophecy is at once a warning and a promise. Imprisonment is coming, but the time of trouble, although sharp, will be short. Two things are to be noted.

First, this is exactly the way in which persecution came. To be a Christian was against the law, but persecution was not constant and continuous. The Christians might be left in peace for a long time, but at any moment a governor might acquire a fit of administrative energy, or the mob might set up a shout to find the Christians—and then the storm burst. The terror of being a Christian was the uncertainty. In those days a Christian was a man who lived with a sword poised over his head.

Second, imprisonment does not sound so bad to us. We might well say: " Imprisonment? Well, that is not as bad as death anyway." But in the ancient world imprisonment was merely the prelude to death. In those days the state would not take the trouble to look after prisoners. A man was only a prisoner until he was led out to die.

SMYRNA
THE CAUSE OF THE TROUBLE

Revelation 2.8-11 (*continued*)

THE instigators of persecution were the Jews. It was from them that the slanders came. Again and again in the narrative of *Acts* we see how the Jews stirred up the authorities against the Christian preachers. It happened at Antioch (*Acts* 13.50); at Iconium (*Acts* 14.2, 5); at Lystra (*Acts* 14.19); at Thessalonica (*Acts* 17.5).

The story of what happened at Antioch shows us how the Jews very often succeeded in moving the authorities to take action against the Christians. There the story says that the Jews stirred up devout and honourable women and the chief men of the city (*Acts* 13.50). Round about the Jewish synagogues there gathered many "god-fearers." These were Gentiles who were not prepared to go the whole way and to become proselytes and to accept the whole of Judaism; but they were attracted by the preaching of the one God instead of the many gods, and they were attracted very specially by the purity of the Jewish ethic and the chastity of Jewish morals as compared with the lust and sexuality of heathen life. In particular women were attracted to Judaism for these very reasons. Often these women were of very high station, the wives of magistrates and governors, and it was through them that the Jews got at the authorities and moved them to persecute. The Jews had their ways—and effective ways they were—of exerting pressure on the authorities to take action against the Christians.

John calls the Jews the *synagogue of Satan*. Here John is taking a favourite expression of the Jews and reversing it. When the people of Israel met together they loved to call themselves "the assembly of the Lord" (*Numbers* 16.3; 20.4; 31.16). The word *synagogue* is in Greek *sunagōgē*, which literally means a coming together, an assembly, a congregation. It is as if John said: " You call yourselves the assembly of God when, in fact, you are the assembly of the devil." Once John Wesley said of certain men who were presenting a crude and cruel and savage picture of God: " Your God is my devil." It is a terrible thing when religion becomes the means of evil, cruel and horrible things. It has happened. In the days of the French Revolution, Madame Roland uttered her famous cry: " Liberty, what crimes are committed in your name! " And there have been tragic times when the same could have been said about religion.

What were the slanders which were levelled against the Christians? There were six ever-recurring slanders.

(i) On the basis of the words of the Sacrament—This is my body, and this is my blood—the story went about that the Christians were cannibals.

(ii) Because the Christians called their common meal the *Agapē*, the Love Feast, it was said that their gatherings were orgies of lust and immorality.

(iii) Because Christianity did, in fact, often split families, when some members of them became Christians and some did not, the Christians were accused of breaking up homes and " tampering with family relationships."

(iv) The heathen accused the Christians of atheism because they could not understand a worship which had no images of the gods, such as they themselves had.

(v) The Christians were accused of being politically disloyal citizens and potential revolutionaries because they would not say: " Caesar is Lord."

(vi) The Christians were accused of being incendiaries because they foretold the end of the world in flames and disintegration.

It was not difficult for maliciously-minded people to disseminate dangerous rumours and slanders about the Christian Church.

SMYRNA
CHRIST'S CLAIM AND CHRIST'S DEMAND

Revelation 2.8-11 (continued)

WE have seen that the Church at Smyrna was a Church which was battling with difficulties and which was threatened with worse to come. It is in view of that that the letter to Smyrna opens with two resounding titles of Christ, titles which tell what Christ can offer to a man confronted with such a situation as faced the Christians at Smyrna.

(i) Christ is the first and the last. In the Old Testament that is a title belonging to God. " I am the first," Isaiah heard God say, " and I am the last " (*Isaiah* 44.6; 48.12). This title has two aspects. To the Christian this is a tremendous promise. Come what will, from the first day of life to the last day of life; happen what will, of all the kaleidoscopic colours and experiences of life; the Risen Christ is with us. We have His word that He is with us alway, even unto the end of the world. Of whom then shall we be afraid? But to the pagans of Smyrna this was a warning. They loved their city; they called it the first in Asia, and they were prepared to argue the claims of Smyrna to the primacy against anyone. They lived in a little world of municipal vanity, where every man was striving to be one better than his neighbours, and to get a step ahead of other people. Everyone wished for the first place, and strove competitively for it. But the Risen Christ said: " I am the first and the last." Here is the death of human pride. Beside the glory of Christ all our human titles are things which are of no importance, and all our human claims become ridiculous. When Julian, the Roman Emperor, had failed in his attempt to put the clock back, and to banish Christianity, and to bring back the old gods, and when he had come to death in the attempt, he said: " To shoulder Christ from out the topmost niche was not for me." The topmost niche belongs to Him who is the first and the last, and beside Him our human claims and ambitions are annihilated.

(ii) Christ is He who was dead and is alive again. The tenses of the verbs here are of the first importance. The Greek word for *was* is *genomenos*, which means rather *became*. It describes what we might call the experience of an episode, a passing phase. Christ became dead; for Him it was a passing phase, an episode through which He passed, something which He experienced and overcame. In the Greek the verb which the Authorized Version translates *is alive* is not a present tense at all, as it seems to be in the English. It is an aorist, and the aorist describes one action done and completed in the past. The right translation is *came to life again*, and the reference is to the event of the Resurrection. The Risen Christ is He who experienced death, who passed into death, through death, and out of death, and who came to life again in the triumphant event of the Resurrection, and who is alive for evermore. Here again there are two aspects, but this time both for the Christian to see.

(*a*) The Risen Christ is one who has *experienced* the worst that life could do to Him. He had died, and He had died in the agony of the Cross. No matter what happened to the Christians of Smyrna, Jesus Christ had been through it before. Jesus Christ can help because He knows what life is like at its worst, and He has experienced the bitterness of death. Nothing has happened to us which has not already happened to Him.

(*b*) The Risen Christ has *conquered* the worst that life can do. He triumphed over pain; He triumphed over the Cross; He triumphed over death. He does not offer what He Himself has not performed; and He offers us through Himself the way to victorious living.

But in this passage there is also a demand, and the demand is for *loyalty*. The demand of the Risen Christ is that His people should be faithful unto death, loyal even when death is the price of loyalty. Loyalty was a quality of which the people of Smyrna knew something, for their city had flung in its lot with Rome, when the greatness of Rome was only a faint, far off possibility, and had never wavered from that loyalty, in fair weather and in foul. There is nothing in this world which can take the place of loyalty. If all the other noble qualities of life were placed in the balance against loyalty, loyalty would outweigh them all. It was R. L. Stevenson's prayer that " in all the chances of fortune, and down to the gates of death " we should be " loyal and loving to one another."

The Risen Christ makes great offers and great demands; and it is only in the strength and courage which He offers that we can meet His demands.

SMYRNA
THE PROMISED REWARD

Revelation 2.8-11 (*continued*)

JESUS CHRIST will be in no man's debt, and out of loyalty to Him there comes His own reward. In this passage two rewards are mentioned.

(i) There is *the crown of life*. Again and again the crown of the Christian is mentioned in the New Testament. Here and in *James* 1.12 it is the crown of *life*. Paul speaks of the crown of *righteousness* (2 *Timothy* 4.8), and of the crown of *rejoicing* (1 *Thessalonians* 2.19). Peter speaks of the crown of *glory* (1 *Peter* 5.4). Paul contrasts the immortal crown of the Christian with the fading crown of laurel which was the prize of the victor in the games (1 *Corinthians* 9.25), and Peter speaks of the crown of amaranth which never fades away (1 *Peter* 5.4).

The *of* in each of these phrases means *which consists of*. It is the crown which consists of glory, which consists of righteousness, which consists of beauty, which consists of life, that is meant. To win the crown of righteousness, or the crown of glory, or the crown of life, is to be crowned with righteousness, to be crowned with glory, to be crowned with life. But we must understand the idea behind this word *crown*. In all cases the word is *stephanos*. In Greek there are two words for *crown*; there is *diadēma*, which means the *royal crown*, and there is *stephanos*, which has usually something to do with *joy* and *victory*. It is not the royal crown which is being offered to the Christian; it is the crown of joy and victory. This word *stephanos* has many associations, and all of them contribute something to the riches of thought behind the word. Let us look at the different kinds of *stephanoi* (that is the plural of *stephanos*) which the ancient world wore.

(*a*) First to the mind comes the victor's crown in the games. Smyrna had games which were famous all over Asia. As in the Olympic Games, most famous of all, the reward of the victorious athlete was the laurel crown. The Christian can win the crown of victory in the contest of life. He can so run the race of life that at the end of it he is the victorious athlete of Christ.

(*b*) When a man had diligently and faithfully performed the work of a magistrate, at the end of his term of office he was granted a crown. The crown is the reward of faithful service. He who throughout life faithfully serves Christ and his fellow-men will receive his crown.

(*c*) The heathen world was in the habit of wearing crowns, chaplets of flowers, at banquets. The crown was the sign of festal joy. At the end of the day, if the Christian is loyal, he will have the joy of sitting at the banquet of God as the guest of God.

(*d*) The heathen worshippers were in the habit of wearing crowns when they approached the temples of their gods. The crown was the sign of entry into the presence of a god. At the end of the day, if he has been faithful, the Christian will have the joy of entering into the nearer presence of God.

THE REVELATION OF JOHN

(e) Lastly, some scholars have seen in this crown a reference to the halo or the nimbus which is round the head of divine beings in pictures. If that is so, it means that the Christian, if he is faithful, will be crowned with the divine life which belongs to God Himself. As John said: " We shall be like Him, for we shall see Him as He is " (I *John* 3.2).

In this life it may be that the Christian's loyalty will bring him also the crown of thorns, but in the life to come it will surely bring him the crown of glory.

(ii) Cyprian uses two great phrases to describe those who are faithful unto death. He describes them as " illustrious with the heraldry of a good name," and he calls them, " the white-robed cohort of the soldiers of Christ." To the faithful another promise is made: they will not be hurt by the *second death*. The *second death* is a mysterious phrase which occurs nowhere in the New Testament outside the *Revelation* (20.6, 14; 21.8). The Rabbis used the phrase; they talked of " the second death whereof the wicked die in the next world." The phrase may have two origins.

(a) Amongst the Jews the Sadducees believed that after death there was absolutely nothing; amongst the Greeks the Epicureans held the same doctrine. This belief finds its place even in the Old Testament for that pessimistic book *Ecclesiastes* is the work of a Sadducee. " A living dog is better than a dead lion; for the living know that they shall die, but the dead know not anything " (*Ecclesiastes* 9.4, 5). For the Sadducees and the Epicureans death was annihilation, obliteration, extinction, the ultimate end beyond which there was nothing. To the orthodox Jew this was too easy, for it meant that for the wise and for the fool the end was the same (*Ecclesiastes* 2.15, 16; 9.2). They, therefore, came to believe that there were, so to speak, two deaths—physical death which every man must undergo, but after that a death which was the judgment of God.

103

(b) This is very closely connected with the ideas which we touched on when we were studying the word *paradise* (2.7). We saw that many of the Jews and of the early Christian thinkers believed that there was an intermediate state into which all men passed, and in which they waited until the time of judgment. If that were so, then indeed there would be two deaths, one the physical death which no man can escape, and the other the spiritual death into which the wicked would enter after the final judgment.

Of such things it is not given to any man to speak with confidence, but, when John spoke of the faithful being unharmed by the second death, he meant precisely the same as Paul meant, when he said that there is nothing in life or in death, in time and in eternity which can separate those who love Him from Jesus Christ. Such a man is safe from all that life can do to him, and safe from all that death can do to him (*Romans* 8.38, 39).

THE LETTER TO PERGAMUM

Revelation 2.12-17

And to the angel of the Church in Pergamum, write:

These things says He who has the sharp two-edged sword.

I know where your home is. I know that it is where the throne of Satan is; and yet you hold fast to my name, and have not denied your loyalty to me, even in the days of Antipas, my faithful martyr, who was killed among you, where Satan has his home.

But I have a few things against you. You have among you some people who hold the teaching of Balaam, who taught Balak to put a stumbling-block before the children of Israel, to eat meat offered to idols, and to commit fornication. So you, too, have those who in the same way hold the teaching of the Nicolaitans. So, then, repent. If you do not, I am coming to you quickly, and I will go to war with them with the sword of my mouth.

Let him who has an ear hear what the Spirit is saying to the Churches. To him who overcomes I will give a share of the hidden manna; and I will give him a white stone, and written on the stone a new name, which no one but him who receives it knows.

PERGAMUM
THE SEAT OF SATAN

Revelation 2.12-17

IT will be noticed that there is a difference in the name of this city in the different translations of the New Testament. The Authorized Version calls it *Pergamos*, while the Revised Version, the American Standard Revised Version, and Moffatt call it *Pergamum*. *Pergamos* is the feminine form of the name, and *Pergamum* is the neuter form of the name; in the ancient world it was known by both forms of the name; but *Pergamum* was much the commoner, and the newer translations are right to prefer it.

Pergamum had a place all its own in Asia. It was not on any of the great roads, as Ephesus and Smyrna were; but historically it was the greatest city in Asia. Strabo called it an illustrious (*epiphanēs*) city, and Pliny called it " by far the most famous city in Asia " (*longe clarissimum Asiae*). The reason for this was that, by the time John was writing, Pergamum had been a capital city for almost four hundred years. Away back in 282 B.C. it was made the capital of the Seleucid kingdom, one of the sections into which the empire of Alexander the Great was broken up. It remained the capital of that kingdom until 133 B.C. In that year Attalus the Third died; and, before he died, he willed his dominions into the possession of Rome. Out of the dominions of Attalus, Rome formed the province of Asia, and Pergamum still remained the capital of the province. There is always something special in the air and atmosphere of a capital city, and Pergamum had enjoyed that distinction for almost four hundred years.

Its geographical position made Pergamum even more impressive. It was built on a tall conical hill, which dominated the valley of the River Caicus, and from the top of which the Mediterranean could be seen, fifteen miles away. Sir William Ramsay, a modern traveller and scholar, describes it thus: " Beyond all other cities in Asia Minor, it gives the traveller the impression of a royal city, the home of authority; the rocky hill on which it stands is so huge, and dominates the broad plain of the Caicus so proudly and so boldly." History and honour indeed gathered around Pergamum. Let us then set down the outstanding characteristics of this regal city.

(i) Pergamum could never achieve the commercial greatness of Ephesus or of Smyrna, but it was a centre of culture which surpassed both these cities. Pergamum was famous for its library, which contained no fewer than 200,000 parchment rolls. In the ancient world it was second only to the unique library of Alexandria. It is interesting to note that the word *parchment* is derived from *Pergamum*. In the ancient world *parchment* was *hē pergamēnē charta*, which means *the Pergamene sheet*; and to this name there attaches a story. For many centuries ancient rolls were written on papyrus. Papyrus is a substance made of the pith of a very large bulrush which grows beside the Nile. The pith was extracted, cut into strips, pressed into sheets, and smoothed. There emerged a substance not unlike brown paper, and this was the substance universally used for writing. In the third century B.C. a Pergamene king called Eumenēs was very anxious to make the library of the city supreme. In order to do so he persuaded—or even bribed—Aristophanes of Byzantium, who was the librarian at Alexandria, to agree to leave Alexandria and to come to Pergamum. Ptolemy of Egypt was enraged at this seduction of his outstanding scholar. He promptly imprisoned Aristophanes, and by way of retaliation he put an embargo on the export of papyrus to Pergamum. Faced with this situation, the scholars of Pergamum invented parchment or vellum, which is made of the skins of beasts, smoothed and polished and prepared for writing upon. In point of fact parchment or vellum is a much superior vehicle for writing, and, although it did not do so for many centuries, it in the end ousted papyrus altogether as a substance for writing upon. Pergamum, then, gloried in its knowledge and in its culture.

(ii) Pergamum was one of the great religious centres in the ancient world. In particular it had two most famous shrines. In the letter of the Risen Christ Pergamum is said to be the place where " Satan's seat " is. Obviously this must refer to something which the Christian Church regarded as particularly evil, and particularly hostile to the Christian faith. Some people have found the reference to Satan's seat explained in Pergamum's religious splendour. Let us then look at Pergamum's two most famous shrines, and let us see if they are adequate to explain this phrase.

(a) Pergamum regarded itself as the custodian and defender of the Greek way of life and the Greek worship of the gods. Round about 240 B.C. Pergamum had won a great victory against the savage invading Galatae or Gauls. Through that victory the hordes of the Galatae were halted. In memory of that victory a great altar to Zeus was built. It was built in front of the Temple of Athene which stood eight hundred feet up on Pergamum's conical hill. It was forty feet high, and it stood on a projecting ledge of rock. It looked exactly like a great seat or throne on the hillside; and all day every day it smoked with the smoke of sacrifices offered to Zeus. Around its base was carved one of the greatest achievements in the world of sculpture, the frieze which showed the Battle of the Giants, in which the gods of Greece were victorious over the giants of the barbarians. It has been suggested that that great, dominating altar was Satan's seat. No doubt the commanding position of that altar made it impossible for any citizen of Pergamum to forget Athene and Zeus. But it is unlikely that even a Christian writer would call that altar and its temple Satan's seat, for even by this time the old Greek gods were anachronisms, and it would not have been worthwhile to waste the powder and shot of Christian invective attacking them.

(b) Pergamum was very particularly connected with the worship of Asclepios. So much so was this the case that Asclepios was known as " the Pergamene god." When Galen was mentioning common and favourite oaths, he said that people commonly swore by Artemis of Ephesus, or Apollo of Delphi, or Asclepios of Pergamum. Asclepios was the god of healing; his temples were the nearest approach to hospitals in the ancient world. From all over the world people, many of them wealthy, flocked to Pergamum for relief for their pains and their diseases. R. H. Charles has called Pergamum " the Lourdes of the ancient world." The task of healing was partly the work of the priests; partly the work of doctors—Galen, second only to Hippocrates in the medical history of the ancient world, was born in Pergamum; and partly the work of the direct and miraculous intervention of Asclepios himself. Was there anything in that worship to move the Christians to call the Temple of Asclepios Satan's seat? There may have been two things.

First, the commonest and most famous title for Asclepios was *Asclepios Sōtēr*, which means Asclepios the Saviour. It might well be that the Christians felt a shudder of horror that the name *Saviour* should be given to anyone other than Jesus Christ, the Saviour of the world.

Second, the emblem of Asclepios was the serpent, which still appears on the cap badge of the Royal Army Medical Corps. Many of the coins of Pergamum have Asclepios' serpent as part of their design. It might well be that any Jew, or any Christian, might regard any religion which took the serpent as its emblem as a Satanic cult. But again this explanation seems unlikely. As it has been pointed out, the Christians would regard the place where men went to be healed—and often were healed—with pity rather than with savage indignation. The worship of Asclepios surely would not give adequate ground for calling Pergamum Satan's seat.

It seems then that we must look elsewhere for the explanation of this phrase.

(iii) Pergamum was the administrative centre of the province of Asia. In spite of the greatness of Ephesus Pergamum still retained the functions of a capital city. That means that Pergamum was the centre of Caesar worship for the province of Asia. We shall have much more to say of Caesar worship later on. But briefly Caesar worship was this. Rome's problem was to find a unifying bond in her vast and heterogeneous Empire. To many countries the government of Rome had brought blessings of prosperity, of peace, and of even-handed justice. Many of the provincials, in fact most of them, were ready and willing to see something divine in the spirit of Rome, and very early—in Smyrna, as we have seen, as early as 195 B.C. —there were temples to *Dea Roma*, the goddess Rome, the spirit of Rome. The spirit of Rome was incarnated in one man, in the Emperor; and so there arose the deification of the Emperor, and the erection of temples to his honour. Again this was not forced upon the people; in many cases it was the people who took the first step. Cities strove for the title of *Neōkoros* of the temple to the Emperor. *Neōkoros* literally means *temple-sweeper*, and proud cities were eager to have this title. Rome saw in the spread of Caesar worship that very unifying principle which she needed; and so it became the law that once a year every Roman citizen should go to the temple of the Emperor, burn a pinch of incense to the godhead of Caesar, and say: " Caesar is Lord." Having done that, the citizen was given a written certificate to prove that he had made this act of worship. Two things have to be noted. First, this was far more an act of political loyalty than it was of religious worship. Second, Rome never intended, and never tried, to make this worship exclusive. Having confessed that Caesar was Lord, the Roman citizen could go and worship any god he chose so long as the worship did not conflict with public decency and order. But the one thing no Christian would say was: "Caesar is Lord." For him Jesus Christ, and none other, was Lord. The Roman government was incapable of understanding this point of view, and Christians were regarded as disloyal and revolutionary citizens, and were, therefore, proscribed and outlawed.

Caesar worship was organised with a provincial centre and an administration like that of a presbytery or diocese. The point here is that Pergamum was the centre of that worship for the province of Asia. First of all Asian cities, before even Smyrna, in 29 B.C. a temple to the godhead of Caesar had been erected in Pergamum; and the worship of Caesar had its centre there. That meant that every Christian in Pergamum was under permanent threat of death. He never knew when the sword would fall. Undoubtedly that is why Pergamum was Satan's seat; it was the place where men must take the name of *Lord* and give it to Caesar instead of to Christ; and to a Christian there could be nothing more devilish and Satanic than that.

And here is the explanation of the beginning of the letter to Pergamum. In the address the Risen Christ is called *He who has the sharp two-edged sword.* Under the Roman government Roman governors were divided into two classes—those who had the *ius gladii,* the right of the sword, and those who had not. Those who had the right of the sword had the power of life and death; on their word a man could be executed on the spot. Humanly speaking the proconsul, who had his headquarters at Pergamum, had the *ius gladii,* the right of the sword, and at any moment he might use it against any Christian; but the letter bids the Christian not to forget that the last word is still with the Risen Christ, who has the sharp two-edged sword. The power of Rome might be satanically powerful; the power of the Risen Lord was greater yet.

PERGAMUM
AN ENGAGEMENT VERY DIFFICULT

Revelation 2.12-17 (continued)

To be a Christian in Pergamum was to face what Cromwell would have called " an engagement very difficult."

We have already seen what a concentration of pagan religion had its centre in Pergamum. There was the worship of Athene and Zeus, with its magnificent altar dominating the city; there was the worship of Asclepios, bringing sick people from far and near; and above all there were the demands of Caesar worship, hanging for ever like a poised sword above the heads of the Christians.

So the Risen Christ says to the Christians of Pergamum: " I know where you stay." The word for *to stay* is here *katoikein*; and it means to have one's home in a place, to have one's permanent residence in a place. This is a very unusual word to use of Christians in the world. Usually the word which is used of Christians is *paroikein*, which means to be a stranger, a sojourner in a place. Peter writes his letter to the *strangers*, the *sojourners*, throughout the provinces of Asia Minor. It is far more usual to think of a Christian as a stranger and a pilgrim than as a permanent resident in any place in the world. But here the matter is being regarded from another point of view. The Christians of Pergamum have their permanent residence, so far as this world is concerned, in Pergamum; and Pergamum is the place where the throne of Satan is, the place where Satan's rule is strongest, the place where Satan exercises most authority. It is there that the Christians of Pergamum have to stay, and have to go on staying, whether they like it or not. They are there, and they cannot get away.

Here is something very important. The principle of the Christian life is not escape, but conquest. It may be that we often feel it would be very much easier to be a Christian in some other place and in some other circumstances, amongst people who are more sympathetic and in a circle where witness is easier; but the duty of the Christian is not to run away, but to witness for Christ where life has set him. We once heard of a girl who was converted in an evangelistic campaign; she was a reporter on a secular newspaper, a position in which Christian witness was by no means easy. Her first step after her conversion was to leave her job, and to get a new job on a small Christian newspaper where she was constantly in the society of professing Christians. It was a strange thing that the first thing that her conversion did for her was to make her run away. The more difficult it is to be a Christian in any set of circumstances, the greater the obligation to remain within these circumstances. The Christians of Pergamum had to be Christians where Satan's throne was, and there they had to stay. If in the early days Christians had run away every time they were confronted with an engagement very difficult, there would have been no chance of a world for Christ.

Further, the Christians at Pergamum proved that it was perfectly possible to be a Christian under such circumstances. Even when martyrdom was in the air they did not flinch or retreat. Of Antipas we know nothing; there is a late legend in Tertullian that he met his death by being placed within a brazen bull and being slowly roasted to death within it. But there is a point in the Greek which is impossible to reproduce in English, but which is intensely suggestive. The Risen Christ calls Antipas my faithful *martus*. Now we have translated *martus* by the English word *martyr*; but *martus* is, in fact, the normal Greek word for *witness*. In the early Church to be a martyr and to be a witness were one and the same thing. *Witness* meant so often *martyrdom*. An early Christian knew quite well what he was doing; as soon as he became a Christian he had made himself liable to death. Here is a rebuke to us. There are so many who are prepared to demonstrate their Christianity in Christian circles, but who are equally prepared to play down their Christianity in circles where Christianity is met with ridicule, with contempt, with indifference or with opposition. The Christian must remember that the word *martus* means equally *martyr* and *witness*, and that Christian witness can be, and often must be, a costly thing.

But we must note still another thing. The Risen Christ calls Antipas *my faithful martus*; and in doing so He gives to Antipas nothing less than His own title. In *Revelation* 1.5 and 3.14 Jesus Christ Himself is called *the faithful martus*, the faithful witness; and to those who are true to Him Jesus Christ gives nothing less than His own honour and His own name. It is easy to be a Christian when it is no trouble to be a Christian; but the greater glory is for the man who accepts the fact that witness and martyrdom go hand in hand.

PERGAMUM
THE DOOM OF ERROR

Revelation 2.12-17 (*continued*)

IN spite of the fidelity of the Church at Pergamum there is error there. There are those who hold the teaching of Balaam, and the doctrine of the Nicolaitans. We have already discussed these people in connection with Ephesus and we shall deal with them again when we come to study the letter of Thyatira. Suffice it at the moment to say, that they sought to persuade Christians that there was nothing wrong with a prudent conformity to the world's standards, and that they urged the Church to use a cautious policy of compromise with the practices and the morals of the world.

The man who is not prepared to be different need not start on the Christian way at all. The commonest word for the Christian in the New Testament is the word *hagios*; and again and again we have noted that the basic meaning of that word is *different* or *separate*. The Temple is *hagios* because it is *different* from other buildings; the Sabbath

day is *hagios* because it is different from other days; God
is supremely *hagios* because in His infinite sinless holiness
He is totally different from men; and the Christian is
hagios because he is different from other men.

We must be very clear what this difference means, for
there is a paradox in it. It is Paul's summons to the
Corinthians that they should be different from the world.
" Come ye out from among them," he urges them (2 *Corinthians* 6.17). Now this difference from the world definitely
does not involve isolation and separation from the world,
nor does it involve contempt of, and hatred for, the world.
This very same Paul, who urges his Christian converts to
come out from among the people of the world, says in
writing to the very same Church: " I am made all things
to all men, that I might by all means save some " (I *Corinthians* 9.22). It was Paul's claim, to use the modern phrase,
that he could get alongside any man; but—and here is the
point—his getting alongside them was *that he might save
some*. It was not a question of bringing Christianity down
to their level; it was a question of bringing them up to the
level of Christianity. The fault of the Nicolaitans was that
they were seeking to adjust Christianity to the level of the
world rather than lift the world to the level of Christianity.
In other words, they were following a policy of compromise
simply and solely to save themselves from trouble they
were afraid and unwilling to face.

It is the word of the Risen Christ that He will come and
make war with them. We must note that He did not say:
" I will go to war with *you* "; He said: " I will go to war
with *them*." The wrath of Christ was not directed against
the whole Church. It was directed against those who were
misleading, deceiving and seducing the Church; for those
who were led astray, for those who were more sinned
against than sinning, He had nothing but pity. The wrath
of Christ is hottest against those who lead others astray.

It is the threat of the Risen Christ that He will make
war against them with *the sword of His mouth*. The Christ

of the sword is a startling idea. Thinking of the past conquerors, and comparing them with Jesus Christ, the poet wrote:

> Then all these vanished from the scene,
> Like flickering shadows on a glass;
> And conquering down the centuries came
> The swordless Christ upon an ass.

What then is the sword of Christ? The writer to the Hebrews speaks of the word of God which is sharper than any two-edged sword (*Hebrews* 4.12). And Paul speaks of "the sword of the Spirit which is the word of God" (*Ephesians* 6.17). The sword of Christ is the word of Christ. In the word of Christ there is *conviction of sin*; in it a man is confronted with the truth, and is thereby confronted with his own failure to know and to obey the truth. In the word of Christ there is *invitation to God*; it convicts a man of sin and then invites him back, not to the judgment, but to the love of God. In the word of Christ there is *assurance of salvation*; it convicts a man of sin, it leads him to the Cross, and it assures him that there is no other name under heaven, given among men, whereby we may be saved (*Acts* 4.12). The conquest of Christ is His power to win men to the love of God.

PERGAMUM
THE BREAD OF HEAVEN

Revelation 2.12-17 *(continued)*

IN this letter the Risen Christ promises two things to the man who overcomes. He promises him a share of the *hidden manna* to eat. Herein is a Jewish conception which has two aspects.

(i) When the children of Israel had no food in the desert God gave them manna to eat (*Exodus* 16.11-15). When the need of the manna passed, the memory of it did not pass. A pot of the manna was taken and was put into the ark and was laid up before God in the Holy of Holies in the taber-

nacle and in the Temple (*Exodus* 16.33, 34; *Hebrews* 9.4).
Early in the sixth century B.C. the Temple which Solomon
had built was destroyed; and the rabbis had a legend that,
when that happened, Jeremiah had hidden away the pot
of manna in a cleft in Mount Sinai, and that, when the
Messiah came, Jeremiah would return and the pot of manna
would be discovered again. Therefore, to a Jew to eat of
the hidden manna meant to enjoy the blessings of the
Messianic age. Jesus was the Messiah, and, therefore,
to a Christian to eat of the hidden manna meant to enter
into the blessedness of the new world which would emerge
when the Kingdom came, and when Jesus opened the
treasures of His blessings to His own.

(ii) But there may be a wider and more general meaning
here than that. Of the manna it is said: " This is the bread
which the Lord hath given you to eat " (*Exodus* 16.15).
The manna is called " corn from heaven " (*Psalm* 78.24);
and it is said to be the " bread of the mighty," that is, of
the angels (*Psalm* 78.25). And here the manna may mean
heavenly food. In that case John would be saying: " In
this world you cannot share with the heathen in their
feasts and in their banquets and on their social occasions;
you cannot sit down to meat which is meat that is part of a
sacrifice that has been offered to an idol. You may think
that you are missing much and that you are being called
upon to give up much. But if you abstain in this world from
these polluted feasts, the day will come when you will
feast in heaven upon heavenly food." If that is so, the
Risen Christ is saying that a man must abstain from the
seductions of earth if he wishes to enjoy the blessings of
heaven.

(iii) There is one possible further interpretation of this.
Some have suggested that the hidden manna is the bread of
God which is given to the Christian at the Sacrament of
the Lord's Supper. John tells us that the Jews said to Jesus
that their fathers had eaten manna in the wilderness, so
receiving bread to eat. And then John goes on to tell

us that Jesus said that God alone could give the true bread from heaven; and that He made the great claim: " I am the bread of life " (*John* 6.31-35). If the hidden manna and the bread of life are the same, then the hidden manna is not only the bread of the Sacrament; it stands for nothing less than Christ, who is the bread of life, and this is a promise that Christ will give to him who is faithful, nothing less than Himself.

PERGAMUM
THE WHITE STONE AND THE NEW NAME

Revelation 2.12-17 (*continued*)

THE final promise of Christ to the faithful in Pergamum is that He will give them the white stone with the new name on it. This is a passage of which there are almost endless interpretations. We shall look at some of them, for each of them has something to add to the picture and the preciousness of it. In the ancient world a white stone might stand for many things, and signify many things.

(i) There was a Rabbinic legend that precious stones fell from heaven along with the manna. The white stone would then simply stand for the precious gifts of God to His people.

(ii) In the ancient world coloured stones were used as counters for working out calculations, as a child strings beads on a wire to count. This would mean that the Christian is reckoned and counted among the number of the faithful.

(iii) In the ancient law courts white and black stones were used for registering the verdict of juries. When the case had been stated for the prosecution and for the defence, the jury expressed their verdict by casting stones into an urn, black stones for condemnation, white stones for acquittal, and the verdict was given according to whether the white or the black stones were in the majority in the voting urn. The white stone, then, stands for acquittal.

This would mean that the Christian is acquitted, justified, in the sight of God, because of the work of Jesus Christ.

(iv) In the ancient world objects called *tesserae* were much used. A *tessera* (the singular form of the Latin word) was a little tablet, made of wood, or metal, or stone; it had writing on it; and, generally speaking, the possession of a *tessera* conferred some kind of right or privilege upon a man. Three of these *tesserae* are of interest, and add something to the picture.

(a) In Rome the great houses had their *clients*. The clients were dependents who received their livelihood free from wealthy citizens. Every morning they received from their patron food and money for the day. And they were often given a *tessera* by which they identified themselves as being clients, and as having the right to the free gifts. This would mean that the Christian is the man who has the right and the privilege to the free gifts for life which Christ can give.

(b) To win a victory at the games was one of the greatest honours that the ancient world could give. Outstanding victors at the games were given, by the master of the games, a *tessera* which in the days to come conferred upon them the right of free entry to all public spectacles, public games, and public entertainments. This would mean that the Christian is the victorious athlete of Christ who receives his prize, and who is a sharer in the honour and the glory of his Lord.

(c) In Rome a great gladiator was the admired hero of all. Often a gladiator had to fight on until he was killed in combat. But if a gladiator had had a specially illustrious and honourable career, if he had been the darling of the crowds in the amphitheatre, when he grew old, he was exempted from all further combats, and he was allowed to retire in honour. Such men were given a *tessera* with the letters SP on it. SP stands for the Latin word *spectatus*, which means *a man whose valour has been proved beyond a doubt*. This would mean that the Christian is the gladiator of Christ, and that, when he has proved his valour in the battle of life, he is allowed to enter into the rest which Christ gives with honour.

(v) In the ancient world a specially happy and successful day was called *a white day*. Plutarch tells that when Pericles was besieging Samos he knew that the siege would be long; he did not wish his army to grow weary; so he divided it into eight parts; every day the eight companies drew lots; one of the lots was a white bean; and the company which drew the white bean was exempt from duty for the day, and could enjoy itself as it wished. From the use of the white bean a happy day came to be called a white day (Plutarch, *Life of Pericles* 64). Pliny in one of his letters tells a friend that that day he had had the joy of hearing in the law courts two magnificent young pleaders, young men in whose hands the future of Roman oratory was safe. And, he says, that experience made that day for him a day marked *candidissimo calculo*, with the whitest of stones (Pliny, *Letters* 6.11). It was said that the Thracians and the Scythians kept in their homes an urn, and for every happy day they threw a white stone into it, and for every unhappy day a black stone; then at the end of their lives the stones were counted, and as the white or the black preponderated, a man was said to have had a wretched or a happy life. This would mean that through Jesus Christ the Christian can have happiness and joy in life, the joy that no man taketh from him (*John* 16.22).

(vi) Along this line of interpretation there is one last possibility, and of them all it is most likely the correct one. One of the commonest of all customs in the ancient world was to carry an amulet or charm. It might be made of a precious metal like gold or silver, or a precious stone like a diamond; but quite often it was nothing more than a pebble. On the pebble there was a sacred name; to know a god's name was to have a certain power over him, to be able to summon him to one's aid in time of difficulty, and to have mastery over the demons. Such an amulet was thought to be doubly powerful and effective, if no one other than the owner knew the name that was inscribed upon it. Most likely what John is saying is: " Your heathen friends—and you did the same in your heathen days— carry amulets and charms, with superstitious inscriptions on them, and they think that their amulets will keep them safe. You need nothing like that; for you are safe in life and in death because you know the name and the nature of the only true God." The trust of the heathen was in a superstitious charm; the trust of the Christian was in the name of God.

PERGAMUM
RENAMED BY GOD

Revelation 2.12-17 (continued)

IT is just possible that we ought to look for the meaning of the new name and the white stone in another direction altogether.

The words *white* and *new* are characteristic of the *Revelation*. R. H. Charles has said in the *Revelation* " white is the colour and livery of heaven." The word that is used does not describe a dull, flat whiteness; it describes a whiteness which glistens and glitters and scintillates like snow in the winter sun. It stands for what we can only call the snow-white, dazzling purity of heaven and God. So in the *Revelation* we find white raiment (3.5); white robes (7.9); white linen (19.8, 14); and the great white throne of God Himself (20.11). White, then, is heaven's colour. Further, in Greek there are two words for *new*. There is the word *neos*, which means new in point of time. A thing can be *neos*, and yet exactly like any number of things; it may simply be a newly-made specimen of a common and ancient thing. On the other hand there is *kainos*, which is not only new in point of time, but also new in point of quality. If a thing is *kainos* it is not only newly made; nothing like it has ever been made before; it introduces to life something hitherto unknown. So in the *Revelation* there is the new Jerusalem (3.12); the new song (5.9); the new heavens and the new earth (21.1); and God makes all things new (21.5). With this in mind two lines of thought have been suggested.

It has been suggested that the white stone is the man himself; that the Risen Christ is promising His faithful ones a new self, a new life, a new character, cleansed of all earthly sins and stains, and glistening with the purity of heaven itself. The white stone, if that be so, is the man himself recreated and made new.

Next, as to the new name—one of the features of the Old Testament is the giving to a man of a new name to mark a new status. So Abram becomes Abraham when the great promise is made to him that he will be the father of many nations, and when he, as it were, acquires a new status in the plan of God for men (*Genesis* 17.5). So after the wrestling at Peniel, Jacob becomes Israel, which means the prince of God, because he had prevailed with God (*Genesis* 32.28). Isaiah hears the promise of God to the nation of Israel: " And the Gentiles shall see thy righteousness, and all kings thy glory; and thou shalt be called by a new name, which the mouth of the Lord shall name " (*Isaiah* 62.2).

This custom of giving a new name to mark a new status was known in the heathen world as well. The name of the first of the Roman Emperors was Octavius; but when he became the first of the Emperors he was given the name Augustus. This very name marked his new status; he was now unique and superhuman and more than man.

A curious superstitious parallel to this comes from peasant life in Palestine. When a person was very ill and in danger of death, he was often given a new name, the name of someone who had lived a long and saintly life, as if the giving of the new name turned him into a new person over whom the illness might lose its power.

If this is the case, then Christ promises a new status to those who are faithful to Him; to them is granted to enter into His glory and to sit in His throne and to become kings and priests to Him.

This is an attractive interpretation. It suggests that the white stone means that Jesus Christ gives to the man who is true to Him a new self and a new character, and clothes him with the purity of heaven; it suggests that the new name means the new status of honour and glory into which the man who has been true to Christ will enter when this life ends and when the next begins.

It remains to say that, attractive as that interpretation is, the view which traces back the white stone and the new name to the use of amulets is more likely to be correct.

THE REVELATION OF JOHN

THE LETTER TO THYATIRA

Revelation 2.18-29

And to the angel of the Church in Thyatira write:

These things says the Son of God, who has eyes like a flame of fire, and whose feet are like beaten brass.

I know your works—I mean your love and your loyalty and your service and your steadfast endurance; and I know that your last works are more than your first.

But I hold it against you that you make no effort to deal with the woman Jezebel, who calls herself a prophetess, and whose misleading teaching causes my servants to commit fornication, and to eat meat offered to idols. I have given her a time within which to repent, and she refuses to repent from her fornication. Behold, I am going to cast her into a bed, and I am going to cast her paramours into great affliction, unless they repent from her deeds; and I will slay her children with death; and all the Churches will know that I am He who searches the inmost desires and thoughts of a man's being; and I will give to each one of you what your works deserve.

To the rest of you in Thyatira, to all those who do not hold this teaching, to such as have not known the depths of Satan, as they call them, I say this— I am not going to put any other burden on you. All I say is, hold on to what you have until I come.

I will give to him who overcomes, and who keeps my works to the end, authority over the Gentiles; and he will smite them with a rod of iron; like vessels of pottery they will be smashed; for this is the authority that I have received from my Father; and I will give him the morning star.

Let him who has an ear hear what the Spirit is saying to the Churches.

THE REVELATION OF JOHN

THYATIRA
THE PERIL OF COMPROMISE

Revelation 2.18-29

THE longest of the seven letters is written to the least important of the seven cities. Pliny dismisses Thyatira as an unimportant town. Nonetheless, as we shall come to see, the problem which faced Thyatira and the danger which threatened Thyatira were the problem and the danger which were universally involved in the position of the Christians in Asia.

Thyatira lies in the long valley which connects the valleys of the Hermus and the Caicus rivers, through which the railway runs today; and it was Thyatira's geographical position which gave it its importance.

(i) Thyatira lay on the road which connected Pergamum with Sardis and which went on to Philadelphia and to Laodicea, the road which linked up with both Smyrna and Byzantium. That was the road by which the imperial post travelled; and it was a road which was crowded with the trade and commerce of Asia and the east. Therefore, first and foremost Thyatira was a great commercial town.

(ii) Strategically the importance of Thyatira was that it was the gateway to Pergamum, and Pergamum was the capital of the province. The first we hear of Thyatira is that it is an armed garrison, manned by a company of Macedonian troops, placed there as an outpost to protect Pergamum. The difficulty was that Thyatira was not capable of any prolonged defence. It lay in an open, easy, smiling valley. There was no height and no hill that could be fortified; and all that Thyatira could ever hope to do was to fight a delaying action until Pergamum could prepare to meet the invaders. Thyatira was, therefore, strategically a most important frontier town, but it was fated never to be able to fight anything other than a delaying action to give Pergamum time.

(iii) Thyatira had no special religious significance. It was not a centre of either Caesar worship or of Greek worship. Its local hero-god was called Tyrimnus and he appears on its coins on horseback armed with a battle-axe and a club. The only notable thing about Thyatira from the religious point of view was that it possessed a fortune-telling shrine, presided over by a female oracle called the Sambathē. Certainly no threat of persecution hung over the Thyatiran Church.

(iv) What, then, was the problem and the danger in Thyatira? We know less about Thyatira than about any other of the seven cities; and we are, therefore, seriously handicapped in trying to reconstruct the situation. The one thing we do know about Thyatira is that it was a great commercial centre. It was specially a centre of the dyeing industry and of the trade in woollen goods. It was from Thyatira that Lydia, the seller of purple, came (*Acts* 16.14). From inscriptions which have been discovered we learn that Thyatira had an extraordinary number of trade guilds. These trade guilds were associations of the people employed in certain trades for their mutual profit and pleasure. We find that there were in Thyatira guilds of workers in wool, leather, linen and bronze, makers of outer garments, dyers, potters, bakers and slave-dealers. Herein, we think, was the problem of the Church in Thyatira. To refuse to join one of these trade guilds would be much the same as to refuse to join a trade union today. It would mean that the person who refused to join had given up all hope of commercial prosperity, and had, in fact, given up all prospect of commercial existence. Why, then, should a Christian not join one of these guilds? These guilds had two characteristics. First, they held common meals. These common meals would very often be held in a temple. Even if they were not held in a temple, they would begin and end with a formal sacrifice to the gods, and the meat eaten at them would be meat which had already been offered to idols. Was it possible for a Christian to participate in a

meal like that? Second, it often happened that these
communal meals were occasions of drunken revelry and of
slack morality. Was it possible for a Christian to enter
into a social occasion like that?

Here was the problem at Thyatira. There was no threat
of persecution; the threat came from inside the Church.
Inside the Church there were those who were asking why
the Christian should not be a member of a trade guild, and
why he should sacrifice his business interests by refusing
membership. Such people would argue that the Christian
was so defended by the Holy Spirit and the presence of
Jesus Christ that he would take no harm by sharing in
the ceremonies and feasts of the trade guilds. In other words,
in Thyatira there was a strong movement, led by the
woman addressed as Jezebel, which pled for compromise
with the world and the world's standards in the interests of
business and commercial prosperity. The answer of the
Risen Christ is unequivocal. With such things the Christian
must have nothing to do.

The problem at Thyatira was the universal problem, the
problem which still meets us today, the problem of how far,
if at all, the Christian may compromise with the world.

THYATIRA
THE STATE OF THE CHURCH IN THYATIRA

Revelation 2.18-29 (continued)

R. H. CHARLES points out that by far the longest of the
seven letters is written to the most unimportant of the
seven cities; but the problem and the evil which were
imperilling the Church at Thyatira were very far from being
unimportant.

Of all the seven letters the letter to Thyatira is the
most enigmatic. Our trouble is that we have so little
definite information about Thyatira, and about the background against which the Church existed there. In the

case of the other cities, we have a store of information about the cities themselves which illumines the letters to them, and which enables us to see what was happening. In the case of Thyatira we have no such information; and it is doubtful if anyone would be willing to claim that he is able to provide a certain interpretation of this letter. In this letter we are presented with a series of four questions —What really was the situation of the Church in Thyatira? Who was this woman Jezebel, who is the centre of the situation? What did she really teach? What do the promises made to the Church at Thyatira really mean?

First, then, let us ask the question, What really was the situation in the Church at Thyatira?

The letter opens with a description of the Risen Christ which has a threat in it. His eyes are like a flame of fire, and His feet are like beaten brass. The description is taken from the description of the angelic messenger in *Daniel* 10.6: " His face was as the appearance of lightning, and his eyes as lamps of fire, and his feet like in colour to polished brass." There is something for awe and terror and reverence here. The flaming eyes must stand for two things. They must stand for the blazing anger against sin in the eyes of the Risen Christ; and they must stand for the awful penetration of that gaze which strips the disguises away and sees into a man's inmost heart. The brazen feet must stand for the inflexible, immovable strength and power of the Risen Christ. A message which begins like that will certainly be no soothing tranquilliser.

But the letter goes on to open in terms of the highest praise. The love and the loyalty and the service and the steadfast endurance of the Church at Thyatira are matters for congratulation. We must note how these great qualities go in pairs. Service is the outcome of love, and steadfast endurance is the product of loyalty. There are at least certain things in which the Church at Thyatira is better now than it was when it began.

Then comes the condemnation of the woman Jezebel and all her ways and all her teaching; and one can hardly avoid the conclusion that she had very considerable influence in the Church at Thyatira.

The necessary conclusion seems to be this. On the surface the Church at Thyatira was a strong and a flourishing Church. If a stranger went into it, he would be impressed with its abounding energy and its generous liberality and its apparent steadfastness. But, for all that, there was something essential missing; there was a canker at the heart of it.

Here is a warning. A Church which is crowded with people and which is a hive of energy and a dynamo of activity is not necessarily a real Church. It is quite possible for a Church to be crowded, because its people come to it to be entertained instead of instructed, and to be soothed and petted instead of to be challenged and confronted with the fact of sin and the offer of salvation. A Church may be so full of energy that it becomes a restless ferment instead of a haven of peace. A Church may be packed with many activities, but in the abounding energy the centre may have been lost, and it may be a highly successful Christian club rather than a real Christian congregation. The state of things in Thyatira is something designed to give us searchingly to think.

THYATIRA
THE SOURCE OF THE ERROR

Revelation 2.18-29 (continued)

THE source of the trouble in Thyatira centred round a woman whom the letter calls Jezebel. Who was this woman? A variety of answers have been given to that question.

(i) We begin with an answer which is very interesting, although it is doubtful if it is possible. The Authorized

Version calls her *that woman Jezebel*. Moffatt translates
"that Jezebel of a woman." The Greek is *tēn gunaika
Iezebel*. There are some few manuscripts which after
gunaika have the word *sou*, which means *your*. Now the
noun *gunē*—the nominative case of the word of which
gunaika is the accusative form—not only means *woman*;
it is also the regular word for *wife*; and if with these
manuscripts we read *tēn gunaika sou Iezebel*, then the
phrase will mean *your wife Jezebel*. Very early on we saw
that the *angel* of the Church may possibly be the *bishop*
of the Church. If, then, the letter is addressed to the
bishop of the Church, and in it there is a reference to
your wife Jezebel, it means that the cause of all the trouble
is the bishop's wife! That, indeed, would be an interesting
sidelight on the early Christian congregations. It would
not be the last time that the wives of church officials were
the sources of trouble in a congregation. But, on the
whole, this interpretation must be rejected, because the
evidence for inserting the word *sou* is not good enough.

(ii) We have already said that one of the few claims
to distinction which Thyatira possessed was that there
was there an oracle called the *Sambathē*, who was a woman
fortune-teller. The Greeks made great use of, and put great
faith in, oracles. The oracle at Delphi was world famous,
and the expression *a Delphic utterance* has become proverb-
ial. It may be that this oracle was a Jewess, for the Jews
in the ancient world went in largely for this business of
fortune telling. There are those who see in the Sambathē
the evil influence which was threatening the Church at
Thyatira; it is perfectly possible that such an oracle
should use her influence to injure the Church, an activity
which would be all the more likely if she was a Jewess.
Again this must be rejected, for it is quite clear that this
woman who is called Jezebel was a member of the Church,
and her influence is being exerted from within.

(iii) There are some few who on no grounds whatever
have identified this Jezebel with Lydia, the seller of purple

from Thyatira, whom Paul met and converted at Philippi. It is suggested that she came back to Thyatira, and became an evil and a domineering influence in the Church, because of her wealth and her business interests. That theory is merely a slander on Lydia.

(iv) The only reasonable conclusion is that we have no idea who this Jezebel was, although we can with certainty trace the kind of person that she was.

That she claimed to be a prophetess is not so very surprising. It is true that Paul would have nothing to do with women speaking in the Church (1 *Corinthians* 14.34). But it is also true that in both the Old and the New Testaments there are prophetesses. In the Old Testament there are Miriam (*Exodus* 15.20); Deborah (*Judges* 4.4); Huldah (2 *Kings* 22.14); and in the New Testament there are Anna (*Luke* 2.36), and the four virgin daughters of Philip (*Acts* 21.9). It was perfectly possible for a woman to emerge as a prophetess within the Church.

This woman is called *Jezebel*, and, therefore, her character and her influence must be discovered in the original Jezebel. There are few women who have acquired such a reputation for wickedness as Jezebel has. She was the daughter of Ethbaal, king of Sidon, and the wife of Ahab (1 *Kings* 16.31). When she came from Sidon, she brought with her her own gods, and caused Ahab and his people to worship Baal. It was not that she would have wished to banish the worship of Jehovah, if the prophets of Jehovah would have accepted Baal *in addition to* Jehovah; she wished to add Baal worship to the worship of the God of Israel. She slew the prophets of the Lord, and at her own table she supported four hundred and fifty prophets of Baal (1 *Kings* 18.13, 19). She was Ahab's evil genius; in particular, she was responsible for the murder of Naboth in order that Ahab might enter into the possession of the ground where Naboth's vineyard stood (1 *Kings* 21). And she left behind her a name for " whoredoms and witchcrafts " (2 *Kings* 9.22). Jezebel was notoriously the immoral woman who had seduced Ahab and Israel from the worship of the true God.

That must mean that the Jezebel of Thyatira was an evil and a seductive influence on the purity of the life and worship of the Christian Church. It must be clearly understood that she had no wish to destroy the Church; but she wished to bring into it new ways and new practices which were, in fact, destructive of the faith. Jezebel was one of these people who wish to alter Christianity to suit themselves, and who think that they can improve upon the teaching of Jesus Christ.

THYATIRA
THE TEACHING OF JEZEBEL—I

Revelation 2.18-29 *(continued)*

THIS Jezebel of a woman is accused of teaching two things—of teaching the Christian people to commit fornication and to eat meat offered to idols.

Let us take the second of these things first, because we can be surer of what it means. One of the great problems of the Christian Church was the problem of meat offered to idols, and it was a problem which met the Christian every day in life. When a man made a sacrifice in a Greek temple, very little of the actual meat was burned on the altar. Sometimes all that was actually burned was a few hairs cut from the forehead of the animal. The priests received a share of the meat of the animal as their perquisite; and the worshipper received the rest. With the meat which he received the worshipper did one of two things. He held a feast of his friends within the temple precincts with the meat. Many festal meals were held in temples. A common form of invitation to a festal meal ran: " I invite you to dine with me at the table of our Lord Serapis." If he did not do that, he could take the meat home, and hold a feast of his friends in his own house. Here was the

Christian problem. Could a Christian go to a feast which was held in a heathen temple? Could he enter the doors of such a place? Could he, in a temple or anywhere else, eat meat which had been offered to idols? Paul discusses this very problem in I *Corinthians* 8-10. We must remember that the ancient world believed intensely in demons; the pagan gods were regarded as demons; and one of the easiest ways for a demon to get into a man was for the demon to settle on the man's food, and thereby to gain an entry to his body. Meat offered to idols had been consecrated and dedicated to pagan gods who were demons. Could a Christian eat such meat? Could he sit at a feast where such meat was set before him? Even if he had Christ within him as the all-powerful antidote to all hurtful things, was it right that by his presence at such a meal, and by his partaking of such meat, he should appear to countenance the worship of idols and of demons and of false gods?

The problem was complicated by the fact that even in the butchers' shops the meat might well have been offered to idols before it was sold to the public. The priests in the temples could not possibly consume all the meat of all the sacrifices which fell to them. They, therefore, sold much of their share to the butchers' shops. Such meat was the best meat. What was a Christian going to do about that? To us this sounds a very remote question; but to the Christians of the early Church, it was something which met them in the ordinary course of life every day.

The Church had no doubt as to where a Christian's duty lay. Abstention from things offered to idols was one of the conditions on which the Gentiles received the right of entry into the Christian Church (*Acts* 15.29). The Church was clear that the Christian must not touch things polluted like that.

The prohibition of meat offered to idols had one far-reaching consequence. It came near to cutting off a Christian from all social fellowship with non-Christians; if a Christian was compelled to abstain from things offered to idols, there were few social occasions, and almost no feasts and banquets which he could share with the heathen world.

This had another consequence which, as we have already said, we think was at the back of the situation in Thyatira. In the ancient world each craft and trade had its guild. These guilds met frequently, and they met for a common meal. Such a meal was at least, in part, a religious ceremony. It would probably meet in a heathen temple; and it would certainly begin with a libation to the gods, and the meal itself would largely consist of meat offered to idols. The official position of the Church meant that a Christian could not attend such a meal. This involved much more than an abstention from social fellowship; it meant that a Christian must commit commercial suicide; for his career as a crafts-man or tradesman was finished if he could not become a member of his guild. It was no longer possible for him to build up a flourishing business; it was probably not even possible for him to be in business at all.

Here, then, is where Jezebel came in. She urged upon the Christians that there was no need for them to cut themselves off from society; she urged that there was no reason why they should not be members of the guilds; she urged that there was no reason for a man to commit commercial suicide because he had become a Christian; she insisted that in the world there was no harm at all in accepting the world's customs and the world's ways. She was eager that the Church should accommodate itself to the world and that it should work out a working compromise with the world. And it must be clear that, when she did so, she was not proceeding on grounds of principle at all; she was simply trying to protect her business interests. The Jezebel of Thyatira was in effect saying that if the standards of the Church and business interests and practices clashed, then the standards of the Church must be abandoned. Jezebel was one of the people who love their business more than they love the Church, and to whom the claims of commercial success speak more loudly than the claims of Christ.

THYATIRA
THE TEACHING OF JEZEBEL—2

Revelation 2.18-29 (*continued*)

IT is the second part of Jezebel's teaching which is not so clear. She is said to teach the people to commit fornication (verse 20); she is urged to repent from her fornication (verse 21); and her paramours and her children are threatened along with her (verses 22, 23). The question is this—Is this reference to fornication to be taken literally, or, is it to be taken in the metaphorical sense which is so common in Scripture? Is this reference to sexual immorality, or, is it to spiritual infidelity to God?

(i) There is no doubt that in Scripture infidelity to God is expressed in terms of fornication and adultery. Israel is the Bride of God (*Isaiah* 54.5; *Jeremiah* 3.20); and in the New Testament the Church is the Bride of Christ (2 *Corinthians* 11.1, 2; *Ephesians* 5.24-28). Again and again in the Old Testament the Israelites are, therefore, said to go " awhoring after strange gods " (*Exodus* 34.15, 16; *Deuteronomy* 31.16; *Psalm* 73.27; *Hosea* 9.1). In the New Testament the age which is unfaithful to Jesus Christ is an " evil and adulterous generation " (*Matthew* 13.39; 16.4; *Mark* 8.38). Is this what is meant here? Is the *fornication* which Jezebel's teaching inculcated a spiritual infidelity to Jesus Christ? Does it mean a drifting away to the worship of heathen gods, or at least a compromise with that worship? If that is the meaning, her *paramours* (verse 22) will be those who are, as we say, flirting with this kind of teaching, and her *children* (verse 23) will be those who have accepted this teaching, and who have followed it.

There is nothing at all impossible in this. The whole tendency of heathenism was to acquire new gods. Heathen religion was seldom exclusive; it seldom insisted that worship must be offered to one god alone. It tended to think that there was very probably something in every religion, and that it was, therefore, prudent to give all the gods a share in worship. Every Roman home had its *lararium*, a little household shrine with the two little *lares*, the guardian gods of the household. In the *lararium* of Alexander Severus, the Roman Emperor, there stood images of Apollonius, Christ, Abraham, Orpheus, and " others of that sort."

It may well be that the teaching of Jezebel was that the Christians did not need to be so exclusive in their worship of Jesus Christ, and, above all, that there was no need for them to refuse to say, " Caesar is Lord," and to burn their pinch of incense. She would argue that there was no harm at all in conforming to the outward rituals and ceremonies of heathen worship. If Christians would be sensible about that, then they would win the heathen much more easily, and would save themselves an immense amount of trouble. If the Christian Church as a whole had accepted that form of teaching, the inevitable consequence would have been that Christianity would have become nothing more than still another of these religions of which the Roman Empire was so full. The claim of Christianity is not that Jesus Christ is one of the Saviours; not even that He is the chief of Saviours; but that He is the only Saviour.

(ii) Are we then to believe that what Jezebel taught was not physical sexual fornication, but that spiritual fornication which was infidelity to Jesus Christ? There is one thing in the letter which militates against that view. We read that the followers of Jezebel claimed to know *the depths of Satan* (verse 24). Some scholars think that this is the Risen Christ's contemptuous description of the false teaching. The real Christian knows what Paul called the deep things of God (I *Corinthians* 2.10); but what Jezebel and her company know is the deep things of Satan. But that will not do, for the letter unmistakably speaks of " the deep things of Satan, as *they* call them." This is quite certainly a reference to a kind of belief that was not uncommon among the heretics. Some of them held that it was a plain duty to experience every kind of sin. The real achievement was to allow the body to wallow in sin and to keep the spirit and the soul entirely unaffected. They argued that it was nothing for a man who had never indulged in pleasure to abstain from pleasure; that it was nothing for a man who had never mixed with lust to abstain from lust; the real achievement was to indulge in pleasure to the limit, and not to be conquered by it. The very indulgence in pleasure was a kind of training of the soul. Those who knew the deep things of Satan were those who had plumbed evil to its depths deliberately in order to experience it. This has got some kind of remote parallel in the old idea that it is necessary for a young man to sow his wild oats. Jezebel may well have been teaching that it was a duty to sin.

What, then, shall we say? It seems to us that in this case all the threads tie up and that there is no necessity to make a choice between views. All the probability is that Jezebel was teaching that a Christian ought to accommodate himself to the world, and ought not so rigidly to reject all the world's practices. She was teaching that there was no need for the Christian to abstain from the usual business and commercial practices; she was teaching that there was no need for the Christian to insist on so high an ethical and moral standard; she was urging the Christians to meet the world half way; in other words she was urging on the Church a spiritual infidelity which was bound to issue in a physical fornication. It is in the mercy of God that the teaching of Jezebel and her like did not become the view of the Church. If that had happened, and if it happens in the days to come, the Church would have become, and will become, a kind of cultured, pleasant paganism. On this Paul said: " Be not conformed to this world, but be ye transformed by the renewing of your mind " (*Romans* 12.2). And

Jesus said the last word on the matter when He said: "No man can serve two masters. . . . Ye cannot serve God and mammon" (*Matthew* 6.24). The old choice is still the new choice: "Choose ye this day whom ye will serve" (*Deuteronomy* 30.19; *Joshua* 24.15).

THYATIRA
PROMISES AND THREATS

Revelation 2.18-29 (*continued*)

THE letter to Thyatira finishes with a series of great threats and great promises. The woman Jezebel has been given all the latitude that the divine mercy can give her. If she does not repent, she will be cast into a bed of sickness, and her paramours and her followers will share her fate. This will prove to all men that indeed the Risen Christ, as the Authorized Version has it, " searches the reins and the hearts." The phrase itself is a translation of *Jeremiah* 11.20. In *Jeremiah* the prerogative of searching the inmost thoughts of men belongs to God; but in the *Revelation*, as so often, the prerogatives of God have become the prerogatives of the Risen Christ.

The *reins* are the *kidneys*; strange as it may seem to us, in Hebrew psychology it was believed that the seat of the emotions was in the lower viscera, the kidneys and the bowels; and the seat of the thoughts was in the heart. So, when the Risen Christ says that He will search the reins and the heart, it means that every emotion and every thought will be open to His gaze.

There is real point here. When we began to study the letter to Thyatira we saw that anyone coming into that Church for the first time would have believed it to be a Church surging with life and energy and fertile and fruitful in every good work. No doubt those who prospered in business because of their compromise with the world were lavish in their liberality. No doubt those who attended the trade guilds gave generously to charitable funds and appeals for the poor. They *looked* like real Christians. No doubt the woman Jezebel seemed to many a fine character. She must have had a command of language and a fine presence to be regarded as a prophetess. And the point here is that the Risen Christ can see beyond the outward disguise. He will know whether or not the repentance is real. He will know whether there are any reservations in her repentance as there are in her Christian loyalty. She may deceive men, but she will not deceive the Risen Christ.

Then to those who are faithful the promise is made. The promise is twofold.

(i) The first part of it comes from *Psalm* 2.8, 9: " Ask of me, and I shall give thee the heathen for thine inheritance, and the uttermost parts of the earth for thy possession. Thou shalt break them with a rod of iron; thou shalt dash them in pieces like a potter's vessel." In Jewish belief and teaching that was a Messianic Psalm, which was a description of the triumph which the Messiah of God would one day enjoy. It is quite true that the Psalm was thinking in the first instance of a conquering Messiah who would smash the heathen, and extend the rule of Israel to the ends of the earth. But there is one thing that we must remember. That Psalm has been one of the great missionary inspirations of the Church. It was to bring that promise true that many and many a missionary went out. Many a missionary claimed that promise: " Ask of me, and I will give thee the heathen for thine inheritance." This Psalm sounds as if it was a promise of the conquest of power; but in the light of Christ it has become a promise of love, and of the gospel to all men.

(ii) The second part of the promise is the promise of the morning star. The very words are lovely, like poetry, but what do they mean? Four main interpretations have been given.

(a) It is taken as a promise of the first resurrection. As the morning star rises after the night, so the Christian will rise after the night of death.

(b) It is taken as the conquest of Lucifer. Lucifer is the devil; he was the angel who was so proud that he rebelled against God and was cast over the battlements of heaven (*Isaiah* 14.12). Now the name *Lucifer* means the *light-bringer*; and Lucifer is the name of the morning star. If that be so, this is a promise of complete power and conquest over Satan and over sin. Satan will not be able to touch the Christian who is true.

(iii) This has been referred to *Daniel* 12.3. There the promise is: " They that be wise shall shine as the brightness of the firmament; and they that turn many to righteousness as the stars for ever and ever." If that be so, the morning star is the glory which will come to those who are righteous, and who have helped and enabled others to walk in the paths of righteousness.

(iv) All these are very lovely, and maybe all are involved in this promise; but we are quite certain that the correct interpretation is this. The *Revelation* itself calls Jesus " the bright and morning star " (*Revelation* 22.16). And the morning star is nothing less than a promise of Christ Himself. If the Christian is true, when life comes to an end he will possess Christ, never to lose Him any more.

THE LETTER TO SARDIS

Revelation 3.1-6

And to the angel of the Church in Sardis, write:

> These things says He who has the seven Spirits of God, and the seven stars.

> I know your works; I know that you have a reputation for life, but that you are dead. Show yourself watchful, and strengthen what remains, and what is going to die. I have not found your works completed before my God. Remember, then, how you received and heard the gospel, and keep it, and repent. If, then, you are not on the watch, I will come as a thief, and you will not know at what hour I will come to you.

> But you have a few people in Sardis, who have not defiled their garments, and they will walk with me in white raiment, because they are worthy. He who overcomes will be thus clothed in white raiment, and I will not wipe his name out of the Book of Life, but I will acknowledge his name before my Father and before His angels.

> Let him who has an ear hear what the Spirit is saying to the Churches.

SARDIS
PAST SPLENDOUR AND PRESENT DECAY

Revelation 3.1-6

SIR W. M. RAMSAY said of Sardis that nowhere was there a greater example of the melancholy contrast between past splendour and present decay. Sardis was a city of degeneration. Let us look at its history, for the letter to Sardis was written in the memory of the history of Sardis.

Seven hundred years before the letter to Sardis was written Sardis had been one of the greatest cities in the world. There the king of Lydia ruled over his empire in oriental splendour and in all the magnificence and luxury of almost unlimited wealth. At that time Sardis was a city of the east, and was hostile to the Greek world, and feared by the Greeks. Aeschylus, the great Greek writer of tragedies, wrote of Sardis: " They that dwelt by Tmolus pledged themselves to cast the yoke on Hellas."

Sardis stood in the midst of the plain of the valley of the River Hermus. To the north of that plain rose the long ridge of Mount Tmolus; from that ridge a series of hills go out like spurs, each of them forming a narrow plateau. On one of these spurs, fifteen hundred feet up, stood the original Sardis. Clearly such a position made Sardis almost literally impregnable. The sides of the ridge were smoothly precipitous; and only where the spur met the ridge of Mount Tmolus was there any possible approach into Sardis, and even that approach was hard and steep. It has been said that Sardis stood like some gigantic watch-tower guarding the Hermus valley. The time came when the narrow space on the top of the plateau was too small for the expanding city; and Sardis grew round the foot of the spur on which the citadel stood. The name Sardis (*Sardeis* in Greek) is really a plural noun, for there were two towns, the town on the plateau and the town in the valley beneath.

The wealth of Sardis was legendary. Through the lower town there flowed the River Pactolus, which was said in the old days to have had gold-bearing waters from which much of the wealth of Sardis came. Greatest of the Sardian kings was Croesus, whose name is still commemorated in the proverb, " As rich as Croesus." It was with him that the power and splendour of Sardis reached its zenith, and it was with him that Sardis plunged to disaster.

It was not that Croesus was not warned where Sardis was heading. Solon, the wisest of the Greeks, came on a visit to Sardis. He was shown the wealth, the splendour, the magnificence and the luxury. He saw the blind confidence of Croesus and his people that nothing could end this splendour; but he also saw that the seeds of softness, of flabbiness and of inevitable degeneration were being sown. And it was then that Solon uttered his famous saying to Croesus: " Call no man happy until he is dead." Solon knew only too well the chances and the changes of life which Croesus had forgotten.

Croesus embarked upon a war with Cyrus of Persia which was the end of the greatness of Sardis. Again Croesus was warned, but he failed to see the warning. To get at the armies of Cyrus he had to cross the River Halys. He took counsel of the famous oracle at Delphi; and he was told: " If you cross the River Halys, you will destroy a great empire." Croesus took it as a promise that he would annihilate the Persians; it never crossed his mind that it was a prophecy that the campaign on which he had embarked would be the end of his own power.

He crossed the Halys, and engaged in battle, and was routed. He was not in the least worried, for he thought that all he had to do was to retire to the impregnable citadel of Sardis, and recuperate and refit and fight again. Cyrus initiated the siege of Sardis, but Croesus and the Sardians were unconcerned. Cyrus waited for fourteen days; then he offered a special reward to anyone who would find an entry into Sardis. The rock on which Sardis was built is friable. It is, in fact, more like close packed dried mud than rock, and it wears away. Today the plateau where Sardis once stood is so narrow a knife-edge that, as Ramsay says, "it takes a steady head and nerve to try to cross it at all." The nature of the rock meant that, although it was precipitous, it developed faults and cracks. For fourteen days, as Herodotus the Greek historian tells the story, Cyrus besieged the city. He then offered a reward to any of his soldiers who could find a way into the impregnable Sardis. A certain Mardian soldier called Hyeroeades had been watching the battlements of Sardis, and at a certain point he had seen a Sardian soldier accidentally drop his helmet over the battlements, and then make his way down the precipice to retrieve it. Hyeroeades knew that there must be a crack in the rock there, by means of which an agile man could climb up. That night he led a party of Persian troops up by the fault in the rock. When they reached the top they found the battlements completely unguarded. The Sardians had thought themselves too safe to need a guard; and so Sardis fell. A city with a history like that knew what the Risen Christ was talking about, when He said: "Watch!"

So, then, Sardis fell to Cyrus, because its defenders thought it too strong to need a guard. There were a few futile attempts at rebellion; but Cyrus followed a deliberate policy. He forbade any Sardian to possess any weapon of war. He ordered them to wear tunics and buskins, that is, actor's boots, instead of sandals. He ordered the Sardians to teach their sons lyre-playing, the song and the dance, and retail trading. Sardis had been flabby already, but the last vestige of spirit was banished from its people, and it became the city of the degeneration.

Sardis vanished from history under Persian rule for two centuries. In due time it surrendered to Alexander the Great, and through him it became a city of Greek culture. And then history repeated itself. After the death of Alexander there were many claimants for the power. Antiochus, who became the ruler of the area in which Sardis stood, was at war with a rival called Achaeus.

THE REVELATION OF JOHN

Achaeus sought refuge in the impregnable Sardis. For a year Antiochus besieged him; and then a soldier called Lagoras repeated the exploit of Hyeroeades. At night with a band of brave men he climbed the steep cliffs. The Sardians had forgotten their lesson. There was no guard there, and once again Sardis fell because it was not upon the watch.

In due time the Romans came. Sardis was still a wealthy city. It was a centre of the woollen trade; and it was claimed that the art of dyeing wool was actually discovered there. It became a Roman assize town. In A.D. 17 it was destroyed by an earthquake which devastated the area. Tiberius, the Roman Emperor, in his kindness remitted all tribute for five years and gave a donation of 10,000,000 sesterces, that is, £400,000, towards rebuilding, and Sardis recovered itself by the easy way.

When John wrote his letter to Sardis, Sardis was wealthy, but Sardis was degenerate. Even the once great citadel was now only an ancient monument on the hill top. There was no life, no spirit there. The once great Sardians were soft, and twice they had lost their city because they were too lazy to watch. And in that enervating atmosphere of degeneration and decay the Christian Church too had lost its vitality and its power, and was a corpse instead of a living Church. The Christian Church in Sardis was a degenerate Church in a degenerate city.

SARDIS
DEATH IN LIFE

Revelation 3.1-6 (continued)

IN the introduction to this letter the Risen Christ is described in two phrases.

(i) He is He who has the seven Spirits of God. We have already come upon this strange phrase in *Revelation* 1.4.

145

It has two aspects of meaning. (a) It denotes the Holy Spirit with His sevenfold gifts, an idea which is founded on the description of the Spirit in *Isaiah* 11.2. The sevenfold gifts are a sevenfold manifestation of the Spirit of God. (b) It denotes the Spirit in His sevenfold operation. There are seven Churches, yet in each of them the Spirit operates with all His presence and with all His power. In each of them His presence is equally full and equally complete. The *seven spirits* signifies the completeness of the gifts of the Spirit, and the universality of the presence of the Spirit.

(ii) He is He who has the seven stars. The stars stand for the Churches and their angels. The Church is the possession of Jesus Christ. It is He who has, who owns, who possesses the Church. Many and many a time men act as if the Church belonged to them, as if they had a right to administer and to govern the Church to suit themselves and their own purposes. But the Church, and every congregation within it, belongs to Jesus Christ, and all who are in the Church are His servants. In any decision regarding the Church, or any part of the Church, the decisive factor must be, not what any man wishes the Church to do, but what Jesus Christ, the Master, the Owner, and the Lord of the Church wishes to be done.

The terrible accusation against the Church at Sardis is that, although it has a reputation for life, it is, in fact, spiritually dead. The New Testament frequently likens sin to death. In the Pastoral Epistles we read: " She that liveth to pleasure is dead while she liveth " (I *Timothy* 5.6), The Prodigal Son, when he comes home, is he who was dead and is alive again (*Luke* 15.24). The Roman Christians, because they have met and accepted Jesus Christ, are men who are alive from the dead (*Romans* 6.13). Paul says that his converts in their pre-Christian days were dead in trespasses and sins (*Ephesians* 2.1, 5). The effect of sin is a kind of death.

(i) Sin is the *death of the will*. If a man accepts the invitations of sin for long enough, the time comes when he cannot accept anything else. Habits grow upon him until he can no longer break them, however much he wishes to do so. Indulgences gain a hold upon him until he can no longer break away from them, even when he hates them. A man comes, as Seneca had it, to hate his sins and to love them at the same time. He comes to a state when he has become the slave of sin, helplessly in its power. There can be few of us who have not experienced the power of some habit into which we have fallen. So great is the power of sin that in the end sin can kill the will.

(ii) Sin is the *death of the feelings*. The process of becoming the slave of sin does not happen, as it were, overnight. The first time a man sins he does so with many a qualm and many a hesitation. The first time a man allows himself a forbidden pleasure he does so with reluctance, and with the idea that this will not happen again. But the day comes, if he goes on taking that which is forbidden, when he does without a qualm and without hesitation that which once he would have been horrified to do, and that which once he did with a tremor and a regret. Sin, as Burns had it, " petrifies the feeling." The tragedy of sin is that it kills the highest part of human nature.

(iii) Sin is the *death of all loveliness*. The terrible thing about sin is that it can take the loveliest things and turn them into ugliness. Through sin the desire for the highest can become the lust for power; the wish to serve can become the intoxication of ambition; the desire of love can become the passion of lust. Sin is the killer of life's loveliness.

It is only by the grace of God that we can escape the death of sin, and rise from that death, when sin has got us into its power.

SARDIS
A LIFELESS CHURCH

Revelation 3.1-6 *(continued)*

THE lifelessness of the Church at Sardis had a strange effect.

(i) The Church at Sardis was untroubled by any heresy. There is no indication that there were any outbreaks of false doctrine or any influx of false teachers at Sardis. The Church at Sardis was too lazily lethargic for the effort of thought. Heresy is always the product of the searching and the seeking mind. Heresy is, in fact, the sign of a Church that is vitally alive. Heresy is the sign that a man has at least tried to think things out for himself. Heresy is usually an unbalanced stressing of one side of the truth. If we overstress the divinity of Christ, we run into that Docetism in which Jesus Christ is a divine figure disguised in what is only a seeming manhood. If we overstress the humanity of Christ, Jesus Christ becomes nothing more than an heroic figure, the best of good men. If we overstress law, we run into the legalism which kills; if we overstress grace, we may run into the antinomianism which believes that grace is so great that sin does not matter. But the fact remains that heresy is the characteristic of the man and of the Church which is not content with a second-hand faith, and a conventional and unthinking acceptance of orthodoxy, but which is compelled to think things out for himself and for itself. There is nothing worse than a state in which a man is orthodox because he is too lazy to think for himself. A man is actually better with a heresy which he holds intensely and personally than with an orthodoxy about which in his heart of hearts he does not care.

(ii) The Church at Sardis was untroubled by any attack from the outside. It was troubled neither by heathen attack and persecution, nor by Jewish slander and calumny. The truth was that the Church in Sardis had ceased to matter. It was so lifeless that it was not worth attacking.

It was not worth expending powder and shot on. The Pastoral Epistles describe those who had drifted away from the true faith by saying that they had a form of godliness, but they denied the power thereof (2 *Timothy* 3.5). As Moffatt translates it: " Though they keep up a form of religion, they will have nothing to do with it as a force." As Phillips puts it: " They will maintain a façade of ' religion,' but their conduct will deny its validity."

When a Church has lost its vital force, it is no longer worth attacking; it is so ineffective that it has ceased to matter in the life of the community.

A truly vital Church will always be under attack. A really live Church will necessarily be the conscience of the community, and because of that there will be many who will wish to silence it, and to eliminate it. " Woe unto you,' said Jesus, " when all men shall speak well of you ! " (*Luke* 6.26). There are some people whose enmity is preferable to their friendship, and whose criticism is preferable to their praise. A Church with a positive message is bound to be a Church to which there will be opposition. The Church and the world remain over against each other. And a Church which has so accommodated itself to the world that the world finds no fault in it is a dead Church.

A Church which is so lethargic as to fail to produce a heresy is mentally dead; and a Church which is so negative as to fail to produce opposition is dead in its witness to Christ.

SARDIS
WATCH!

Revelation 3.1-6 (*continued*)

IF anything is to be rescued from the impending ruin of the Church in Sardis the one necessity is that Christians there should be upon the watch. They must wake from their deadly lethargy, and they must watch. No commandment appears more frequently in the New Testament than the commandment to watch.

(i) Watchfulness should be the constant attitude of the Christian life. " It is high time," says Paul, " to awake out of sleep " (*Romans* 13.11). " Watch ye, stand fast in the faith," he urges (I *Corinthians* 16.13). As it has been said: " Eternal vigilance is the price of liberty," and, even so, eternal watchfulness is the price of salvation.

(ii) The Christian must be on the watch against the wiles of the devil (I *Peter* 5.8). The history of Sardis had its vivid examples of what happens to the garrison whose watch is slack. The Christian is under continual attack by the powers which seek to seduce him from his loyalty to Christ, and from the right way. Often these attacks are subtle and concealed. He must, therefore, be for ever on the watch.

(iii) The Christian must be on the watch against temptation. " Watch and pray," said Jesus, " that ye enter not into temptation " (*Matthew* 26.41). Temptation waits for our unguarded moments, and then it attacks. A moment of passion may relax a man's self-control. A slackening of will may relax a man's resolution to have nothing to do with evil. A weariness of body or spirit may reduce a man's resistance power. A time of over-confidence may prove a time of ruin. In the Christian life there must be unceasing vigilance against temptation.

(iv) Repeatedly the New Testament urges the Christian to be on the watch for the coming of his Lord. " Watch, therefore," said Jesus, " for ye know not what hour your Lord shall come." " What I say unto you, I say unto all, watch " (*Matthew* 24.42, 43; *Mark* 13.37). " Let us not sleep, as do others," writes Paul to the Thessalonians. " Let us watch and be sober " (I *Thessalonians* 5.6). No man knows the day and the hour when for him eternity will invade time. " The last day is a secret," says Augustine,

" that every day may be watched." A man should live every day, as if every day was his last day.

(v) The Christian must be on the watch against false teaching and against false teachers. In Paul's last address to the elders of Ephesus he warns them that grievous wolves will invade the flock from outside, and from inside men will arise to speak perverse things. " Therefore," he says, " watch ! " (*Acts* 20.29-31).

(vi) Nor must the Christian forget, that, even as he must watch for Jesus Christ, Jesus Christ is watching him. " I have not found your works completed," says the Risen Christ, " before my God." Here two great truths meet us. (*a*) Christ is looking for something from us. We so often regard Jesus Christ as the one to whom we look for things; we look to Him for His strength, His help, His support, His comfort. But we must never forget that He is looking for our love, our loyalty and our service. Christianity must never be regarded as a one-way traffic in which we look for everything and give nothing. Christ is looking to us for the service and the love which we can give. (*b*) The things a man must do lie to his hand. The old saying is true: " Fate is what we must do; destiny is what we are meant to do." The Christian does not believe in an inescapable fate; but he does believe in a destiny which he can accept or refuse. From everyone of us Jesus Christ is looking for something; and for everyone of us there is something to do.

SARDIS
THE IMPERATIVES OF THE RISEN LORD

Revelation 3.1-6 (continued)

IN verse 3 of this passage we have a series of imperatives.

(i) The Risen Christ says: " *Remember* how you received and heard the gospel." In this case the imperative is the present imperative, and it means: " Keep on remembering;

remember every day; never allow yourself to forget."
The Risen Christ is telling the lethargic Sardians to remember the enthusiasm and the thrill with which they first
heard the message and the good news of the gospel. It is a
fact of life that there are certain things which sharpen
memory which has grown dull. When we return to a
graveside, the sorrow from which the years has taken the
edge grows piercingly poignant again. When we return
to some place where we had some great experience, the
sight of that place rekindles the thrill which has passed,
and brings back the intensity of feeling which has been
blunted by time. Ever and again the Christian must stand
before the Cross, that he may remember again what God
has done for him.

(ii) The Risen Christ says: " *Repent* ! " In this case the
imperative is an aorist imperative, which describes one
definite action. In the Christian life there must be a decisive
moment, when a man decides to be done with the old way,
and to begin on the new way; when he decides surgically
to excise the old things, and to put on the new things;
when he makes the complete turn, and sets out towards
Christ, instead of drifting away from Christ. Every man
must realize that Christianity is neither drifting nor
procrastination, but decision.

(iii) The Risen Christ says: " *Keep* the commands of
the gospel." Here again we have a present imperative,
which indicates continuous action. It means: " Never stop
keeping the commands of the gospel; keep them and
observe them day and daily; walk continually in the
Christian way." Here is a warning against what we might
call " spasmodic Christianity." Too many of us are Christian
one day and un-Christian the next. Too many of us are
capable of the greatest nobility at one moment, and the
greatest lapse into meanness and disloyalty the next.
Too many of us are capable sometimes of an almost sacrificial kindness, and sometimes of an almost brutal selfishness. The command of the Risen Christ is that consistently

and continuously, day in and day out, we should keep and observe the commands and demands of the gospel.

(iv) Finally, there is the command *to watch*. There is an old Latin saying that "the gods walk on feet that are wrapped in wool." Their approach is silent and unobserved, until all unexpectedly a man finds himself suddenly and without warning facing eternity. But that cannot happen if every day in life a man lives in the shadow of eternity, if every day in life he lives in the presence and in the company of Christ. He who walks hand-in-hand with Christ cannot be taken unawares by the coming of Christ.

SARDIS
THE FAITHFUL FEW

Revelation 3.1-6 (*continued*)

IN verse 4 there shines through the darkness a ray of hope. Even in Sardis there are the faithful few. God in His mercy searches for the good even more than He searches for the evil. When Abraham is pleading with God for Sodom, he appeals to God: "To slay the righteous with the wicked, that be far from Thee" (*Genesis* 18.25). God searches with patience to find the faithful few. In the old story of the kings, Abijah alone of all the sons of Jeroboam was spared, because in him there was found some good thing toward the Lord God of Israel (I *Kings* 14.13). God never abandons His search for the faithful few, and they are never lost to His sight in the mass of the wicked.

It is said of the faithful that they "have not defiled their garments." James spoke with respect and admiration of the man who kept himself "unspotted from the world" (*James* 1.27). There are two possible pictures here.

(i) In the heathen world no worshipper was allowed to approach a temple of the gods with soiled and unclean clothes. A white robe was the necessity of approach to God. For the heathen this was an external thing. But this may describe the man who has kept his soul clean so that he can enter into the presence of God, and not be ashamed.

(ii) Swete thinks that the white garments stand for the profession a man made at baptism; and that the phrase describes the man who has not broken his baptismal vows. It is to be remembered that at this stage in the Church's history baptism was adult baptism, and at baptism a man took his own spontaneous and personal pledge to Jesus Christ. This is all the more likely because it was common at baptism to clothe a man, after he had emerged from the water, in clean white robes, which were symbolic of the cleansing of his life. The man who is faithful to his pledge will, beyond a doubt, some day hear God say: " Well done ! "

To those who have been true the promise is that they will walk with God. Again there is a double background here.

(a) There may be a heathen background. At the Persian court the king's most trusted favourites were given the privilege of walking in the royal gardens with the king, and were called " The Companions of the Garden." Those who have been true to God will some day walk with God in the Paradise of God.

(b) There may be a reference and an allusion to the old story of Enoch. Of Enoch it is said: " And Enoch walked with God, and he was not; for God took him " (*Genesis* 5.22, 24). Enoch walked with God on earth, and continued to walk with God in the heavenly places. The man whose walk with God is close on earth will but enter into a nearer companionship with God when the end of life comes to him.

SARDIS
THE THREEFOLD PROMISE

Revelation 3.1-6 (*continued*)

To those who have been faithful comes the threefold promise.

(i) They will be clothed with white raiment. It is said

of the righteous that " they shall shine forth as the sun in the Kingdom of their Father " (*Matthew* 13.43); and it is said of God Himself that He covers Himself with light as with a garment (*Psalm* 104.2). For what then do the white robes stand ?

(*a*) In the ancient world white robes stood for *festivity*. " Let thy garments be always white," said the preacher, " and let thy head lack no ointment " (*Ecclesiastes* 9.8). The white robes may stand for the fact that the faithful will be guests at the banquet of God.

(*b*) In the ancient world white robes stood for *victory*. On the day when a Roman triumph was being celebrated, all the citizens clad themselves in white. The city itself was called *urbs candida*, the city in white. The white robes may stand for the reward of those who have won the victory, and who receive the reward of God.

(*c*) In any land and time white is the colour of *purity*, and the white robes may stand for the purity whose reward it is to see God. " Blessed are the pure in heart, for they shall see God " (*Matthew* 5.8).

(*d*) It has been suggested that the white robes stand for *the resurrection bodies* which the faithful will some day wear. They who are faithful will share in that very whiteness of light which is the garment of God Himself.

We need not make a choice between these various meanings of the white robes; we may well believe that they are all included in the greatness of the promise.

(ii) Their names will not be wiped out of the Book of Life. The Book of Life is a conception which occurs often in the Bible. Moses is willing to be wiped out of the book which God has written, if by his sacrifice he can save his people from the consequence of their sin (*Genesis* 32.32, 33). It is the hope of the Psalmist that the wicked will be blotted out of the book of the living (*Psalm* 69.28). In the time of judgment those who are written in the book will be delivered (*Daniel* 12.1). The names of Paul's fellow-labourers for

God are written in the book of life (*Philippians* 4.3). He who is not written in the book of life is cast into the lake of fire (*Revelation* 20.15); only they who are written in the Lamb's book of life shall enter into blessedness (*Revelation* 21.27).

In the ancient world a king kept a register of his citizens. If a man committed a crime against the state, or when he died, his name was erased from the book of citizens. To have one's name written in the book of life is to be numbered amongst the faithful citizens of the Kingdom of God; it is to be included with those who belong to God.

(iii) Jesus Christ will confess their names before His Father and the angels. It was Jesus' promise that, if a man confessed Him before men, He would confess him before His Father; and if a man denied Him before men, He would deny Him before His Father (*Matthew* 10.32, 33; *Luke* 12.8, 9). Jesus Christ is for ever true to the man who is true to Him.

THE LETTER TO PHILADELPHIA

Revelation 3.7-13

And to the angel of the Church in Philadelphia, write:

These things says He who is holy, He who is true, He who has the key of David, He who opens and no man will shut, and shuts and no man opens. I know your works. Behold, I have set before you a door which stands open, and which no man shuts, because you have a little strength, and because you have kept my word, and have not denied my name. Behold, I will give you those who belong to the synagogue of Satan, who call themselves Jews, and who are not, but who lie. Behold, I will make them come and kneel before your feet, and they will know that I have loved you. Because you have kept my command to endure, I, too, will keep you safe from the hour of testing, which is to come upon the whole inhabited world, to test those who dwell upon the earth. I am coming quickly. Hold on to what you have, that no one may take your crown.

I will make him who overcomes a pillar in the temple of my God, and he will go out no more; and I will write upon him the name of my God, and the name of the city of my God, of the new Jerusalem, which is coming down from heaven from my God, and my new name.

Let him who has an ear hear what the Spirit **is** saying to the Churches.

PHILADELPHIA
CITY OF PRAISE

Revelation 3.7-13

PHILADELPHIA was the youngest of all the seven cities. It was founded by colonists from Pergamum under the reign of Attalus the Second, who ruled in Pergamum from 159 to 138 B.C. *Philadelphos* is the Greek word for *one who loves his brother*. Such was the love of Attalus for his brother Eumenes that he was called Philadelphos, and it was after him that Philadelphia was named.

Philadelphia was founded for a special purpose and with a special intention. It was situated where the borders of Mysia, Lydia and Phrygia met. It was a border town. But it was not as a garrison town that Philadelphia was founded, for there was little danger there. It was founded with the deliberate intention that it might be a missionary of Greek culture and the Greek language to Lydia and Phrygia; and so well did it do its work that by A.D. 19 the Lydians had forgotten their own Lydian language and were all but Greeks. Sir W. M. Ramsay says of Philadelphia that it was " the centre for the diffusion of Greek language and Greek letters in a peaceful land, and by peaceful means." That is what the Risen Christ means when he speaks of the open door that is set before Philadelphia. Three centuries before Philadelphia had been given an open door to spread Greek ideas in the lands beyond; and now there has come to it another great missionary opportunity, an open door to carry to men who never knew it the message of the love of Jesus Christ.

But Philadelphia had one great characteristic which has left its mark upon this letter. Philadelphia was on the edge of a great plain called the *Katakekaumenē*, which means The Burned Land. The *Katakekaumenē* was a great volcanic plain, which bore the marks of the lava and the ashes of the volcanoes then extinct. That had its advantages. Such land is fertile; and Philadelphia was the centre of a great grape-growing area, and a famous producer of wines. But that situation had its perils, and these perils had left their mark more deeply on Philadelphia than on any other city. In A.D. 17 there came a great earthquake, the earthquake which destroyed Sardis, and ten other cities. In the other cities the earthquake was over and done with; but in Philadelphia the tremors went on for years. Strabo describes Philadelphia as a " city full of earthquakes." Now it often happens that, when a great earthquake shock comes, people meet it with courage and with self-possession; but it is frequently the case that ever-recurring minor shocks over a long period drive people to sheer panic. That is what happened in Philadelphia. Strabo describes the scene. Shocks were an everyday occurrence. Great gaping cracks appeared in the walls of the houses. Now one part of the city was in ruins, now another. Most of the population lived outside the city in huts, and feared even to go on the city streets lest they should be killed by falling stones and masonry. Those who still dared to live in the city were reckoned mad; they spent their time shoring up the shaking buildings, and every now and then fleeing to the open spaces for safety. These terrible days in Philadelphia were never wholly forgotten, and people in it ever waited subconsciously for the ominous tremors of the ground, ready to flee for their lives to the open spaces. People in Philadelphia well knew what gratefulness and security lay in a promise that " they would go out no more." A promise like that meant for them the security their hearts desired.

But there is more of Philadelphia's history than that in this letter. When this earthquake devastated Philadelphia, Tiberius was as generous to Philadelphia as he had been to Sardis. Philadelphia was grateful, and in gratitude it changed its name to Neocaesarea—the New City of Caesar. Later in the time of Vespasian Philadelphia was in gratitude to change its name again to Flavia, for Flavius was the family name of the Emperor Vespasian. It is true that neither of these new names lasted, and the name Philadelphia came back. But the people of Philadelphia well knew what it was to receive " a new name." The history of Philadelphia is written into this letter.

Of all the cities Philadelphia receives the greatest praise, and it was to show that it deserved it.

In later days Philadelphia became a very great city; but there came the time when the Turks and Mohammedanism flooded across Asia Minor. When every other town had fallen, Philadelphia stood erect. For centuries it was a free Greek Christian city amidst a pagan people. Philadelphia was the last bastion of Asian Christianity, and it was not till midway through the fourteenth century that Philadelphia fell. And to this day there is a Christian bishop and a thousand Christians in Philadelphia. With the single exception of Smyrna the other Churches are in ruins, but Philadelphia still stands holding aloft the banner of the Christian faith.

PHILADELPHIA
TITLES AND CLAIMS

Revelation 3.7-13 (*continued*)

IN the introduction to this letter the Risen Christ is called by three great titles, each of which has implicit in it a tremendous claim.

(i) He is called He who is holy. The great significance of this is that the word Holy is the name and the title and the description of God Himself. " Holy, holy, holy is the Lord of hosts," was the song of the seraphs which Isaiah heard (*Isaiah* 6.3). " To whom will ye liken me, or shall I be equal? saith the Holy One " (*Isaiah* 6.3). " I am the Lord, your Holy One, the creator of Israel, your King " (*Isaiah* 43.15). All through the Old Testament God is the Holy One; and now that title is taken and given to the Risen Christ. We must remember the meaning of the word *holy* (*hagios*). It means *different, separate from*. God is holy, because He is different from men; He has that quality of life and being which men can never have by themselves and which belongs to Him alone. To say that Jesus Christ is holy is to say that He shares nothing less than the life and the being of God.

(ii) He is called *He who is true.* In Greek there are two words for *true.* There is *alēthēs,* which means *true* in the sense that a true statement is different from a false statement. That which is *alēthēs* may be unhesitatingly believed as the truth. There is *alēthinos,* which means *real* or *genuine,* as opposed to that which is shadowy and unreal and, as it were, a substitute and imitation of reality. It is the second of these words which is used here. Jesus is *alēthinos.* In Him is reality. When we are confronted with Jesus Christ, we are confronted with no shadowy outline and image of the truth, but with the truth itself. In Him we are confronted with no imitation of life, but with real life itself. In Him we are confronted, not with a substitute for divinity and godhead, but with the genuine reality of God Himself. When we are confronted with Jesus Christ, our guessings and our gropings after truth are gone; the dim shadows of God are past; here is truth, reality, God Himself.

(iii) He is *He who has the key of David, He who opens and no man will shut, and shuts and no man opens.* We may first note that the key is *the symbol of authority.* Here is the picture of Jesus Christ as the one who has the final authority which no one can question.

But behind this there is an Old Testament picture. Hezekiah had a faithful steward called Eliakim, who was over all his house, and who alone could admit to the presence of the king. Isaiah heard God say of this faithful Eliakim: " The key of the house of David will I lay upon his shoulder; so he shall open, and none shall shut; and he shall shut, and none shall open " (*Isaiah 22.22*). It is this picture which is in John's mind. Jesus, and Jesus alone, has complete authority to admit to the new Jerusalem, the new city of David; He alone can admit to the presence of God, just as the faithful steward can admit to the presence of the king. As the *Te Deum* has it: " Thou didst open the kingdom of Heaven to all believers." He is the new and living way into the presence of God. Through Jesus Christ the door to God is unlocked, and He has the key to the Kingdom.

PHILADELPHIA
THE OPEN DOOR

Revelation 3.7-13 *(continued)*

BEFORE we go on to think of *the open door*, we may note that in verses 8 and 9 there is a problem of punctuation. In the early Greek manuscripts there was no punctuation at all, and punctuation has to be supplied. The problem is that the words " because you have a little strength, and because you have kept my word, and have not denied my name," can go equally well with what precedes them, or with what follows them. These words may express, either, the reason why the door stands open before the Christians of Philadelphia, or, the reason why they will be given those who belong to the synagogue of Satan. There can be no certain decision about how these words are to be taken; either connection gives excellent sense; we have taken them with the words which precede them, but they can go equally well with the words which follow them.

It is the great promise of the Risen Christ that He has set before the Christians of Philadelphia an open door which no man can ever shut. What is the meaning of this open door ?

(i) It may be the door of missionary opportunity. Writing to the Corinthians of the work which lies ahead of him, Paul says: " A great and effectual door is opened unto me " (I *Corinthians* 16.9). When he came to Troas, a door was opened to him by the Lord (2 *Corinthians* 2.12). He asks the Colossians to pray that a door of utterance may be opened for him (*Colossians* 4.3). When Paul came

back to Antioch he told how God had opened the door of
faith to the Gentiles (*Acts* 14.27). This meaning is particularly appropriate for Philadelphia. We have seen how
Philadelphia was a border town, standing where the boun-
daries of Lydia, Mysia and Phrygia met, and how in the old
days it had been founded with the definite idea that it
should be a missionary of the Greek language and Greek
culture to the barbarous peoples beyond. Philadelphia
was on the road which led from the coast of Smyrna, passed
through Philadelphia, went out to Phrygia and the main
mass of Asia Minor, and on to the east. It was on the road
of the imperial postal service, which left the coast at
Troas, came to Philadelphia *via* Pergamum, Thyatira and
Sardis, and joined the great road out to Phrygia. The armies
of Caesar travelled that road; the caravans of the merchant-
men travelled that road; and now that road was beckoning
the missionaries of Christ. And now there lies before
Philadelphia a still greater missionary task; there stands
before it the open door through which the gospel of Christ
can be carried to the regions beyond. Two things emerge
here. (*a*) There is a door of missionary opportunity before
every man, and he need not go overseas to find it. Within
the home, within the circle in which we move, within the
parish in which we reside, there are those to be won for
Christ. To use that door of opportunity is at once our
privilege and our responsibility. (*b*) In the way of Christ
the reward of work well done is more work to do. Philadelphia had proved faithful, and the reward for her fidelity
was still more work to do for Christ. Not ease, but high
endeavour, is the reward which Christ offers.

(ii) It has been suggested that the door which is set
before the Philadelphians is none other than Jesus Himself.
" I am the door," said Jesus (*John* 10.7, 9); and so the door
which stands open before Philadelphia may be the door in
Christ to the very presence of God.

(iii) It has been suggested that the door is the door to
the Messianic community. With Jesus Christ the new age

came; the new kingdom of David was inaugurated; and, just as in the ancient kingdom Eliakim had the keys to admit to the royal presence, so in the new kingdom Jesus has the keys, and is the door, to admit to the kingdom of the elect of God.

(iv) Apart from all these things, it remains true that for any man the door of prayer is ever and always open. Any man may enter in at the door of prayer, and find himself within the presence of God. That, indeed, is a door which no man can ever shut, and it is a door which, indeed, Jesus Christ opened, when He assured men of the seeking love of God the Father.

We may be very sure that the door of opportunity and the door of prayer ever stand open, inviting the Christian to enter in.

PHILADELPHIA
INHERITORS OF THE PROMISE

Revelation 3.7-13 (*continued*)

In verse 9 the promise and the prophecy of the Risen Christ is that some day the Jews, who hate and slander the Christians, will come and kneel before them. This is an echo of an expectation of the Jews which finds frequent expression in the Old Testament.

One of the great expectations of the Jews was that in the new age, when God broke in to vindicate His people, all nations would come and do humble homage to the Jews. This is a promise which recurs again and again in *Isaiah*. " The sons of them that afflicted thee shall come bending unto thee; and all that despised thee shall bow themselves down at the soles of thy feet " (*Isaiah* 60.14). " The labour of Egypt, the merchandise of Ethiopia and of the Sabeans, men of stature, shall come over unto thee, and they shall be thine; they shall come after thee; in chains they shall come over, and they shall fall down unto thee " (*Isaiah*

45.14). "Kings shall be thy nursing fathers, and their queens thy nursing mothers; they shall bow down to thee with their faces towards the earth, and lick up the dust of thy feet" (*Isaiah* 49.23). Zechariah has a vision of the day, when all men of all nations and languages shall turn to Jerusalem, when "they will take hold of the skirt of him that is a Jew, saying, We will go with you; for we have heard that God is with you" (*Zechariah* 8.22, 23). It was the Jewish expectation that the day would come when all things would be given unto them.

Now it was the Christian belief that the Jewish nation, as a nation, had lost its place in the plan of God, and that that place had passed to the Church. A Jew in God's sense of the term was not now one who could claim racial descent from Abraham, but one of any nation who had made the same venture of faith as Abraham (*Romans* 9.6-9). The Church was the Israel of God (*Galatians* 6.16). It was, therefore, now true that all the promises which had been made to Israel had been inherited by the Church. It was to the Church of Christ that one day all men of all nations would humbly make their submission; and among them would come the Jews themselves. This promise is a reversal of all that the Jews had expected; they had expected that all nations would kneel before them; but the day was to come when they with all nations would kneel before Christ.

That is what the Philadelphian Church would see, at least in its beginnings, if its members were faithful. Up until now they had been faithful. In the sentence, "You have kept my word, and have not denied my name," both the verbs are in the aorist tense, which describes one definite act in past time; and the implication of that is that there had been some time of trial and persecution and peril out of which the Philadelphian Church had emerged triumphantly true and victorious. They may have only a little strength; their resources may be small; as men reckon power, their power may be little; but, if they are faithful they will see the dawn of the day of the triumph of Christ.

Though few and small and weak your bands,
    Strong in your Captain's strength,
Go to the conquest of all lands;
    All must be His at length.

That which must keep a Christian faithful is the vision of a
world for Christ, for the coming of such a world depends
on the fidelity of the individual Christian.

PHILADELPHIA
THOSE WHO KEEP ARE KEPT

Revelation 3.7-13 (*continued*)

IT is the promise of the Risen Christ that he who keeps
will be kept. " You have kept my commandment," He says,
" therefore, I will keep you." Jesus Christ will be in no
man's debt. and loyalty has its sure reward. In verse 10
in the Greek the phrase *my command to endure* is highly
concentrated. Literally, it is *the word of my endurance.*
And the real meaning is that the promise is to those who
have practised the same kind of endurance as Jesus practised
and displayed in His earthly life. When we ourselves are
called upon to show endurance, the endurance of Jesus
Christ supplies us with three things. First, it supplies us
with an example. And, second, it supplies us with an
inspiration. We must walk looking unto Him, who for the
joy that was set before Him endured the cross despising the
shame (*Hebrews* 12.1, 2) and the sight of the endurance of
Jesus Christ is at once our pattern and our inspiration.
But, third, the endurance of Jesus Christ is the guarantee
of His sympathy with us, when we are called upon to
endure. " In that He Himself has suffered, being tempted,
He is able to succour them that are tempted " (*Hebrews*
2.18). We know that our trust is in one who has gone through
it, and who is able to help others who are going through it.

In verse 2 we are back again amidst beliefs which are
characteristically Jewish. As we have so often seen, the

Jews divided time into two ages. There is the present age which is wholly bad, and wholly under the domination of evil; and there is the age to come, which is wholly good and wholly under God. In between the two there was the terrible time of disintegration when the present world will pass away in shattered destruction, and when judgment will fall upon the world, and when all that is against God will be obliterated. It is to that terrible time that John refers. Even in the days when the world, as men know it, is crashing in ruins, those who are faithful to Christ will be brought through the destruction to the ultimate glory beyond.

The word of the Risen Christ is that there is nothing which can separate from Him. Even when time comes to an end, and when the world as we know it ceases to exist, he who is faithful to Christ will still be safe in the keeping of Christ.

PHILADELPHIA
PROMISE AND WARNING

Revelation 3.7-13 (*continued*)

In verse 11 there is promise and warning combined.

The Risen Christ tells them that He is coming quickly. It has well been said that in the New Testament the Coming of Christ is continually used for two purposes.

(i) It is used as *a warning to the heedless*. Jesus Himself spoke the parable which tells of the wicked servant, who thought that his master was not coming back, and who took advantage of his master's absence to conduct himself evilly, and to whom the master made a sudden and unexpected return, which brought judgment and condemnation (*Matthew* 24.48-51). Paul warns the Thessalonians of the terrible fate which awaits the disobedient and the unbelieving when the Lord Jesus shall be revealed from heaven, and when He will take swift and final vengeance on His enemies (2 *Thessalonians* 1.7-9). Peter warns his people that they will give account for their deeds to Him who comes to judge the quick and the dead (I *Peter* 4.5). In the New Testament the idea of the Coming of the Lord is used to warn the man who thinks that he can do what he likes that the day of reckoning comes, and that ultimately judgment awaits him.

(ii) It is used as a *comfort to the oppressed*. James urges patient endurance on his people because the coming of the Lord is drawing near (*James* 5.8); soon their distresses will be at an end. The writer to the Hebrews urges patience, for soon He that shall come will come, and He will not delay (*Hebrews* 10.37). The idea is that, if Christ's people will only endure a little longer, the time of rescue is coming near.

So in the New Testament men used the idea of the Coming of Christ as a warning to the heedless, and as a comfort to the oppressed. It is quite true that, in the literal sense, Jesus Christ did not come back to those who were so warned and exhorted. But what is true is that no man knows when eternity will invade his life, and when God will bid him rise and come; and that, too, must warn the careless to prepare to meet his God, and cheer the oppressed with the thought of the coming glory of the faithful soul.

But there is another warning here. The Risen Christ bids the Philadelphians to hold to what they have, that no one may take their crown (verse 11). It is not a question of someone stealing their crown. It is a question of God taking their crown from them and giving it to someone else, because they were not worthy to wear it. R. C. Trench makes a list of people in the Bible who lost their place to someone else, because they had shown that they were not fit to hold it. Esau lost his place to Jacob (*Genesis* 25.34; 27.36). Reuben, the eldest son of Jacob, unstable as water, lost his place to Judah (*Genesis* 49.4, 8). Saul lost his place to David (I *Samuel* 16.1, 13). Shebna lost his place to Eliakim (*Isaiah* 22.15-25). Joab and Abiathar lost their places to Benaiah and Zadok (I *Kings* 2.25). Judas lost his place in the apostolic band to Matthias (*Acts* 1.25, 26). The Jews lost their place to the Gentiles (*Romans* 11.11).

There is tragedy here. It sometimes happens in life that a man is given a task to do, that he is selected and chosen for that task, and that he goes towards that task with the highest hopes; but it begins to be seen that he is too small for the task, and that the task is too big for him; that he is not worthy of the trust which has been reposed in him; that he has not got it in him to rise to the height of the challenge which has been given to him. When that happens, the man is removed from the task, and it is given to someone else. That, too, can happen with the tasks of God. God has a task for every man; but it may be that the man proves himself unfit for the task; and then the task is given to another, and the man who has failed must lose his crown. It is blessedly true that even out of failure a man can still redeem himself—but only if he casts himself upon the grace of Jesus Christ. Only when we walk close with Christ, can we carry out the task that God has given us; and, if in our folly and pride we attempt the task and fail in it, only in the grace of Christ can we begin again, and find even in our failure a stepping-stone to higher things.

PHILADELPHIA
MANY PROMISES

Revelation 3.7-13 (*continued*)

IN verse 12 we come to the promises of the Risen Christ to those who are faithful, and in this case they are many, and most of them would paint pictures which would be very vivid and very real to the people of Philadelphia.

(i) The faithful Christian will be a pillar in the Temple of God. A pillar of the Church is a great and honoured support of the Church. Peter and James and John were the pillars of the early Church in Jerusalem (*Galatians* 2.9).

Abraham, said the Jewish Rabbis, was the pillar of the world. Like a strong pillar, the faithful Christian is built into the very fabric of the Church of God.

(ii) The faithful Christian will go out no more. There may be something of two meanings here. (*a*) This may be a promise of security. We have seen how for years Philadelphia and its citizens were terrorized by recurring earthquakes and tremors of the earth, and how, when such times came, they fled out into the open country to escape the collapsing buildings and the falling masonry, and how when the tremors ended they came uncertainly back. For them life was a process of going out and coming back; it was lived in an atmosphere of insecurity. The promise is that in Christ there will be no more of that. There is for the faithful Christian the promise of a settled serenity in the peace which Jesus Christ can give. (*b*) Some scholars think that what is here promised is fixity of moral character. In this life even the best of us is sometimes good and sometimes bad. We have relapses into the forbidden things, and we have times of which we are ashamed. But he who is faithful will in the end come to a time when he is like a pillar fixed in the Temple of God, when he has conquered evil, when he has defeated the tempter, and when goodness has become the constant atmosphere of his life. If this is the meaning, this phrase describes the life of untroubled goodness which is lived when, after the battles of earth, we reach the presence of God.

(iii) Jesus Christ will write upon the faithful Christian the name of His God. There may be three pictures here. (*a*) In the cities of Asia Minor, and in Philadelphia, when a priest had for a life-time faithfully discharged his duties, men honoured him, when he died, by erecting a new pillar in the temple in which he had served, and by inscribing his name, and the name of his father, upon it. This then would describe the lasting honour which Christ pays to His faithful ones. (*b*) It is just possible that here there is a reference to the custom of branding a slave with the initials of his owner. Just as the master puts a mark upon a slave to show that the slave belongs to him, just as sheepmasters have their own brand upon their sheep that all men may recognize them as theirs, so God will put His mark upon His faithful ones. Whichever picture is behind this, the sense is that the faithful ones will wear the unmistakable badge of God. (c) It is just possible that here we have an Old Testament picture. When God told to Moses the blessing which Aaron and the priests must pronounce over the people, He says: " They shall put my name upon the children of Israel " (*Numbers* 6.22-27). It is the same idea again; it is as if the mark of God was upon Israel, so that all men may know that they are His people.

(iv) On the faithful Christian the name of the new Jerusalem, the city of God, is to be written. That stands for the gift of citizenship in the city of God to the faithful Christian. According to Ezekiel the name of the recreated city of God was to be *The Lord is there* (*Ezekiel* 48.35). And the faithful ones will be citizens of the city and the kingdom where there is always the presence of God.

(v) On the faithful Christian Christ will write His own new name. The people of Philadelphia knew all about taking a new name. When in A.D. 17 a terrible earthquake devastated their city, Tiberius, the Roman Emperor, dealt kindly with them, remitting taxation, and making them a generous gift to rebuild their city; and in their gratitude the Philadelphians for a time called their city Neocaesarea, the New City of Caesar; and later when again Vespasian was kind to them, they called their city Flavia, for that was the family name of Vespasian. So Jesus Christ will mark His faithful ones with His new name; what that name was we need not even speculate, for no man knows it (*Revelation* 19.12). But in the time to come, when Christ has conquered all, His faithful ones will bear the badge which shows that they are His and that they share His triumph.

THE LETTER TO LAODICEA

Revelation 3.14-22

And to the angel of the Church in Laodicea, write:

> These things says the Amen, the witness on whom you can rely, and who is true, the moving cause of the creation of God.

> I know your works; I know that you are neither cold nor hot. Would that you were cold or hot! So, because you are tepid, and neither cold not hot, I will vomit you out of my mouth. Because you say, I am rich, and I have acquired riches, and I need nothing, and are quite unaware that it is you who are the wretched and the pitiable one, the poor and the blind and the naked one, I advise you to buy from me gold, that has been refined by fire, that you may be rich, white raiment that you may be clothed, and that the shame of your nakedness may not be openly displayed, and eye-salve to anoint your eyes, that you may see.

> I rebuke and discipline all those whom I love. Be eager, therefore, and repent.

> Behold, I am standing at the door and knocking. If anyone hears my voice and opens the door, I will come in and will have my meal with him, and he with me.

> I will give to him who overcomes to sit with me in my throne, even as I also overcame, and took my seat with my Father in His throne.

> Let him who has an ear hear what the Spirit is saying to the Churches.

LAODICEA
THE CHURCH CONDEMNED

Revelation 3.14-22

LAODICEA has the grim distinction of being the only Church of which the Risen Christ has nothing good to say.

In the ancient world there were at least six cities called Laodicea, and the Laodicea of the *Revelation* was called Laodicea on the Lycus to distinguish it from the others. It was founded about 250 B.C. by Antiochus of Syria, and it was named after his wife Laodicē. Laodicea's importance was due entirely to its position. The road from Ephesus to the east and to Syria was the most important road in Asia. That road began at the coast at Ephesus and it had to find a way to climb up to the central plateau which was 8,500 feet up. It set out along the valley of the River Maeander until it reached what were known as the Gates of Phrygia. Beyond these gates lay a broad valley where Lydia, Phrygia and Caria met. The road into that valley taken by the Maeander was a narrow, rocky, precipitous gorge, through which no road could pass. The road, therefore, detoured through the Lycus valley and climbed up to the plateau by that way. In that valley Laodicea stood. It was literally astride the great road to the east. That road went straight through Laodicea, entering by the Ephesian Gate and leaving by the Syrian Gate. That in itself would have been enough to make Laodicea one of the great commercial and strategic centres of the ancient world. And originally Laodicea had been a fortress; but as a fortress it had the serious handicap that all its water supply had to come by underground aqueduct from springs no less than six miles away, a perilous situation for a town besieged. Two other roads passed through the gates of Laodicea. There was the road from Pergamum and the Hermus Valley to Pisidia and Pamphylia and to the coast at Perga. And the road from eastern Caria to central and west Phrygia also passed through Laodicea.

As Sir W. M. Ramsay says: " It only needed peace to make Laodicea a great commercial and financial centre." That peace came with the dominion of Rome. In the previous days of unsettlement Laodicea had been a comparatively small town, but when the Roman peace gave it its opportunity it became, as Pliny called it, " a most distinguished city."

Laodicea had certain characteristics which have left their mark on the letter written to it.

(i) It was a great banking and financial centre. When Cicero was travelling in Asia Minor it was at Laodicea that he cashed his letters of credit. Laodicea was one of the wealthiest cities in the world. In A.D. 61 Laodicea was devastated by an earthquake; but so rich and independent were its citizens that they refused any help from the Roman government, and out of their own resources and by their own efforts rebuilt their city. Tacitus, the Roman historian, writes: " One of the most famous cities of Asia, Laodicea, was in that same year overthrown by an earthquake, and, without any relief from us, recovered itself by its own resources " (Tacitus, *Annals*, 14.27). No wonder that Laodicea could boast that it was rich and had amassed wealth and had need of nothing. Laodicea was so wealthy that it did not even need God.

(ii) It was a great centre of clothing manufacture. The sheep which grazed round Laodicea were famous for their soft, violet-black, glossy wool. It mass-produced cheap outer garments. It was specially connected with a tunic called the *trimita*, so much so, indeed, that it was sometimes called Trimitaria. Laodicea was so proud of the garments it produced that it never realized that it was naked in the sight of God.

(iii) It was a very considerable medical centre. Thirteen miles to the west, between Laodicea and the Gate of Phrygia, there stood the temple of the Carian god Men. At one time that temple was the social, the administrative and the commercial centre of the whole area. Until less than a hundred years ago great markets were regularly held on the site of that temple. In particular the temple was the centre of a medical school. That medical school was transferred to Laodicea itself. So famous were its doctors that the names of some of them appear on the coins of Laodicea. Two of them were called Zeuxis and Alexander Philalethes. This medical school was famous for two things throughout the world. It was famous for ointment for the ears; and it was famous for ointment for the eyes. The Authorized Version speaks of eye-*salve*. The word for *salve* is *kollurion*, which literally means *a little roll of bread*. The reason for the word is that this famous *tephra Phrygia*, Phrygian powder, was exported all over the world in solidified tablet form, and the tablets were in the shape of little rolls. Laodicea was so conscious of its medical skill in the care of the eyes that it never realized that in the sight of God it was spiritually blind.

The words of the Risen Christ arise directly from the prosperity and the skill in which Laodicea took so much pride, and which had in the minds of its citizens, and even of its Church, eliminated the need for God.

(iv) We may add one final fact about Laodicea. It was in an area where there was a very large Jewish population. So many Jews emigrated to this area that the Rabbis inveighed against the Jews who sought the wines and baths of Phrygia. In 62 B.C. Flaccus the governor of the province was alarmed at the amount of currency which the Jews were exporting in the payment of the Temple tax which every Jew paid. He put an embargo on the export of currency. The result was that twenty pounds weight of gold were seized as contraband in Laodicea and one hundred pounds weight in Apameia in Phrygia. That amount of gold would be equal to 15,000 silver *drachmae*. The Jewish Temple tax amounted to half a shekel, which would be the equivalent of one shilling and sixpence, which is equal to two *drachmae*. This, then, means that in the district there were at least 7,500 male Jews apart from women and children. In the city of Hierapolis, six miles away from Laodicea, there was a " Congregation of Jews " which had power to levy and to retain fines, and an archive office where Jewish legal documents were specially kept. There can have been few areas where the Jews were wealthier and more influential.

Such, then, was Laodicea, the city which was too prosperously wealthy to have any real need of God.

LAODICEA
THE CLAIMS OF CHRIST

Revelation 3.14-22 (continued)

OF all the seven Churches that of Laodicea is most unsparingly condemned. For it there is no word of praise; in it there is no redeeming feature. It is interesting to note that the third century work *The Apostolic Constitutions* (8.46) says that Archippus was the first Bishop of the Church in Laodicea. Now when Paul was writing to the neighbouring Church of Colossae, he says sternly: " Say to Archippus, Take heed to the ministry which thou hast received in the Lord, that thou fulfil it " (*Colossians* 4.17). It would seem that Archippus was somehow failing in his duty, and needed a sharp reminder. That was thirty years before the *Revelation* was written; but it may be that as long ago as that the rot had set in in the Church in Laodicea, and that an unworthy pastor and an unsatisfactory and unfaithful ministry had sown the seeds of degeneration there.

As in all the letters, the introduction begins with a series of great titles of Jesus Christ.

(i) He is the Amen. This is a strange title. It may go back to either of two origins. (*a*) In *Isaiah* 65.16 God is called the God of truth; but in the Hebrew God is there called by the strange name the *God of Amen*. The word Amen is the word which is often put at the end of a solemn statement or affirmation in order to guarantee and to emphasize its truth. So, then, if God is called the God of Amen, it means that He is utterly to be relied upon; that His words are unquestioningly to be accepted; that His promises are always true. This, then, would mean that Jesus Christ is the One whose words and promises are true beyond all doubt. (b) In John's gospel Jesus' statements often begin: " Verily, verily, I say unto you " (e.g. *John* 1.51; 3.3, 5, 11). The Greek of that phrase is: " Amen, Amen, I say unto you." It is possible that when Jesus Christ is called the Amen it is a reminiscence of His own way of speaking. The meaning would be the same; it would mean that Jesus is the one whose statements are true, and whose promises can be relied upon.

(ii) He is the witness on whom we can rely and who is true. R. C. Trench well points out that a witness must satisfy three essential conditions. (a) He must have seen with his own eyes that of which he tells. (b) He must be absolutely honest, so that he repeats with accuracy that which he has heard and seen. (c) He must have the ability to tell what he has to say, so that his witness may make its true impression on those who hear. Jesus Christ perfectly satisfied these exacting conditions. He can tell of God, because He came from God. We can rely on His words for He is the Amen, whose words are true. He is able to tell His message, for never man spake as this man. Jesus Christ is the perfect witness of the things of God to men.

(iii) As the Authorized Version has it, He is the beginning of the creation of God. This is a phrase about which we must be careful, for, as it stands in English, it is ambiguous. To say that Jesus is the beginning of creation could mean, either, that He was the first person to be created, or, that He was the moving cause of all creation, He who began the process of creation and who initiated the work of creation, as R. C. Trench put it, " dynamically the beginning." There is no doubt at all that it is the second meaning which is intended here. The word for beginning is *archē*. In early

Christian writings we read that Satan was the *archē* of death, that is to say, that death took its source and origin in him; or that God is the *archē* of all things, that is, that all things find their beginning and origin in God.

The connection of the Son with creation is frequently made in the New Testament. John begins his gospel by saying of the Word: " All things were made by Him, and without Him was not anything made that was made " (*John* I.3). " By Him," says Paul, " were all things created " (*Colossians* I.15, 18). The insistence on the part of the Son in creation was due to the emergence of heretics who explained sin and disease by saying that the world had been created, not by the true God, but by a false and inferior God. It is the Christian insistence that this world is the creation of God, and that the sin and the sorrow of it are not the fault of the Creator, but are caused by the disobedience of men. As the Christian sees it, the God of creation and the God of redemption are one and the same.

LAODICEA
NEITHER ONE THING NOR ANOTHER

Revelation 3.14-22 (continued)

THE condemnation of Laodicea begins with a picture of almost crude vividness; because the Laodiceans are neither cold nor hot, they have about them a kind of nauseating quality, which will make the Risen Christ vomit them out of His mouth.

The exact meaning of the words is to be noted. The word for *cold* is *psuchros*; and it can mean cold to the point of freezing. *Ecclesiasticus* (43.20) speaks of the *cold* (*psuchros*) north wind which makes the ice congeal upon the waters. The word for hot is *zestos*; and it means hot to boiling point. The word for *tepid* is *chliaros*. Things which are tepid often have a nauseating effect. Hot food can be appetising and cold food can be appetising, but tepid food will often make the stomach turn. Directly opposite Laodicea, on the other bank of the Lycus, and in full view, stood Hierapolis. Hierapolis was famous for its hot mineral springs. The white lime-encrusted cliff over which the hot springs flowed was one of the first things to meet the eye, when anyone looked out across the river from Laodicea. Often these hot mineral springs with their chemical content are nauseating in their taste and in their smell. They make the person who drinks them want to be physically sick. That is the way in which the Church at Laodicea affected the Risen Christ. Here, indeed, is something to make us think.

(i) The one attitude which the Risen Christ unsparingly condemns is the attitude of indifference. It has been said that an author can write a good biography if he loves his subject, or if he hates his subject, but not if he is coldly and detachedly indifferent to his subject. Of all things indifference is the hardest to combat. If a man feels intensely about something in one direction, it is at least possible to persuade him to feel intensely in the other direction. But if a man has lost the ability to feel intensely at all, then it is very difficult to do anything with him. Indifference is like a kind of icy death in which everything has ceased to matter. The problem of modern evangelism is not hostility to Christianity; it would be better if it were so. The problem is that to so many Christianity and the Church have ceased to have any relevance at all, and men regard them with complete indifference, and indifference is the hardest of all barriers to break down. It can only be broken down by the actual demonstration in life that Christianity is a power to make life strong and a grace to make life beautiful.

(ii) The one impossible attitude to Christianity is neutrality. To be neutral to Jesus Christ is to be an obstacle to Jesus Christ. Jesus Christ works through men; and the man who remains completely detached in his attitude to Jesus Christ has by that very fact refused to undertake the work which is the divine purpose for him, and is, therefore, not on the way, but in the way. The man who will not help Christ is necessarily a hindrance to Christ; and the man who will not submit to Christ has necessarily resisted Christ. If we appeal for a person's love, and the answer of that person is that he does not care one way or another, then obviously love stands frustrated and defeated.

(iii) Hard as it may sound, the meaning of this terrible threat of the Risen Christ is that it is better not even to start on the Christian way than it is to start and then to slip and drift into a conventional and meaningless Christianity of respectability. It is better not even to start on what Trench calls " the grand experiment of the gospel," than it is to start and drift into a religion which means nothing at all. No leader desires followers with reservations; no leader finds any value in a loyalty which has turned into indifference. The fire must be kept burning. There is an unwritten saying of Jesus: " He who is near me is near the fire." And the way to "maintain the spiritual glow" (*Romans* 12.11, Moffatt) is to live ever close to Christ.

LAODICEA
THE WEALTH THAT IS POVERTY

Revelation 3.14-22 (*continued*)

THE tragedy of Laodicea was that it was convinced of its own wealth, and blind to its own poverty. Humanly speaking, and judging by human standards, anyone would say that there was not a more prosperous town in Asia Minor than Laodicea. Spiritually speaking, and judging by divine standards, the Risen Christ declares that there was not a more poverty-stricken community in Asia Minor than Laodicea. Laodicea prided itself on three things; and each of these three sources of pride is taken in turn and shown at its true value.

(i) Laodicea prided itself on its financial wealth. It

was the banking centre of Asia Minor; it was so wealthy that, when it was devastated by the earthquake in A.D. 61, it refused to accept any state aid to help in its rebuilding. Laodicea was rich and had acquired wealth and had need of nothing—so it thought. The Risen Christ advises Laodicea to buy gold tried and refined in the fire. It may be that that gold tried in the fire stands for faith for it is thus that Peter describes faith (I *Peter* 1.7). Wealth can do much, but there are things that wealth can never do. Wealth cannot buy happiness; wealth cannot give a man health either of body or of mind; wealth cannot bring comfort in sorrow; wealth cannot bring fellowship in loneliness. If all that a man has to meet life with is wealth, then he is poor indeed. But if a man has a faith which is tried and refined in the crucible of experience, then there is nothing which he cannot face, and he is rich indeed.

(ii) Laodicea prided itself on its clothing trade. The garments made in Laodicea were famous over all the world, and the wool of the sheep of Laodicea was a luxury article which all men knew. But, says the Risen Christ, Laodicea is spiritually naked; if it wants really to be clothed it must come to Him for what He can offer. The Risen Christ speaks of " the shame of the nakedness of Laodicea." This would mean even more in the ancient world than it means to us. In the ancient world to be stripped naked was the worst humiliation and shame. It was thus that Hanun treated the servants of David (2 *Samuel* 10.4). The threat to Egypt is that Assyria will lead her people naked and barefoot (*Isaiah* 20.4). It was Ezekiel's threat to Israel that her enemies would strip her of her clothes (*Ezekiel* 16.37-39; 23.26-29; cp. *Hosea* 2.3, 9; *Micah* 1.8, 11). The threat which God told Nahum to tell to the disobedient people was: " I will show the nations thy nakedness, and the kingdoms thy shame " (*Nahum* 3.5). On the other hand to be clothed in fine raiment was the greatest honour. Pharoah honoured Joseph by clothing him in vestures of fine linen (*Genesis* 41.42). Daniel is clothed in scarlet by

Belshazzar (*Daniel* 5.29). The royal apparel is for the man whom the king honours (*Esther* 6.6-11). When the prodigal son returns, it is the best robe that is put upon him (*Luke* 15.22).

Laodicea prides itself on the magnificent garments it produces, but spiritually it is naked, and nakedness is shame. The Risen Christ urges it to buy white raiment from Him. What is the white raiment? It may well stand for the beauties of life and character which only the grace of Christ can give. There is little point in a man adorning his body, if he has nothing wherewith to adorn his soul. Not all the clothes in the world will beautify a person whose nature is twisted and whose character is ugly. That which man can put on without will never compensate for that which God can give within.

(iii) Laodicea prided itself on its famous eye-salve; it was exported all over the world as a sovereign remedy for diseases of the eye. But the very facts of the case show the blindness of Laodicea, for Laodicea was blind to its own poverty and its own nakedness. R. C. Trench says: " The beginning of all true amendment is to see ourselves as we are," and for that Laodicea was far too blind. All eye-salves in the ancient world caused the eyes to smart at their first application, and Laodicea had no wish to see itself as it was. Only He who is the light of the world can enable us to see; and to see Him in His holiness, and ourselves in our sin, is the first step to salvation.

LAODICEA
LOVE'S CHASTISEMENT

Revelation 3.14-22 (*continued*)

VERSE 19 is a verse whose teaching runs throughout the whole of Scripture. " I rebuke and discipline all those whom I love." There is one very lovely thing about the way this is put. This is a quotation from *Proverbs* 3.12, but in the quotation one word is altered. In the Greek of the Septuagint the word for *love* is *agapan*; *agapan* indicates the unconquerable attitude of benevolence and goodwill which nothing can turn to hate; but it is a word which maybe has more of the head than the heart in it; but in the quotation the Risen Christ changes *agapan* to *philein*, and *philein* is the word of the warmest and the most tender affection. We might get the atmosphere of the whole phrase better, if we paraphrased it: " It is the people who are dearest to me on whom I exercise the sternest discipline." The Bible is full of the discipline which love must always exercise over those whom it loves.

Let us first take the word *rebuke*; the Greek word is *elegchein*, and it describes, not simply rebuke, but the kind of rebuke which compels a man to see the error of his ways and to admit that he was wrong. *Elegchos* is the corresponding noun, and Aristotle defines it thus: " *Elegchos* is the proof that a thing cannot be otherwise than we say." The most vivid example of this kind of rebuke is the way in which Nathan opened David's eyes to his sin, when David had arranged the death of Uriah that he might possess Bathsheba (2 *Samuel* 12.1-14). To rebuke a man in this sense does not mean to scold and storm and rail at him; it does not mean simply to unleash a flood of angry words at him, however just and righteous the anger may be; it means so to speak to a man that he is compelled to see the error of his ways, to admit how wrong he was, and to amend his life and conduct. The rebuke of God is not so much punishment as it is illumination.

Let us now see how the idea of discipline runs through the Bible.

It is very characteristic of the teaching of *Proverbs*. " He that spareth his rod hateth his son; but he that loveth him chasteneth him betimes " (*Proverbs* 13.24). " Withhold not correction from the child; for, if thou beatest him with the rod he shall not die. Thou shalt beat him with the rod, and shalt deliver his soul from hell" (*Proverbs* 23.13, 14). " Faithful are the wounds of a friend " (*Proverbs* 27.6). " The rod and reproof give wisdom; but a child left to himself bringeth his mother to shame. . . . Correct thy son and he shall give thee rest; yea, he shall give delight unto thy soul " (*Proverbs* 29.15, 17). " Blessed is the man whom Thou chastenest, O Lord, and teachest him out of Thy law " (*Psalm* 94.12). " Behold, happy is the man whom God correcteth; therefore, despise not the chastening of the Almighty " (*Job* 5.17). " We are chastened of the Lord that we should not be condemned with the world " (I *Corinthians* 11.32). " Whom the Lord loveth He chasteneth, and scourgeth every son whom He receiveth. If ye endure chastening, God dealeth with you as with sons; for what son is he whom the father chasteneth not? But, if ye be without chastisement, whereof all are partakers, then are ye bastards, and not sons " (*Hebrews* 11.7, 8). " He that loveth his son will continue to lay stripes upon him, that he may have joy of him in the end. He that chastiseth his son shall have profit of him and shall glory of him among his acquaintances " (*Ecclesiasticus* 30.1). It is, in fact, God's final punishment to leave a man alone. " Ephraim is joined to his idols; let him alone " (*Hosea* 4.17). As R. C. Trench has it: " The great Master-builder squares and polishes with many strokes of the chisel and hammer the stones which shall find a place at last in the walls of the heavenly Jerusalem. . . . It is the crushed grape, and not the untouched, from which the costly liquor distils." It is the fact of life that there is no surer way of allowing a child or young person to end in ruin, than to allow him to do as he likes. It is the fact of life that the best athlete and the finest scholar receive the hardest and the most demanding training. The discipline of God is not something which we should resent, but something for which we should be devoutly thankful.

LAODICEA
THE CHRIST WHO KNOCKS
Revelation 3.14-22 *(continued)*

IN verse 20 we have one of the most famous pictures of Jesus in the whole New Testament. "Behold," says the Risen Christ, "I am standing at the door and knocking." This picture has been derived from two different sources.

(i) It has been taken as a warning that the end is near, and that the Coming of Christ is at hand. The Christian must be like the man who is ready to open whenever he hears his Lord knocking (*Luke* 12.36). When the signs come, the Christian will know that the last time is near, even at the doors (*Mark* 13.29; *Matthew* 24.33). The Christian must live well and live in love because the judge is standing at the door (*James* 5.9). It is quite true that the New Testament uses this picture to express the imminence of the coming of Christ. If that is the picture here, then this phrase contains a threat and a warning, and tells men to have a care for Jesus Christ the Judge and King is at the door.

(ii) We cannot say that that meaning is impossible, and yet it does not seem to fit the context, for the whole atmosphere of the passage is not so much warning and threat as it is yearning and love. It is much better to take this saying of Christ as expressing the appeal of the lover of the souls of men. The origin of the passage is much more likely to be in the tenderest of all passages in *Solomon's Song* when the lover stands at the door of his beloved and pleads with her to open to him. "It is the voice of my beloved that knocketh saying, Open to me my sister, my love, my dove, my undefiled" (*Solomon's Song* 5.2-6) Here is Christ the lover knocking at the door of the hearts of men. And in this picture we see certain great truths of the Christian religion.

(*a*) We see the pleading of Christ. Christ stands at the door of the human heart and knocks. The one unique new fact that Christianity brought into this world is the fact

THE REVELATION OF JOHN

that God is the seeker of men. No other religion has the vision of a seeking God. In his book *Out of Nazareth* Donald Baillie cites three witnesses to the uniqueness of this amazing conception of a seeking God. Montefiore, the great Jewish scholar, said that the one thing which no Jewish prophet and no Jewish Rabbi ever conceived of is the " conception of God actually going out in quest of sinful men, who were not seeking Him, but who were turned away from Him." It would be great enough to think of a God who accepted men when they came back; it was beyond belief to think of a God who actually went out and searched. The National Christian Council of Japan in a document which sought to set out the distinctive difference of Christianity from all other religions found that difference in, " Man not seeking God, but God taking the initiative in seeking man." Baron von Hugel, the great German theologian, used to love to quote a thing that St. Bernard away back in the twelfth century used often to say to his monks. He used to say that, " However early they might wake and rise for prayer in their chapel on a cold mid-winter morning, or even in the dead of night, they would always find God awake before them, waiting for them—nay, it was He who had awakened them to seek His face."

Here there is the picture of the seeking God, the knocking Christ, Christ the supplicant lover, Christ searching for sinful men, who did not want Him. Surely love can go no further than that.

(b) We see the offer of Christ. As the Authorized Version has it, " I will come in and sup with him." The word translated sup is *deipnein*, and its corresponding noun is *deipnon*. The word is very significant. The Greeks had three meals in the day. There was *akratisma*, breakfast, which was no more than a piece of dried bread dipped in wine. There was *ariston*, the midday meal. A man did not go home for it; it was simply a picnic snack eaten by the side of the pavement, or in some colonnade, or in the city square, a meal eaten in the passing. There was *deipnon*; this was the

evening meal; it was the main meal of the day; people
lingered and sat long and talked over it, for the day's
work was done; there was time now for unlimited and
unhurried fellowship together. It was the *deipnon* that
Christ would share with the man who answered His knock.
This was no hurried meal, no visit in the passing, no hasty,
conventional call; it was the meal where people lingered in
fellowship together. This was not " a brief glance, a passing
word." The promise is of intimate friendship with Christ.
If a man will open the door, Jesus Christ will come in, and
linger long with him.

(iii) We see human responsibility. Christ knocks; a man
can answer, or refuse to answer, that knock. Christ does not
break in; He must be invited in. Even on the Emmaus
road, " He made as if He would have gone further "
(*Luke* 24.28). Jesus Christ will never force Himself on any
man; He must be an invited guest. Holman Hunt was
right when in his famous picture *The Light of the World* he
painted the door of the human heart with no handle on the
outside, for that door can only be opened from within.
As R. C. Trench has it: " Every man is lord of the house
of his own heart; it is his fortress; he must open the gates
of it," and he has " the mournful prerogative and privilege
of refusing to open." The man who refuses to open is
" blindly at strife with his own blessedness." He is a
" miserable conqueror."

Christ pleads; Christ offers; but it is all to no avail if a
man will not open the door, and bid Him enter.

LAODICEA
THIS MEANS YOU

Revelation 3.14-22 (*continued*)

THE promise of the Risen Christ to the victor is that the
victor will sit with Christ in His own victorious throne.
We will get the picture right, if we remember that the

eastern throne was more like a couch than a single seat. The victor in life will share the throne of the victorious Christ.

Every letter finishes with the words: " Let him who has an ear hear what the Spirit is saying to the Churches." This saying does two things.

(i) It individualizes the message of the letters. It says to every man as he listens to the words of the Risen Christ: " This means you." So often we listen to a message which comes through a preacher and apply it to everyone but ourselves. In our heart of hearts we believe that the stern words cannot possibly be meant for us; and the promises are too good to be true for us. But this phrase says to every one of us: " All these things are meant for *you*."

(ii) It generalizes the message of the letters. It means that the message of these letters was not confined to the people in the seven Churches nineteen hundred years ago, but that through them the Spirit is speaking to every man in every generation.

We have set these letters carefully against the local situations to which they were addressed; we have set them in their contemporary history; but their message is not local and temporary; it is eternal; and in them the Spirit still speaks to us as we read them today. Their criticisms demand that we should search our own souls; and their promises demand that we should lift up our own hearts; for the Christ who lived in them is the Christ who is alive for evermore, and who is still alive today.

THE OPENING HEAVENS AND THE OPENING DOOR

Revelation 4.1

> After this I saw, and, behold, a door in heaven was standing open, and there came to me the voice that I had heard before, speaking to me like the sound of a trumpet, and the speaker said: " Come up here, and I will show you the events which must follow these things."

In chapters 2 and 3 we saw the Risen Christ walking amidst His Churches upon earth, and now the scene changes from the earth to the court of heaven.

A door was opened in heaven for the seer. There are two possibilities here. (a) It may be that the seer is thought of as already being in heaven, and the door is a door opening in heaven into still more secret and still more holy parts of heaven. (b) It is very much more likely that the door is a door from earth to heaven. Primitive Jewish thought conceived of the sky as a vast solid dome, like the dome of some great church, set like a roof upon a square flat earth; and the idea here is that beyond the dome of the sky there is heaven, and a door is opened in that dome to give the seer entry into heaven. He is given the right of entry beyond the dome of the sky into the heaven above.

In the early chapters of the *Revelation* there are three doors, and they are three of the most important doors in life.

(i) There is *the door of opportunity*. " Behold," said the Risen Christ to the Church at Philadelphia, " I have set before you an open door " (*Revelation* 3.8). That was the door of the glorious opportunity by which the message of the gospel could be taken to the regions beyond. God sets before every man his own door of opportunity.

(ii) There is *the door of the human heart*. " Behold," says the Risen Christ, " I stand at the door and knock " (*Revelation* 3.20). That is the door which a man may open, or refuse to open. At the door of every heart there comes the knock of the nail-pierced hand.

(iii) There is *the door of revelation*. " I saw a door in heaven standing open," says the seer. God offers to every man the door which leads to the knowledge of Himself, and to the knowledge of life eternal.

More than once the New Testament speaks of the heavens *being opened*; and it is of the greatest significance to see the object of that opening.

(i) There is the opening of the heavens for *vision*. That is what Ezekiel saw. " The heavens were opened and I saw visions of God " (*Ezekiel* I.I). God sends to those who seek Him, and to those who wait upon Him, the vision of Himself and of His truth.

(ii) There is the opening for *the descent of the Spirit*. When Jesus was baptized by John, He saw the heavens opened and the Spirit descending upon Himself (*Mark* I.10). When a man's own mind and soul seek upwards, the Spirit of God descends to meet them. God always meets the seeking mind far more than half way.

(iii) There is the opening for *the revelation of the glory of Christ*. It was the promise of Jesus to Nathanael that he would see the heaven open, and the angels of God ascending and descending upon the Son of Man (*John* I.51). Some day the heavens will open to disclose the glory of Christ; and inevitably that day will bring joy to those who have loved Christ, and amazement and fear to those who have despised Him.

THE THRONE OF GOD

Revelation 4.2, 3

> Immediately, I fell under the influence of the Spirit; and, behold, a throne stood in heaven, and there was One seated on it. And He who was seated on the throne was like a jasper stone and a sardian to look at; and there was a rainbow circling round the throne, like an emerald to look at.

WHEN the seer entered the door into heaven, he fell into an ecstasy; he was in a state of spiritual exaltation; he was lifted up above himself and beyond himself.

In heaven he saw a throne and God on the throne. The throne of God is a common Old Testament picture. The prophet said: " I saw the Lord sitting on His throne, and all the host of heaven standing by him " (I *Kings* 19.22). The Psalmist has it: " God sitteth upon the throne of His holiness " (*Psalm* 47.8). Isaiah saw the Lord " sitting upon a throne, high and lifted up " (*Isaiah* 6.I). In the

Revelation the throne of God is mentioned in every chapter except chapters 2, 8, and 9. The throne of God stands for the majesty of God; here is the awesome picture of God the King of the Universe, God in His might and majesty and power. When Handel was asked how he had come to write the magnificent music of the *Messiah*, his answer was: " I saw the heavens opened and God upon His great white throne."

John saw One seated upon the throne. There is something very interesting here. John makes no attempt to describe God in any human shapes or forms. As H. B. Swete says, " He rigorously shuns anthropomorphic details." He describes God in " the flashing of gem-like colours," but he never mentions any kind of shapes or forms. It is the Bible's way to see God in terms of light. The Pastorals describe God as " dwelling in the light that no man can approach unto " (I *Timothy* I.16). And long before that the Psalmist had spoken of God who covers Himself with light as a garment (*Psalm* 104.2).

John sees his vision in terms of the lights which flash from precious stones. We do not know what exactly these stones were, for the ancients described precious stones in names which do not always correspond to their modern names. The three names here are the jasper, the sardian and the emerald. One thing is certain; these stones were, as it were, typical of the most precious stones. Plato mentions the three of them together as representative of precious stones (Plato, *Phaedo* III E). These three stones were part of the rich array of the King of Tyre (*Ezekiel* 28.13); they were among the precious stones on the breastplate of the High Priest (*Exodus* 28.17); and they were among the stones which were the foundations of the Holy City (*Revelation* 21.19). Apart from anything else, these stones stand symbolically for the most precious and costly things of which a man can conceive.

The *jasper* is nowadays a dull opaque stone, but in the ancient world it seems to have been a translucent rock crystal, through which the light would come with an almost unbearable scintillation. There are some who think that here it means a diamond, and it is not impossible that it is so. The *sardian*, so-called because it was said to be found mainly near Sardis, was a blood-red stone; it was a gem which was frequently used to have engravings incised on it; it may correspond to the modern carnelian. The *emerald* is most likely the green emerald which we know.

The picture of the presence of God which John saw was like the blinding flash of a diamond in the sun, with the dazzling blood-red of the sardian; and these flashed through both the more restful green of the emerald, for in that way alone could the eye bear to look upon the sight. There may well be symbolism here.

It may well be that the *jasper* stands for the unbearable white brightness of the *purity* of God; that the blood-red *sardian* stands for the avenging *wrath* of God; and that the gentle green of the *emerald* stands for the *mercy* of God, by which alone we can meet the purity and the justice of God.

THE TWENTY-FOUR ELDERS

Revelation 4.4

> And in a circle round the throne I saw twenty-four thrones, and seated upon the thrones twenty-four elders, clothed in white garments, with golden crowns upon their heads.

WE now approach one of these difficult passages for which the *Revelation* is notorious. We approach the passage in which we meet the twenty-four elders, and then the four living creatures; and we have to try to identify them. In this, and in all such passages, we shall set down such explanations as we think most probable, and in most cases there will be more than one, for there are many passages in the *Revelation* about the explanation of which it is not possible to speak with dogmatic certainty.

We find the twenty-four elders frequently appearing in the *Revelation*. Let us set down the facts about them. They sit around the throne, clothed in white robes and wearing crowns (4.4; 14.3); they cast their crowns before the throne (4.10); they continually worship and praise (5.11, 14; 7.11; 11.16; 14.3; 19.4); they bring to God the prayers of the saints (5.6); one of them encourages the seer, when he is sad (5.5); and one of them acts as interpreter of one of the visions (7.13). We may note five lines of explanation.

(i) In the Old Testament there are indications of a kind of council or senate surrounding God. The prophet sees God sitting on His throne and all the host of heaven standing by Him on His right hand and on His left (I *Kings* 19.22). In *Job* the sons of God come to meet with God (*Job* 1.6; 2.1). Isaiah speaks of God reigning in glory among His elders (*Isaiah* 24.23). In the old *Genesis* story of the garden, the accusation against Adam is that he has eaten of the fruit of the forbidden tree and has, in the curious phrase of God, become one *of us* (*Genesis* 3.22). In primitive thought God had His council or His senate surrounding Him. It may be that the idea of the elders has something to do with this.

(ii) When the Jews were in Babylon, they could not avoid coming into contact with Babylonian ideas. And it might well be that sometimes they would incorporate Babylonian ideas into their own thinking, especially if there was some initial resemblance. The Babylonians, in fact, had twenty-four star gods, for the worship and the power of the stars was a part of Babylonian religion and imagery; and it has been suggested that the twenty-four Babylonian star gods became in Jewish thought twenty-four angels who surrounded the throne of God, and that the elders stand for these.

(iii) We now move on to explanations which we think are very much more likely. There were so many priests in Israel that they could not possibly serve in the Temple all at the one time, so they were divided into twenty-four different courses, as the Old Testament tells (I *Chronicles* 24.7-18). Each of these courses had its president, and they were known as elders of the priests. Sometimes they were called princes, or governors, of the house of God (I *Chronicles* 24.5). It is suggested that the twenty-four elders stand symbolically for the twenty-four courses of the priests. They present the prayers of the faithful to God (*Revelation* 5.6), and that is priestly work. The Levites were similarly divided into twenty-four courses for the work of the Temple and they praised God with harps and psalteries and cymbals (I *Chronicles* 25.9-31), and the elders also have their harps (*Revelation* 5.8). So the twenty-four elders may stand for the heavenly ideal of the earthly worship of the priests and Levites in the Temple in Jerusalem. They present the perfect heavenly worship of which the worship on earth is a faint and pale copy.

(iv) It has been suggested that the twenty-four elders stand for the twelve patriarchs and the twelve apostles combined. In the Holy City, the new Jerusalem, the names of the twelve patriarchs are on the twelve gates and the names of the twelve apostles are on the foundation stones of the wall. The patriarchs and the apostles are the joint foundation of the Church, and it may be that the twenty-four elders represent them.

(v) We think that the likeliest explanation of all is that the twenty-four elders are the symbolic representatives of the faithful people of God. Their white robes are the robes which are promised to the faithful (*Revelation* 3.4), and their crowns (*stephanoi*) are the crowns which those who are faithful unto death are to receive (*Revelation* 2.10). The thrones are the thrones which Jesus promised to those who forsook all and followed Him (*Matthew* 19.27-29). The description of the twenty-four elders fits well with the promises made to the faithful.

The question will then be, Why twenty-four? It is here that we must take in what is right in the explanation, which identified the twenty-four elders with the patriarchs and the apostles. There are now twenty-four because the Church is composed of Jews *and* Gentiles. There were originally twelve tribes, but now it is as if the tribes had been doubled, and the Kingdom of God contains double measure, Jew and Gentile in one. H. B. Swete says that the twenty-four elders stand for the Church *in its totality*. We remember that this is a vision, not of what yet is, but of what shall be; and the twenty-four elders stand as representatives of the whole Church which one day in glory will praise and worship in the presence of God Himself.

AROUND THE THRONE

Revelation 4.5, 6a

> And flashes of lightning and voices and peals of thunder were coming forth from the throne. There were seven torches of fire burning before the throne, and these are the seven Spirits of God. And in front of the throne there was what I can only call a sea of glass like crystal.

HERE John adds more details to his mysterious and awe-inspiring picture of heaven. The voices are the voices of the thunder; and thunder and lightning are often connected with the voice and the manifestation of God. In the vision of Ezekiel lightning comes out of the fiery haze around the throne (*Ezekiel* 1.13). The Psalmist tells how the voice of the thunder of God was heard in the heavens, and the lightnings lightened the world (*Psalm* 77.18). God sends His lightning unto the ends of the earth (*Job* 37.4). But that which is primarily in the mind of John is the description of Mount Sinai as the people waited for the giving of the Law: " There were thunders and lightnings and a thick cloud upon the mount, and the voice of the trumpet exceeding loud " (*Exodus* 19.16). Here John is using the imagery which is regularly connected with the presence of God.

THE REVELATION OF JOHN

The seven torches are the seven Spirits of God. We have
already met the seven Spirits before the throne (*Revelation*
1.4; 3.1) and we saw that the Spirits stand for the sevenfold
gift of the Spirit, and for the action of the Spirit in every
Church. We may note that there are those scholars who
see Babylonian influence here also. For the Babylonians
the seven planets were also divine and were within the
presence of God; it would be very natural to liken the
planets to torches; and it has been suggested that this
imagery is Babylonian in its origin.

The " glassy sea " has exercised a strange fascination
over the minds of many people, for instance, of the hymn-
writers. It has first to be noted that the Greek does not
say that there was a sea of glass before the throne; it says
that there was " as it were a sea of glass "; there was
something which was beyond all description, but which
could be likened only to a great sea of glass. Where did
the seer get this picture of the sea of glass?

(i) He may have got it from a conception which is in
the most primitive thought of the Old Testament. We
have already seen that the firmament is conceived of as a
great solid dome arching over the earth. Beneath it there
is the earth, and above it there is the heaven. The creation
story speaks of the waters under the firmament and the
waters *above* the firmament (*Genesis* 1.7). The Psalmist
calls upon the waters that are above the heavens to praise
the Lord (*Psalm* 148.4). The belief was that above the
firmament, in the heavens, perhaps as the kind of floor of
heaven there was a great sea. Further, it was on that sea
that God had set His throne. The Psalmist says of God that
He set the beams of His chambers upon the waters (*Psalm*
104.3). It may be that John is finding his picture in the
old picture of the sea above the firmament with the throne
of God, as it were, built upon it.

(ii) It may be that John's time in Patmos gave him the
idea of this picture. H. B. Swete suggests that John saw a
vast surface which flashed back the light, " like the Aegean

196

Sea, when on summer days John looked upon it from the heights of Patmos." John had often seen the sea like a sea of molten glass, when he was in Patmos, and maybe his picture was born from that.

(iii) There is still a further possibility. According to the *Koran* (Sura 27) Solomon had in his palace a floor of glass which was exactly like a sea. So like a sea was it that, when the Queen of Sheba came to visit him, when she began to cross it she picked up her skirts thinking that she had to wade through water. It may just possibly be that John is thinking of the throne of God set in a glass-floored palace. That was the kind of luxury palace the richest potentates of earth possessed, and John may be transferring the imagery to heaven.

(iv) There is one other remote possibility. John says, as all translators translate it, that the glassy sea was like *crystal* (*krustallon*); but *krustallon* could mean *ice*; and then the idea would be an expanse which shimmered and glittered like an ice-field. It is a magnificent picture, but it can hardly be the real picture because neither John nor his people, living in Asia Minor, would ever have seen such a scene, and it would have meant nothing to them.

There are three things which we can say that this sea like shining glass does symbolize.

(i) It undoubtedly symbolizes *preciousness*. In the ancient world glass was usually dull and semi-opaque, and glass as clear as crystal was as precious as gold. In *Job* 28.17 gold and glass are mentioned together as examples of precious things.

(ii) It undoubtedly symbolizes *dazzling purity*. The blinding light reflected from the glassy sea would be too much for the eyes to look direct upon, like the purity of God.

(iii) It undoubtedly symbolizes *great and immense distance*. The throne of God was in the immense distance, as if at the other side of a great sea. Swete writes of " the vast distance which, even in the case of one who stood in the

THE REVELATION OF JOHN

door of heaven, intervened between himself and the throne of God."

One of the greatest characteristics of the writing of the seer is the reverence which, even in the heavenly places, never dares to be familiar with God, but paints its picture in terms of light and distance.

THE FOUR LIVING CREATURES

Revelation 4.6b-8

> And, between the throne and the elders, in a circle round the throne, were four living creatures, full of eyes in front and behind. The first living creature was like a lion; the second living creature was like a calf; the third living creature had what appeared to be a man's face; the fourth living creature was like an eagle in flight. The four living creatures had each of them six wings; and around and within they were full of eyes. Night and day they never rested from saying:
>> Holy, holy, holy is the Lord, the Almighty, who was, and who is, and who is to come.

HERE in the four living creatures we come to another of the symbolic problems of the *Revelation*. The four living creatures appear frequently in the heavenly scene; so let us begin by collecting what the *Revelation* itself says about them. They are always found near and around the throne and near the Lamb (4.6; 5.6; 14.3). They have six wings and they are full of eyes (4.6, 8). They are constantly engaged in praising and in worshipping God (4.8; 5.8; 5.14; 7.11; 19.4). They have certain functions and duties to perform. They invite the dreadful manifestations of the wrath of God to appear upon the scene (6.1; 6.7). One of them hands over the vials of the wrath of God (15.7).

Although there are quite definite differences, there can be little doubt that we find the ancestors of these living creatures in the visions of Ezekiel. In Ezekiel's vision the four living creatures each have four faces—the faces of a

man, a lion, an ox, and a calf. And they uphold the firmament (*Ezekiel* 1.6, 10, 22, 26); in *Ezekiel* it is the felloes
of the wheels which are full of eyes (*Ezekiel* 1.18). In *Ezekiel*
we have all the details of the picture in the *Revelation*,
although the details are differently allocated and arranged.
But in spite of the differences the family resemblance is
clear.

In *Ezekiel* the four living creatures are quite definitely
identified with the *cherubim*. (It is to be noted that *-im*
is the Hebrew plural ending; *cherubim* is simply *cherubs*
and *seraphim* is simply *seraphs*; the Hebrew *-im* is simply
the plural ending which corresponds to the English *-s*).
Let us, then, examine the Old Testament to find the picture
of the cherubim which it contains. The identification is
made in *Ezekiel* in *Ezekiel* 10.20, 22. The cherubim were
part of the decoration of Solomon's Temple, in the place of
prayer and on the walls (1 *Kings* 6.23-30; 2 *Chronicles* 3.7).
The cherubim were represented on the hanging veil which
shut off the Holy of Holies from the Holy Place (*Exodus*
26.31). There were two cherubim on the lid of the ark,
which is called the mercy-seat; and they were so placed
and represented that they faced each other, and their wings
swept over to form a kind of canopy over the mercy-seat
(*Exodus* 25.18-21). One of the commonest pictures of God
is to picture God as sitting between the cherubim, and it is
thus that God is often addressed in prayer (2 *Kings* 19.15;
Psalm 80.1; 99.1; *Isaiah* 37.16). God is represented as
flying on the cherubim and on the wings of the wind
(*Psalm* 18.12). It is the cherubim who guard the way to the
Garden when Adam and Eve had been banished from it
(*Genesis* 3.24). In the later books, which were written
between the Testaments, such as *Enoch*, the cherubim are
the guardians of the throne of God (*Enoch* 71.7).

From all this picture one thing emerges clearly—the
cherubim are angelic beings whose place in the heavenly
scheme is close to God, and who are the guardians of the
throne of God.

THE FOUR LIVING CREATURES

Revelation 4.6b-8 (continued)

WHAT, then, do these four living creatures symbolize?

(i) They are clearly part of the scenery and the imagery of heaven, and they are not figures whom the writer of the *Revelation* created, but whom he inherited from previous visions and pictures. They may well originally have come from Babylonian sources, and they may have originally stood for the four principal signs of the Zodiac, and for the four winds coming from the four quarters of heaven. But, even if that is so, the John who wrote the *Revelation* was not aware of that, and he used them simply as part of the imagery of heaven in which he had been brought up.

(ii) How, then, did John himself think of the symbolism of these living creatures? We think that in this Swete offers the right explanation. The four living creatures stand for everything that is noblest, strongest, wisest, and swiftest in nature. Each of them has the pre-eminence in his own particular sphere and world. The lion is supreme among beasts; the ox is supreme among cattle; the eagle is supreme among birds; and man is supreme among all creatures. The lion is the king of beasts, the noblest of them all. The labouring ox is the strongest of beasts. The eagle is the swiftest of all birds. And man is the wisest in all creation. So, then, the beasts represent all the greatness and the strength and the beauty of nature. Here we see nature praising God. In the verses which are to follow we see the twenty-four elders praising God; and when we put the two pictures together we get the complete picture of both nature and man engaged in constant praise and adoration of God. " The ceaseless activity of nature under the hand of God is a ceaseless tribute of praise." The idea of nature praising God is one which occurs in the Old Testament more than once. " The heavens declare the glory of God; and the firmament showeth His handiwork. Day unto day uttereth speech and night unto night showeth knowledge " (*Psalm* 19.1, 2). " Bless the Lord all His works in all places of His dominion " (*Psalm* 103.22). The whole of *Psalm* 148 is a magnificent summons to the whole of nature to join in praising God.

There is a great and tremendous truth here. The basic idea behind this is that anything in this world which is fulfilling the function for which it was created is praising God. One of the basic conceptions of Stoicism was that in everything there was a spark of God; that which gives every living thing life is the fact that in it there resides a *scintilla*, a spark, of God. " God," said Seneca, " is near you, with you, within you; a holy spirit sits within us." As Gilbert Murray points out, the sceptics laughed at this, and sought to make a fool of the whole idea. " What," said the sceptic, " God in worms? God in dung beetles? " " Why not? " demanded the Stoic. Cannot an earthworm serve God? Do you suppose that it is only a general who is a good soldier? Cannot the lowest private and camp attendant fight his best and give his life for the cause? Happy are you, if you are serving God, and carrying out His purpose as faithfully as an earthworm. That which carries out the function for which it was created is in the very action praising and adoring and worshipping God.

This is a thought which opens out the most magnificent vistas. The humblest and the most unseen activity in the world can be the true worship of God. The worship of God is not the preserve of liturgy and technically religious activities and intellectual pursuits. Work and worship literally become one. Man's chief end is to glorify God and to enjoy Him for ever; and man carries out that function when he does that which God sent him into the world to do, and the same great truth applies to every living creature. Work well done rises like a hymn of praise to eternal God.

This means that the doctor on his rounds, the scientist in his laboratory, the teacher in his classroom, the musician at his music, the artist at his canvas, the shop assistant at his counter, the typist at her typewriter, the housewife in her kitchen—all who are doing the work of the world, as it should be done, are joining in a great act of worship and a great act of harmony and praise. Not only every service of worship in the Church, but every day and every task in the day should be prefixed by the words: " Let us worship God. Let us praise God."

THE SYMBOLISM OF THE LIVING CREATURES

Revelation 4.6b-8 (*continued*)

IT was not long before the early Church found certain symbolisms in the living creatures. In particular they found in the living creatures symbolisms of the four Gospels; it was held that each of the living creatures was the symbolic representation of one of the Gospels. More than one scheme was worked out and there is no agreement between the schemes. The special interest of this is that the symbolism of representing the four Gospels by the four living creatures is often to be found in stained-glass windows in churches.

The earliest and the fullest identification was made by Irenaeus about A.D. 170. He held that the four living creatures represented four aspects of the work of Jesus Christ, which in turn are represented in the four Gospels.

The *lion* symbolizes the powerful and effective working of the Son of God, His leadership and His royal power. The *calf* signifies the sacrificial and priestly side of His work, for the calf is the animal of sacrifice. The *man* symbolizes His incarnation, His advent as a human being. The *eagle* represents the gift of the Holy Spirit, hovering with His wings over the Church. Now *John* represents " the original, effective and glorious generation of the Son from the Father," and tells how all things were made by Him. *John* is, therefore, symbolized by the *lion*. *Luke*, begins with the picture of Zacharias the priest, and tells the story of the fatted calf killed for the finding of the younger son. *Luke* represents the priestly side of the work

of Christ; and is, therefore, symbolized by the *calf*. *Matthew*
begins by giving us the human descent and genealogy of
Jesus, thus stressing his humanity. " The character of
a humble and meek man is kept up throughout the whole
gospel." *Matthew* is the gospel of the humanity of Christ;
and is, therefore, symbolized by the man. *Mark* begins
with a reference to the Spirit of prophecy coming down
from on high upon men, for he begins with a reference
to the prophet Isaiah. " This points to the winged aspect
of the Gospel." He shows us Christ made man, and then
sending His divine Spirit over all the earth, protecting us
with His wings; and, therefore, the *eagle* symbolizes Mark.

Irenaeus goes on to say that the fourfold form of the
beasts represents the four principal covenants which God
made with the human race. The first covenant was made
with Adam, prior to the flood. The second was made with
Noah, after the flood. The third consisted of the giving of
the Law to Moses. The fourth is that which renovates man
in Christ, " raising and bearing men upon its wings into
the heavenly kingdom."

So, then, in Irenaeus the identifications are:

Matthew = the man	Mark = the eagle
Luke = the ox	John = the lion.

But, as we have said, there were a variety of different
identifications, and we list the others.

The scheme of Athanasius was:

Matthew = the man	Mark = the calf
Luke = the lion	John = the eagle.

The scheme of Victorinus was:

Matthew = the man	Mark = the lion
Luke = the ox	John = the eagle.

The scheme of Augustine was:

Matthew = the lion	Mark = the man
Luke = the ox	John = the eagle.

It may be said that on the whole Augustine's identifications
became the most commonly accepted, because they fit the

THE REVELATION OF JOHN

facts. *Matthew* is best represented by the *lion*, because in it Jesus is depicted as The Lion of Judah, the One in whom all the expectations and dreams of the prophets came true. *Mark* is best represented by the *man*, because it is the nearest approach to a factual report of the human life of Jesus. *Luke* is best represented by the *ox*, because it depicts Jesus as the sacrifice for all classes and conditions of men and women everywhere. *John* is best represented by the *eagle*, because of all birds the eagle flies highest and is said to be the only living creature which can look straight into the sun; and *John* of all the gospels reaches the highest heights of thought.

THE SONG OF PRAISE

Revelation 4.6b-8 (*continued*)

NIGHT and day the living creatures never rested from their doxology of praise:

> Holy, holy, holy is the Lord, the Almighty,
> Who was, and Who is, and Who is to come.

Here there is set out the sleepless praise of nature. As it has been put: "Man rests on the Sabbath, and in sleep, and in the end in death, but the course of nature is unbroken and unbroken in praise." There is never any time when the world God made is not praising God.

> As o'er each continent and island
> The dawn leads on another day,
> The voice of prayer is never silent,
> Nor dies the strain of praise away.

It is to be noted that the doxology seizes on three aspects of God.

(i) It praises God for *His holiness* (cp. *Isaiah* 6.3). Again and again we have seen that the basic idea of holiness is difference. That which is holy is different; it is separate from the common things; it belongs to another order of life and of being. That is supremely true of God. God is

204

different from men. It is precisely there that there is the reason why we are moved to prayer to, and adoration of, and praise of, God. If God were like us, if He were simply an outsize and glorified human person, we could not praise. As the poet had it: " How could I praise, if such as I could understand? " The very mystery of God, the very difference of God, moves us to awed admiration in His presence, and to amazed love that that greatness should stoop so low for us men and for our salvation.

(ii) It praises *His omnipotence*. God is the Almighty. The people to whom the *Revelation* was written are under the threat of the Roman Empire; they are under a threat from a power which no person and no nation had ever successfully withstood. Think what it must have meant to them to be sure that behind them there stood no one less, and no one other than, the Almighty. The very giving of that name to God affirms the certainty of the ultimate triumph and the present safety of the Christian; not a safety which meant release from trouble, but a safety which made a man safe in life and in death.

(iii) It praises *His everlastingness*. Empires might come and empires might go; God lasts for ever. Men might try to obliterate the faith in God; but no one can obliterate an everlasting God. Here is the triumphant affirmation that God endures unchanging amidst the opposition and the enmity and the rebellion of men. Mortal men and things may rise and perish, but, " God endures unchanging on."

GOD, THE LORD AND CREATOR

Revelation 4.9-11

When the living creatures shall give glory and honour and thanksgiving to Him who is seated on the throne, and who lives for ever and ever, the twenty-four elders shall fall down before Him who is seated on the throne, and worship Him who lives for ever and ever, and cast their crowns before the throne, and say:

> It is right, our Lord and God, that you should
> receive the glory and the honour and the power,
> for you have created all things, and through your
> will all things exist, and have been created.

HERE is the other section of the choir of thanksgiving.
We have seen that the living creatures stand for nature in
all its greatness; and we saw that the twenty-four elders
stand for the great united Church in Jesus Christ. So when
the living creatures and the elders unite in praise, it
symbolizes nature and the Church both praising God.
There are commentators who have made difficulty here.
In verse 8 we have just read that the praise of the living
creatures is unceasing by day and night; in this passage
the picture is of separate bursts of praise at each of which
the elders fall down and worship. But surely to say that
there is an inconsistency here is unimaginative criticism.
We do not look for strict logic in the poetry of adoration.

Here John uses a picture which the ancient world would
know well. He says that the elders cast their crowns before
the throne of God. In the ancient world that was the sign
of complete submission. When one king surrendered to
another king, he cast his crown at the victor's feet. Sometimes the Romans carried with them an image of their
emperor, and, when they had reduced a monarch to submission, there was a ceremony in which the vanquished
one had to cast his crown before the emperor's image.
The picture looks on God as the conqueror of the souls
of men; and on the Church as the body of people who have
surrendered to God, and who have completely abdicated
their power to Him, and who have accepted Him as Master
and Lord. There can be no Christianity without submission.

The doxology of the elders praises God on two counts.

(i) God is Lord and God. Here is something which would
be even more meaningful to John's people than it is to us.
The phrase for Lord and God is *kurios kai theos*; and that
very phrase was the official title of Domitian, the Roman
Emperor. The Roman Emperor claimed to be *Lord and*

God. It was, indeed, because the Christians would not acknowledge that claim that they were persecuted and killed. Simply to call God *Lord and God* was a triumphant confession of faith, an assertion that, for the Christian, God holds the first place in all the universe, and none can take it from Him.

(ii) God is Creator. It is through God's will and purpose that all things existed in the purpose of God, even before they were created, and were in the end brought into actual being. It is well that we should remember that man has acquired many powers, but he does not possess the power to create. He can alter and rearrange; he can make things out of already existing materials; but only God can create something out of nothing. And that great truth means that in the realest sense everything in the world belongs to God, and that there is nothing that a man can handle which God has not given to him.

THE ROLL IN THE HAND OF GOD

Revelation 5.1

> And in the right hand of Him who was seated on the throne I saw a roll written on the front and on the back, and sealed with seven seals.

WE must, as far as we can, try to visualize the scene and the picture which John is drawing.

We must first note the source and origin from which the picture came into the mind of John. The picture is taken from the vision of Ezekiel; " And, when I looked, behold, an hand was sent unto me; and lo, a roll of a book was therein; and he spread it before me; and it was written within and without; and there was written therein lamentations and mourning and woe " (*Ezekiel* 2.9, 10). It was the vision of Ezekiel which gave shape and pattern to the vision of John.

We must further note that it was a *roll* and not a *book* which was in the hand of God. In the ancient world, down to the second century A.D., the form of literary work was the roll, not the book. The roll was made of papyrus, which we shall later go on to describe. Papyrus was manufactured in single sheets about ten inches by eight. The sheets were joined together horizontally when a great deal of writing had to be done. The writing was in narrow columns about three inches long, with margins of about two and a half inches at the top and at the bottom, and with about three-quarters of an inch between the columns. The roll commonly had a wooden roller at each end. It was held in the left hand, unrolled with the right, and, as the reading went on, the part in the left hand was rolled up again. We may get some idea of the dimensions of a roll from the following statistics. 2 and 3 *John*, *Jude* and *Philemon* would occupy one sheet of papyrus; *Romans* would require a roll 11½ feet long; *Mark*, 19 feet; *John*, 23½ feet; *Matthew*, 30 feet; *Luke* and *Acts*, 32 feet. The *Revelation* itself would occupy a roll 15 feet long. It was such a roll that was in the hand of God. Two things are said about this roll.

(i) It was written *on the front and on the back*. We have said that the roll was made of papyrus. Papyrus was a substance made from the pith of a bulrush which grew in the delta of the Nile. The bulrush was about fifteen feet high, with six feet of it below the water; and it was as thick as a man's wrist. The pith was extracted. It was cut into thin strips with a very sharp knife. A row of strips was laid vertically; on the top of them another row of strips was laid horizontally; the whole was then moistened with Nile water and glue; it was then pressed together. The resulting substance was beaten with a mallet and then smoothed with pumice stone; and there emerged a substance not unlike brown paper. From this description it will be seen that on one side the grain of the papyrus would run horizontally; that side was known as the *recto*; and on that side the writing was done, as it was easier to write on the side on which the lines of the writing ran with the lines of the fibre of the papyrus. The side on which the fibres ran vertically was called the *verso*, and was not so commonly used for writing.

But papyrus was an expensive substance. Its quality varied and the price varied with the quality from fourpence to over a shilling for a single sheet. So, if a person had a great deal to write, he wrote on the front and on the back of the sheet. A sheet written on the back, on the *verso*, was called an *opisthograph*, that is, a sheet written behind; and when a person did so use his papyrus sheets, it showed that he had a tremendous amount of material to set down. Juvenal talks of a young tragedian walking about with the papyrus manuscript of a tragedy on Orestes written on both sides; it was a lengthy production! The roll in God's hand was written on both sides. That is to show how much it contained; there was so much on it that *recto* and *verso* alike were taken up with the writing. The story of the roll was a long and a crowded story.

(ii) It was *sealed with seven seals*. That may indicate either of two things. (*a*) When a roll was finished, it was fastened with threads, and the threads were sealed at the knots. The one ordinary document that was sealed with seven seals was a will. Under Roman law the seven witnesses to a will sealed it with their seals, and it could only be opened when all seven, or their legal representatives were present. So, then, the roll may be what we might describe as God's will, God's testamentary disposition, God's final settlement of the affairs of the universe. (*b*) It is more likely that the seven seals stand simply for profound secrecy. The contents of the roll are so secret, so pre-eminently the knowledge of God alone, so hidden from all prying and peering eyes, that the roll is sealed with seven seals. In the Gospels we read how the tomb of Jesus was sealed to keep it safe (*Matthew* 27.66). The apocryphal Gospel of Peter says that it was sealed with seven seals. It was so sealed to make it quite certain that no unauthorized person could possibly open it. So, then, the roll in the hand of God is sealed seven times to show that its contents must remain a profound secret to all but God Himself.

In the picture, then, there is a papyrus roll in the hand of God. It contains such an amount of material that it is written on the *recto* and on the *verso*, on the front and on the back; and it is sealed with seven seals, either because it is God's final disposition of the affairs of the world, or, because it is so secret that none but God may dare to open it.

GOD'S BOOK OF DESTINY

Revelation 5.2-4

> And I saw a strong angel proclaiming in a great voice: " Who is good enough to open the roll, and to loosen its seals? " And there was no one in heaven, or on earth, or under the earth, who was able to open the roll or to look at it; and I was weeping sorely because there was no one who was found to be good enough to open the roll or to see it.

As John looked at God with the roll in His hand, there came a challenge from a strong angel. A strong angel appears again in 10.1 and 18.21. In this case the angel had to be strong so that the challenge of his voice might reach throughout the whole universe. The summons of the angel was that anyone who was worthy of the task should come forward and open the book.

Now we must clearly ask the question what the book was. There is no doubt that the book is the book of the divine decrees; it is the book of the destinies of the world; it contains the record of that which is to happen in the last times; it is, if we like to put it so, the book of history written in advance. That there was such a book, or such tablets of God, is a common conception in Jewish thought. It is common in the *Book of Enoch*. In that book Uriel the archangel says to Enoch in the heavenly places: " O Enoch, observe the writing of the heavenly tablets, and read what is written thereon, and mark every individual fact." Then Enoch goes on: "And I observed everything on the heavenly tablets, and read everything which was written thereon, and understood everything, and read the book of all the deeds of men and of all the children of flesh that will be upon the earth to the remotest generations" (I *Enoch* 81.1, 2). In the same book Enoch has a vision of the Head of Days on the throne of His glory, "and the books of the living were opened before Him" (I *Enoch* 47.3). Enoch declares that he knows the mystery of the holy ones, because "the Lord showed me and informed me, and I have read in the heavenly tables" (I *Enoch* 106.19). On these tables he saw the history of the generations which were still to come (I *Enoch* 107.1). So, then, the idea is that God has a book in which the history of time to come is already written.

When we are seeking to interpret the meaning of this idea, it is well to remember that it is vision and poetry, and that it would be a great mistake to take it, as it were, too literally. It does not mean that everything is fixed and settled long ago, that we are in the grip of an iron determinism and an inescapable fate, that, do what we like, what will be, will be. What it does mean is that God has a plan, a purpose, a design for the universe; that there is a goal and a consummation ahead; and that the purpose of God will be in the end worked out.

> God is working His purpose out, as year succeeds to year:
> God is working His purpose out, and the time is drawing near—
> Nearer and nearer draws the time—the time that shall surely be,
> When the earth shall be filled with the glory of God, as the waters cover the sea.

In response to the challenge of the angel no one came forward. There was none who was good enough to open the roll. And at this John in his vision fell to weeping sorely. There were two reasons for his tears.

(i) In 4.1 the voice had made the promise to him: " I will show these things which must be hereafter." It now looked as if the promise could not be kept, and as if it had been frustrated. The seer weeps because the promised vision, as he thinks, is not to be.

(ii) But there is a deeper reason for his sorrow. It seemed to him that there was no one in the whole universe to whom God could tell His secrets and reveal His mysteries. Here, indeed, was a terrible thing. Here was a world so lost in iniquity that there was no one in it who could receive the voice of God. Long ago Amos had said: " Surely the Lord God will do nothing, but He revealeth His secret unto His servants the prophets " (*Amos* 3.7). But here was a tragic situation in which there was no one in the world who was good enough to receive the prophetic vision. Here was a world so far from God that there was none able to receive the message of God.

For John that problem was to be triumphantly solved in the emergence of the Lamb. But behind this problem there lies a great and a challenging truth. God cannot deliver a message to men unless there be a man fit to receive it. Here there is the very essence of the problem of communication. It is the problem of the teacher; he cannot teach truth which his scholars are unable to receive. It is the problem of the preacher; he cannot deliver a message to a congregation totally incapable of comprehending it. It is the eternal problem of love; love cannot tell its truths, cannot give its gifts, to those who are incapable of hearing and receiving. The need of the world is for men and women who will keep themselves sensitive to God; men and women who are ever ready to learn; men and women who refuse to let the activities of earth dull them to the realities of heaven; and who refuse to let the many voices of the world render them incapable of hearing the still small voice of God. God has a message for the world in every generation; but that message cannot be delivered until there is found a man who is capable of receiving it. And day by day we either fit or unfit ourselves to receive the message of God.

THE LION OF JUDAH AND THE ROOT OF DAVID

Revelation 5.5

> And one of the elders said to me: " Stop weeping. Behold the Lion of the tribe of Judah, the Root of David, has won such a victory that He is able to open the book and its seven seals."

WE are now approaching one of the greatest and most dramatic moments in the *Revelation*, the emergence of the Lamb in the centre of the scene. But before we reach that moment, certain things lead up to it.

John has been weeping because there is none to whom God may reveal His secrets and His purposes. There comes to him one of the elders, acting as the messenger of Christ, and saying to him: " Stop weeping." These were words which were more than once on the lips of Jesus in the days of His flesh. That is what Jesus said to the widow of Nain when she was mourning her dead son (*Luke* 7.13); and that is what Jesus said to Jairus and his family when they were lamenting for the little girl whom they believed to be dead (*Luke* 8.52). The comforting voice of Christ is still speaking in the heavenly places.

Swete has an interesting comment on this. John was weeping, and yet his tears were quite unnecessary. Human grief is often needless, and it often springs from insufficient knowledge. If we had patience to wait and to trust, we would see that God has His own solutions for the situations which bring us tears.

The elder tells John that there is One who has won such a victory that He is able to open the book and to loosen the seals. That one is Jesus Christ. What does it mean to say that Jesus Christ can open the book and loosen the seals? It means three things. It means that because of His victory over death and over all the powers of evil, and because of His complete obedience to, and fidelity to, God, He is able to *know* God's secrets; He is able to *reveal* God's secrets; and it is His privilege and duty to *preside over* and to *control* the things which shall be. Because of what Jesus did, He is the Lord of truth and the Lord of history. He is now called by two great titles.

(i) He is the *Lion of Judah.* This title goes back to Jacob's final blessing of his sons before his death. In that blessing he calls Judah " a lion's whelp " (*Genesis* 49.9). If Judah himself is a lion's whelp, then it is fitting to call the greatest member of the tribe of Judah *The Lion of Judah.* In point of fact this title in the books written between the Testaments became a messianic title. 2 *Esdras* speaks of the figure of a lion and says: " This is the Anointed One, that is, the Messiah " (2 *Esdras* 12.31). The strength and the power of the lion, his undoubted place as the king of beasts, make him a fitting emblem of the all-powerful Messiah, whom the Jews awaited.

(ii) He is the *Root of David.* This title goes back to Isaiah. There the prophecy is that there will come forth a rod out of the stem of Jesse, and a root of Jesse who shall be an ensign to the people (*Isaiah* 11.1, 10). Jesse was the father of David, and this means that Jesus Christ was the Son of David, the promised Messiah.

So, here we have two great titles. They are titles which are particularly Jewish. They have their rise and origin in the Old Testament, and in the Jewish pictures of the coming Messiah; and they lay it down that Jesus Christ triumphantly performed the work of the Messiah, and is, therefore, able to know and to reveal the secrets of God, and to preside over the working out of the purposes of God in the events of history.

THE LAMB

Revelation 5.6

> And I saw a Lamb standing in the midst of the throne
> and of the four living creatures, and in the midst of
> the elders. It still bore the marks of having been
> slain. It had seven horns and seven eyes, which are
> the seven Spirits of God despatched to all the earth.

HERE is the supreme moment of this vision—the emergence
of the Lamb in the scene of heaven. When we try to visualize this scene, it is possible to think of it in two ways.
Either, we may think of the four living creatures forming
a circle around the throne, and the twenty-four elders
forming a wider circle with a larger circumference, with the
Lamb standing between the inner circle of the four living
creatures and the outer circle of the twenty-four elders;
or, and we think that this is much more likely, what John
is saying is that the Lamb was the centre of the whole
scene, as it were, in the very centre of the stage, the focus
of every eye.

The idea of the Lamb is one of the great characteristic
ideas of the *Revelation*. In the *Revelation* Jesus Christ is
called the Lamb no fewer than twenty-nine times. There
is a point in the Greek which shows that the writer of the
Revelation wished to underline that this was a new concep-
tion, as indeed it was. The word he uses for *Lamb* is not
used of Jesus Christ anywhere else in the New Testament.
In other places in the New Testament Jesus is called the
Lamb. John the Baptist pointed to Him as the Lamb of
God who takes away the sin of the world (*John* 1.29, 36).
Peter speaks of the precious blood of Christ, as of a lamb
without blemish and without spot (I *Peter* 1.19). In
Isaiah 53.7, in the chapter so dear to Jesus and to the early
Church, we read of the lamb brought to the slaughter.
But in all these cases the word is *amnos*, whereas the word
that the writer of the *Revelation* uses is *arnion*. *Arnion*
is the word that Jeremiah uses, when he says: " I was
like a *lamb* or an ox that is brought to the slaughter "

(*Jeremiah* 11.19). By using this word *arnion*, and by using it so often, John wishes us to see that this is a new picture and a new conception which he is bringing to men.

(i) The Lamb still bears the marks of having been slain. There we have the picture of the sacrifice of Christ, still visible in the heavenly places. Here is the picture of the pain and the torment, the shame and the humiliation, the death and the Cross, wherein the Lamb of God was God's perfect sacrifice for the sin of men. Even in the heavenly places Jesus Christ is the one who loved us and who gave Himself for us, the one who gave His life a ransom for many, the one whose life and whose death were the perfect and the all-availing sacrifice.

(ii) But there is another side to this, and it is the other side which faces us with the great paradox. This same Lamb, with the marks of sacrifice still on it, is the Lamb with the seven horns and the seven eyes.

(*a*) The seven horns stand for omnipotence. In the Old Testament the horn stands for two things. First, it stands for sheer *power*. In the blessing of Moses the horns of Joseph are like the horns of unicorns and with them he will push the people together to the ends of the earth (*Deuteronomy* 33.17). Zedekiah, the prophet, made iron horns as a sign of promised triumph over the Syrians (I *Kings* 22.11). The wicked is warned not to lift up his horn (*Psalm* 75.4). Zechariah sees the vision of the four horns which stand for the nations who have scattered Israel (*Zechariah* 1.18). Here is the picture of power which cannot be withstood. Second, it stands for *honour*. When Hannah had a child, it is her glad cry that her horn is exalted in the Lord (I *Samuel* 2.1). It is the confidence of the Psalmist that in the favour of God our horn shall be exalted (*Psalm* 89.17). The good man's horn shall be exalted with honour (*Psalm* 112.9). God exalts the horn of His people (*Psalm* 148.14). The horn stands for the honour which God gives to His own. Third, we must add still another strand to this picture. In the time between the Testaments the great

heroes of Israel were the Maccabees; they were the great
warriors who were the saviours and liberators of the
nations; and they are represented as horned lambs
(1 *Enoch* 90.9).

Here is the great paradox; the Lamb bears the sacrificial
wounds upon it; but at the same time it is clothed with the
very might of God which can now shatter and break its
enemies. The Lamb has *seven* horns; we have already
seen that the number *seven* stands for completeness and
perfection; the power of the Lamb is perfect, full, complete,
beyond withstanding.

(*b*) The Lamb has seven eyes, and the eyes are the Spirits
which are despatched into all the earth. The picture comes
from *Zechariah*. There the prophet sees the seven lamps
which are " the eyes of the Lord, which run to and fro
through the whole earth " (*Zechariah* 4.10). It is a strange
and an eerie picture; but quite clearly it stands for the
all-seeing omniscience of God. In an almost crude way
it says that there is no place on earth which is not under
the eye of God, and which God does not see. So, then, the
seven eyes, and the Spirits sent out to the ends of the earth,
stand for the omniscience of the Lamb, His perfect knowledge, and His presence everywhere among men.

Here, indeed, is a truly tremendous picture of Christ.
He is the fulfilment of all the hopes and dreams of Israel,
for He is the Lion of Judah and the Root of David. He is the
one whose sacrifice availed for men, and who still bears the
marks of it in the heavenly places. But the tragedy has
turned to triumph, and the shame has turned to glory,
and He is the one with all power and all knowledge, whose
all-conquering might none can withstand, and whose
all-seeing eye none can escape.

There are few passages of Scripture which show at one
and the same time what Swete called " the majesty and the
meekness " of Jesus Christ, and which in the one picture
combine the humiliation of His death and the glory of His
risen life.

MUSIC IN HEAVEN

Revelation 5.7-14

And the Lamb came and received the roll from the right hand of Him who was seated on the throne. When it had received the roll, the four living creatures fell before the Lamb, and so did the twenty-four elders, each of whom had a harp and golden bowls laden with incenses, which are the prayers of God's dedicated people. And they sang a new song and this is what they sang:

> Worthy are you to receive the roll, and to open its seals, because you were slain, and so at the price of your life blood you bought for God those of every tribe and tongue and people and race, and made them a kingdom of priests to our God, and they will reign upon the earth.

And I saw, and I heard the voice of many angels, who were in a circle round the throne, and the living creatures, and the elders; and their number was ten thousands of ten thousands and thousands of thousands, and they were singing with a great voice:

> The Lamb which has been slain is worthy to receive the power and the riches and the wisdom and the strength and the honour and the glory and the blessing.

And I heard every created creature which was in the heaven and upon the earth and beneath the earth and on the sea and all things in them saying:

> Blessing and honour and glory and dominion for ever and ever to Him who sits upon the throne and to the Lamb.

And the four living creatures said, Amen; and the elders fell down and worshipped.

It is necessary to set this passage down in full, and to look at it as a whole, before we begin to deal with it in detail. R. H. Charles quotes Christian Rossetti on this passage: "Heaven is revealed to earth as the homeland of music." Here is the greatest chorus of praise the universe can ever hear. The praise comes, as it were, in three waves. First, there is the praise of the four living creatures and of the twenty-four elders. Herein we see all nature and all the

Church combining to praise the Lamb. Second, there is the praise of the myriads of angels. As John looks, he sees, not only the four living creatures and the twenty-four elders. He sees in a great surrounding circle, and far beyond it, myriads and myriads of angels, beyond the counting, all singing praise to the Lamb. Here is the picture of all the inhabitants of heaven lifting up their voices in their shout of praise. Third, he sees every created creature, in every part of the universe, to its deepest depth and its widest circle and its farthest corner, singing in praise.

Here is praise taken up in an ever-widening series of circles. It is like some tremendous chorus in which the orchestra and choir, part after part, is brought in, until the chorus swells out in full volume with every part shouting its praise in a great climax until, as it were, it reaches an unparalleled fortissimo.

Here there is the truth that heaven and earth and all that is within them is designed and purposed for the praise of Jesus Christ. The final dream of the universe is a universe praising Christ; and it is our privilege to lend our voices and our lives to this vast chorus of praise, for that chorus is necessarily incomplete so long as there is one voice missing from it.

THE PRAYERS OF THE SAINTS

Revelation 5.8

THE first section in the chorus of praise is the song of the four living creatures and the twenty-four elders; and, as we have seen, they represent all that is in nature and all that is in the universal Church.

The picture of the elders is interesting. They have harps. Amidst the Jews the harp was the traditional instrument to which the Psalms were sung. " Praise the Lord with harp," says the Psalmist (*Psalm* 33.2). " Sing unto the Lord with the harp; the harp, and the voice of a psalm "

(*Psalm* 98.5). " Sing unto the Lord with thanksgiving; sing praise upon the harp unto our God " (*Psalm* 147.7). The harp simply stands for the music of praise as the Jews knew that music.

But the second picture of the elders is even more interesting. They have golden bowls, full of incense, and the incense is the prayers of God's dedicated people. The likening of prayers to incense comes also from the *Psalms*. " Let my prayer be set before Thee as incense; and the lifting up of my hands as the evening sacrifice," says the Psalmist (*Psalm* 141.2). But the significant thing is the idea of intermediaries in prayer, the idea that the prayers of men are brought to God by what we might call celestial bearers of them. In the later Jewish literature this idea of heavenly intermediaries bringing the prayers of the faithful to God is very common. In the *Testament of Dan* (6.2) we read: " Draw near unto God and to the angel that intercedeth for you, for he is a mediator between God and man." In this literature we find many such angels.

Chief of them all is Michael, the archangel, " the merciful and long-suffering " (I *Enoch* 40.9). He is said daily to come down to the fifth heaven to receive men's prayers and to bring them to God (3 *Baruch* 11). In *Tobit* it is the archangel Raphael who brings the prayers of men to God; Raphael says to Tobit: " I am Raphael, one of the seven holy angels, who present the prayers of the saints, and who go in and out before the glory of the Holy One " (*Tobit* 12.15). It is Gabriel who tells Enoch: " I swear unto you that in heaven the angels are mindful of you before the glory of the Great One " (I *Enoch* 104.1). Sometimes it is the guardian angels who bring the prayers of men to God; and it is said that at certain definite times each day the doors are open so that the prayers may be received (*Apocalypse of Paul* 7.10). Sometimes all the angels, or, as *Enoch* calls them, The Watchers, are engaged in this task. It is to " the Holy Ones of Heaven " that the souls of men complain, with their cry for justice (I *Enoch* 9.3). It is the duty of the Watchers of heaven to intercede for men (I *Enoch* 15.2). As we have seen, the angels are mindful of men for good (I *Enoch* 104.1). Sometimes, it would seem, the blessed dead share in this task. The angels and the holy ones in their resting-places intercede and pray for the children of men (I *Enoch* 39.6). The idea of heavenly intermediaries to bring the prayers of men to God is thus very common in later Jewish thought. There are certain things to be said about this belief.

(i) From one point of view it is an uplifting thought. We are, so to speak, not left to pray alone. The hosts of heaven and the unseen cloud of witnesses are there to assist our prayers. No prayer can be altogether heavy-footed and leaden-winged which has all the citizenry of heaven behind it to help it to rise to God.

(ii) From another point of view it is all quite unnecessary. No intermediary is needed; before us there is set an open door which no man can ever shut; for us there is a new and living way even into the Holiest of Holies across which no man can put a barrier. No man's prayers need any assistance, for God's ear is open to catch the faintest whisper of appeal.

(iii) The whole conception of intermediaries arises from a line of thought which has met us before. As the centuries went on, the Jews became ever more impressed with the transcendence of God, the distance of God, the difference between God and men. Such was this difference that they began to believe that there never can be any direct contact and communication between God and man, that there must be angelic intermediaries to bridge this vast and infinite gulf. That is exactly the feeling that Jesus Christ came to take away, for He came to tell us that God " is closer to us than breathing, nearer than hands or feet." He came to be the living way by which for every man, however humble, the door to God is open.

It may be that we shall find comfort in the idea that angelic hands bear our prayers to God; it may be that—even better—we shall be sure that we need no such aid.

THE NEW SONG

Revelation 5.9

THE song that the four living creatures and the elders sang was a *new song*. The phrase *a new song* is very common in the *Psalms*; and there it is always a song for the new mercies of God. " Sing unto Him a new song," says the Psalmist (*Psalm* 33.3). God took the Psalmist out of the fearful pit and from the miry clay, and set his foot on a rock, and put a new song in his mouth, to praise God (*Psalm* 40.3). " O sing a new song to the Lord, for He hath done marvellous things " (*Psalm* 98.1; cp. 96.1). " I will sing a new song unto Thee, O Lord " (*Psalm* 144.9). " Praise ye the Lord. Sing unto the Lord a new song, and His praise in the congregation of saints " (*Psalm* 149.1). But the nearest parallel in the Old Testament comes from *Isaiah*. There God declares new things, and the prophet calls upon men to sing unto the Lord a new song (*Isaiah* 42.9, 10). The new song is the consequence of the new creation.

The new song is always a song for new mercies of God; and the song will be noblest of all when it is a song for the mercies of God in Jesus Christ.

One of the characteristics of the *Revelation* is that it is the book of new things. There is the new name (2.17; 3.12); there is the new Jerusalem (3.12; 21.2); there is the new song (5.9; 14.3); there are the new heavens and the new earth (21.1); and there is the great promise that God makes all things new (21.5).

One most significant thing is to be noted. Greek has two words for *new*. There is *neos*, which means *new in point of time*, but not necessarily new in point of quality. A thing which is *neos* is a thing which has been recently produced, but it may be only a new specimen of a kind of thing which has been in existence for a long time. There is *kainos*, which means *new in point of quality*. *Kainos* describes a thing which has not only been recently produced it describes a thing the like of which has never existed before.

The significance of this is that Jesus Christ brings into life a quality which has never existed before. He brings into life a new joy, a new thrill, a new strength, a new peace. Something begins to live in the world and in life which Christless eyes have never seen and never can see.

That is why the supreme quality of the Christian life is a kind of sheen and radiance. It has been said that " the opposite of a Christian world is a world grown old and sad." About the Christian life there is an eternal youth and an eternal joy, for God is always bringing into life that new quality of life itself which He alone can give through Jesus Christ.

THE SONG OF THE LIVING CREATURES AND OF THE ELDERS

Revelation 5.9, 10

LET us begin by setting down this song:

> Worthy are you to receive the roll, and to open its seals, because you were slain, and so at the price of your life blood you bought for God those of every tribe and tongue and people and race, and made them a kingdom of priests to our God, and they will reign upon the earth.

The praise that is rendered to the Lamb by the four living creatures and by the elders is rendered to Him because He died. In this song there is summed up the results for us of the death of Jesus Christ.

(i) The death of Jesus Christ was a *sacrificial* death. That is to say, it was a death with purpose in it. The death of Jesus Christ was not an accident of history; it was not even the tragic death of a good and an heroic man in the cause of righteousness and of God; it was not merely a disaster caused by human sin and rebellion; it was a sacrificial death. Now the object of sacrifice is to restore the lost relationship between God and man; and it was for that reason, and with that purpose, *and with that result,* that Jesus Christ died.

(ii) The death of Jesus Christ was an *emancipating* death. From beginning to end the New Testament is full of the idea of the liberation of mankind achieved by Jesus Christ. He gave His life a ransom (*lutron*) for many (*Mark* 10.45). He gave Himself a ransom (*antilutron*) for all (I *Timothy* 2.6). He redeemed us—literally *bought us out from* (*exagorazein*)—from the curse of the law (*Galatians* 3.13). We are redeemed (*lutrousthai*) not by any human wealth, but by the precious blood of Jesus Christ (I *Peter* 1.19). Jesus Christ is the Lord that bought us (*agorazein*) (2 *Peter* 2.1). We are bought with a price (*agorazein*) (I *Corinthians* 6.20; 7.23). The New Testament consistently declares that it cost the death of Jesus Christ to rescue man from the dilemma and the slavery into which sin had brought him. The New Testament has no "official" theory of how that effect was achieved; but of the effect itself it is in no doubt whatever.

(iii) The death of Jesus Christ was *universal* in its benefits. It was for men and women of every tribe and tongue and people and race. There was a day when the Jews could hold that God cared only for the Jews of all the peoples of the earth, and that He wished for nothing but the destruction and the obliteration of other peoples, but in Jesus Christ we meet a God who so loves *the world*. The death of Christ was for all men, and, therefore, it is the task of the Church to tell all men of it.

(iv) The death of Jesus Christ was an *availing* death. Jesus did not die for nothing and for no purpose. In this song three aspects of the work of Christ are singled out.

(a) He made us *kings*. He opened to men the royalty of sonship of God. Men have always been sons of God by creation; but now there is a new sonship of grace open to every man. Man's humanity becomes clad with the royalty of God's divinity.

(b) He made us *priests*. In the ancient world the priest alone had the right of approach to God. When a Jew entered the Temple, he could make his way through the Court of the Gentiles, through the Court of the Women, into the Court of the Israelites; but into the Court of the Priests he could not go. For any ordinary man it was thus far and no farther. But Jesus Christ opened the new and the living way for all men to God. Every man becomes a priest in the sense that every man has the right of access to God.

(c) He gave us *triumph*. His people shall reign upon the earth. This is not political triumph or material lordship. It is the secret of victorious living under any circumstances. " In the world ye shall have tribulation, but be of good cheer: I have overcome the world " (*John* 16.33). In Christ there is victory over self, victory over circumstance, and victory over sin.

When we think of what the death and life of Jesus Christ have done for men, it is no wonder that the living creatures and the elders burst into praise of Him.

THE SONG OF THE ANGELS
Revelation 5.11, 12
> And I saw, and I heard the voice of many angels, who were in a circle round the throne and the living creatures and the elders; and their number was ten thousands of ten thousands and thousands of thousands; and they were saying with a great voice:
>> The Lamb, which has been slain, is worthy to receive the power and the riches and the wisdom and the strength and the honour and the glory and the blessing.

Now the chorus of praise is taken up by the unnumbered hosts of the angels of heaven. In a great outer circle round the throne and the living creatures and the elders stand the multitude of the angels, and they begin their song. We have repeatedly seen how John takes his language from the Old Testament; and here there is in his memory David's great blessing and thanksgiving to God:

> Blessed be Thou, Lord God of Israel, our Father, for ever and ever. Thine, O Lord, is the greatness and the power and the glory and the victory and the majesty; for all that is in the heaven and the earth is Thine; Thine is the kingdom, O Lord, and Thou art exalted as head over all. Both riches and honour come of Thee, and Thou reignest over all; and in Thine hand is power and might; and in Thine hand it is to make great, and to give strength unto all (I *Chronicles* 29.10-12).

The great thanksgivings and blessings of the past all resound in the angel song.

The song of the living creatures and of the elders told of the work of Christ in His death; now the angels sing of the possessions of Christ in His glory. Let us look at them one by one. There are seven great possessions which belong to the Risen Lord.

(i) To him belongs the *power*. Paul called Jesus, " Christ the power of God " (I *Corinthians* 1.24). Here is the confidence in the effectiveness of Jesus Christ. He is not one who can plan but never achieve; He is not one who can dream and never realize the dream. To Him belongs the power. We can say triumphantly: of Him " He is able.'

(ii) To Him belongs the *riches*. " Though He was rich," says Paul, " yet for your sakes He became poor " (2 *Corinthians* 8.9). Paul speaks of " the unsearchable riches of Christ " (*Ephesians* 3.8). There is no promise that Jesus Christ has made that he does not possess the resources to carry out. There is no claim on Him which He cannot satisfy. There is no request and petition which is too great to bring to Him. To Him belong the resources to meet every demand.

(iii) To Him belongs the *wisdom*. Paul calls Jesus Christ " the wisdom of God " (I *Corinthians* 1.24). Jesus Christ has the wisdom to know the secrets of God; He has the wisdom to know the way of life; in Him there is the divine knowledge of God and the practical knowledge of the solution of the problems of life.

(iv) To Him belongs the *strength*. Christ is the strong one who can disarm the powers of evil, and who can overthrow Satan (*Luke* 11.22). To use our modern idiom, there is no situation with which Jesus Christ cannot cope. His strength is able to overcome all the powers which array themselves against Him.

(v) To Him belongs the *honour*. The day comes when to Him every knee shall bow, and when every tongue shall confess that He is Lord (*Philippians* 2.11). The day comes when He will be enthroned in the hearts of men. One of the strange things is that even those who are not Christian honour Christ by freely admitting that in His teaching alone there lies the hope of this distracted world.

(vi) To Him belongs the *glory*. As John has it: " We beheld His glory, the glory as of the only begotten of the Father, full of grace and truth " (*John* 1.14). Glory is that which by right belongs to God and to God alone. To say that Jesus Christ possesses the glory is to do nothing less than to say that He is divine and that He shares the rights and privileges of God.

(vii) To Him belongs the *blessing*. Here is the inevitable climax of it all. All these things Jesus Christ possesses, and every one of them He uses in the service of the men for whom He lived and died. He does not clutch His possessions to Himself; He does not use them for Himself; He pours them out for men. And, therefore, there rises to Him from all the redeemed the blessing and the thanksgiving for all that He has done. And that blessing and that thanksgiving are the one gift that we who have nothing can give to Him who possesses all.

THE REVELATION OF JOHN

THE SONG OF ALL CREATION

Revelation 5.13, 14

> And I heard every created creature which was in the heaven, and upon the earth, and beneath the earth, and on the sea, and all things in them, saying:
>
>> Blessing and honour and glory and dominion for ever and ever to Him who sits upon the throne and to the Lamb.
>
> And the four living creatures said, Amen; and the elders fell down and worshipped.

Now the chorus of praise goes so far that it cannot go farther, for it reaches throughout the whole of the universe and the whole of creation. All through the world there is one vast song of praise to the Lamb. We may note one very significant thing here. In this chorus of praise God and the Lamb are joined together; they both receive it, and they both share it. Nothing could better show the height of John's conception of Jesus Christ. In the praise of creation he sets Christ by the side of God.

In the song itself there are two things to note.

The creatures which are in the heaven add their praise. Who are they? More than one answer has been given to that question, and each answer is lovely in its own way. It has been suggested that the reference is to the birds of the air; the very singing of the birds is a song of praise. It has been suggested that the reference is to the sun, the moon and the stars; the heavenly bodies in their shining day and night are praising God. It has been suggested that the phrase gathers up and includes every possible being in heaven—the living creatures, the elders, the myriads of angels and every other heavenly being. It may well be that we should not try to define the phrase, but that we should leave it to include and to contain all.

The creatures which are beneath the earth add their praise. That can only mean the dead who are in Hades, and here is something totally new. In the Old Testament

228

the idea is that the dead, those who are in Sheol, those in the pit, in Hades, are separated altogether from God and man, and live a gray, ghostly, shadowy existence. "In death there is no remembrance of Thee. In the grave who shall give Thee thanks?" (*Psalm* 6.5). "Shall the dust praise Thee? Shall it declare Thy truth? What profit is there in my blood, when I go down to the pit?" (*Psalm* 30.9). "Shall Thy loving-kindness be declared in the grave? or Thy faithfulness in destruction? Shall Thy wonders be known in the dark? And Thy righteousness in the land of forgetfulness? Wilt Thou show wonders to the dead? Shall the dead arise and praise Thee?" (*Psalm* 88.10-12). "The grave cannot praise Thee, death cannot celebrate Thee; they that go down into the pit cannot hope for Thy truth" (*Isaiah* 38.18). Here in the *Revelation* is a vision which sweeps all this away. Not even the land of the dead is beyond the reign of the Risen Christ. Even from beyond death the chorus of praise rises to Him.

The picture here is an all-inclusive picture of all nature praising God. There are in Scripture many magnificent pictures of the praise of God by nature. In the Old Testament itself there is *Psalm* 148. But the noblest song of praise of all comes from the Apocrypha. In the Greek Old Testament there is an addition to *Daniel*. It is called *The Song of the Three Children*, and it is sung by Ananias, Azarias, and Misael, as Shadrach, Meshach and Abed-nego are there called, before they enter the burning fiery furnace. It is long, but it is one of the world's great poems, and we must quote in full the part of it in which they call upon nature to praise God.

> O ye sun and moon, bless ye the Lord:
> Praise and exalt Him above all for ever.
> O ye stars of heaven, bless ye the Lord:
> Praise and exalt Him above all for ever.
> O every shower and dew, bless ye the Lord
> Praise and exalt Him above all for ever.
> O all ye winds, bless ye the Lord:
> Praise and exalt Him above all for ever.

O ye fire and heat, bless ye the Lord:
Praise and exalt Him above all for ever.
O ye winter and summer, bless the Lord:
Praise and exalt Him above all for ever.
O ye dews and storms of snow, bless ye the Lord:
Praise and exalt Him above all for ever.
O ye nights and days, bless the Lord:
Praise and exalt Him above all for ever.
O ye light and darkness, bless the Lord:
Praise and exalt Him above all for ever.
O ye cold and heat, bless the Lord:
Praise and exalt Him above all for ever.
O ye ice and cold, bless ye the Lord:
Praise and exalt Him above all for ever.
O ye frost and snow, bless ye the Lord:
Praise and exalt Him above all for ever.
O ye lightnings and clouds, bless ye the Lord:
Praise and exalt Him above all for ever.
O let the earth bless the Lord:
Praise and exalt Him above all for ever.
O ye mountains and little hills, bless ye the Lord:
Praise and exalt Him above all for ever.
O all ye herbs of the field, bless ye the Lord:
Praise and exalt Him above all for ever.
O all things that grow on the earth, bless ye the Lord:
Praise and exalt Him above all for ever.
O ye fountains, bless ye the Lord:
Praise and exalt Him above all for ever.
O ye seas and rivers, bless ye the Lord:
Praise and exalt Him above all for ever.
O ye whales and all that move in the waters, bless
    ye the Lord:
Praise and exalt Him above all for ever.
O all ye fowls of the air, bless ye the Lord:
Praise and exalt Him above all for ever.
O all ye beasts and cattle, bless ye the Lord:
Praise and exalt Him above all for ever.
O all ye creeping things of the earth, bless ye the
    Lord:
Praise and exalt Him above all for ever.
O ye children of men, bless ye the Lord:
Praise and exalt Him above all for ever.

THE REVELATION OF JOHN

Very closely parallel with this is the hymn which we know as St. Francis' hymn:

> All creatures of our God and King,
> Lift up your voice and with us sing
>   Alleluia, Alleluia!
> Thou burning sun with golden beam,
> Thou silver moon with softer gleam,
>   O praise Him, O praise Him,
>   Alleluia, Alleluia, Alleluia!
>
> Thou rushing wind that art so strong,
> Ye clouds that sail, in heaven along,
>   O praise Him, Alleluia!
> Thou rising morn in praise rejoice,
> Ye lights of evening find a voice.
>
> Thou flowing water, pure and clear,
> Make music for Thy Lord to hear,
>   Alleluia, Alleluia!
> Thou fire so masterful and bright,
> That givest man both warmth and light.
>
> Dear mother earth, who day by day
> Unfoldest blessings on our way,
>   O praise Him, Alleluia!
> The flowers and fruits that in thee grow,
> Let them His glory also show.
>   O praise Him, O praise Him,
>   Alleluia, Alleluia, Alleluia!

The vision of John was a song of praise rising from everything in creation to God and to the Lamb.

NOTES